Table of Contents - Level 4

Just like the last booklet, the 4A book is filled with both new and old. We will keep working on FRACTIONS and take our understanding of them to a whole new level. AREA and PERIMETER are also here, so we do not forget which is which. We also will be getting deep into the study of PRIME NUMBERS, which are of incredible importance, and introduce us to some of the most interesting and difficult questions in the world of mathematics. We hope you enjoy solving this book at least as much as we enjoyed creating it.

Aaron Renert and the entire Renert Mathematics team

1. On your mark...
2. Get set
3. Solve the a-MAZE-ing squirrel→
4. Go!

INTELLIGENT LEARNING
RENERT

Stay #sharp by reviewing what you learned

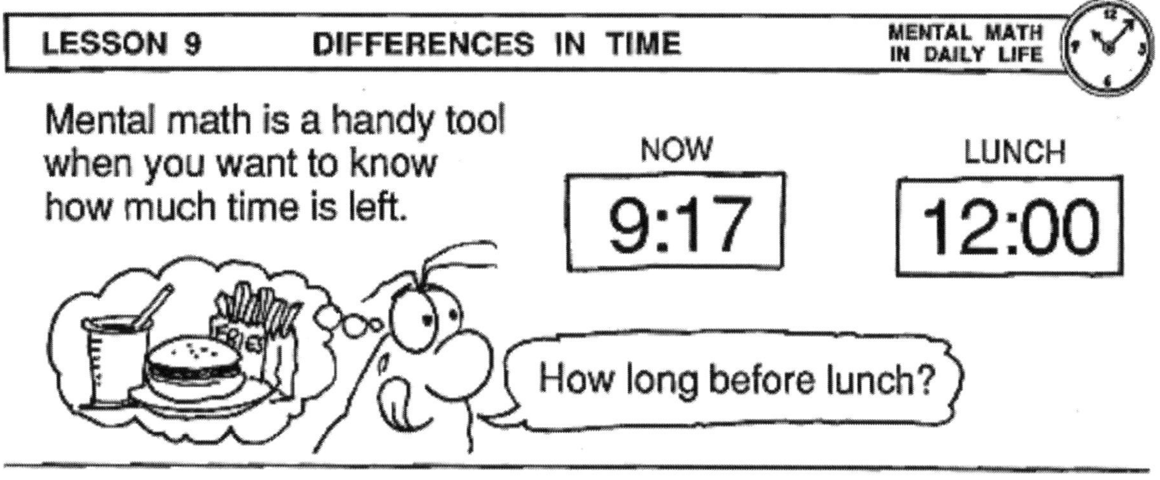
LESSON 9
DIFFERENCES IN TIME
MENTAL MATH IN DAILY LIFE
Mental math is a handy tool when you want to know how much time is left.
NOW
9:17
LUNCH
12:00
How long before lunch?

To figure the difference between two times, add on in steps.

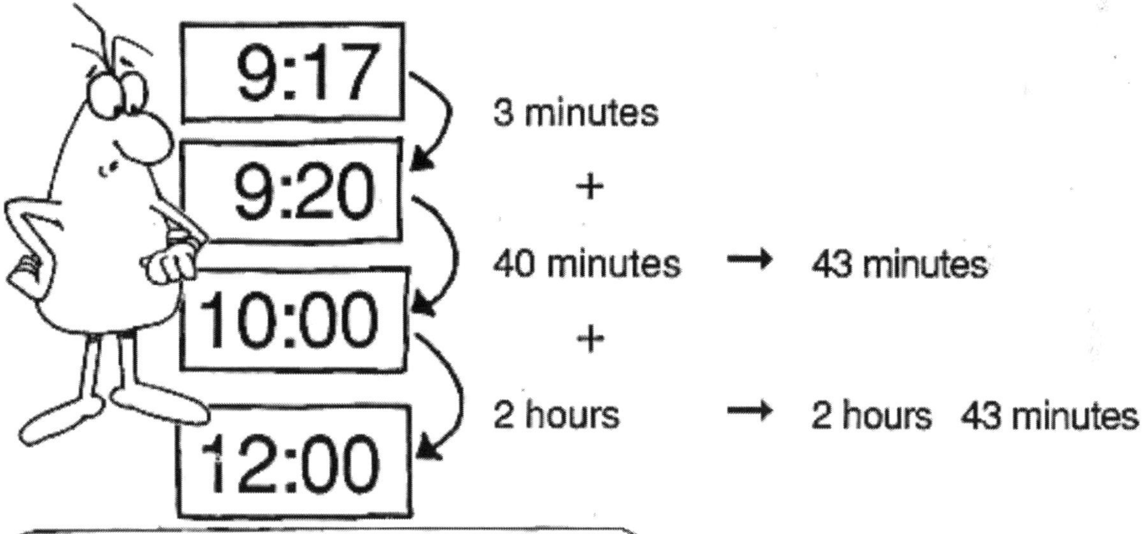
9:17
9:20
10:00
12:00
3 minutes
+
40 minutes → 43 minutes
+
2 hours → 2 hours 43 minutes

TRY THESE IN YOUR HEAD.
Figure the difference by adding on.

1.	9:20 A.M.	10:00 A.M.	**6.**	9:15 A.M.	1:45 P.M.
2.	12:30 P.M.	3:00 P.M.	**7.**	8:50 A.M.	10:05 A.M.
3.	6:55 P.M.	9:00 P.M.	**8.**	5:15 P.M.	7:30 P.M.
4.	8:15 A.M.	12:15 P.M.	**9.**	3:35 A.M.	12:00 noon
5.	3:20 P.M.	8:50 P.M.	**10.**	2:15 P.M.	11:00 P.M.

POWER BUILDER A

1. From 9:00 A.M. to 10:40 A.M. = ________
2. From 7:30 P.M. to 10:40 P.M. = ________
3. From 2:10 P.M. to 9:25 P.M. = ________
4. From 8:25 A.M. to 11:45 A.M. = ________
5. From 12:15 P.M. to 6:30 P.M. = ________
6. From 11:20 A.M. to 4:30 P.M. = ________
7. From 7:35 A.M. to 11:45 A.M. = ________
8. From 1:05 P.M. to 8:55 P.M. = ________
9. From 3:15 P.M. to 9:45 P.M. = ________
10. From 7:45 A.M. to 10:55 A.M. = ________
11. From 2:45 P.M. to 5:20 P.M. = ________
12. From 3:30 P.M. to 8:45 P.M. = ________
13. From 5:10 A.M. to 11:05 A.M. = ________
14. From 7:35 P.M. to 8:20 P.M. = ________
15. From 5:25 P.M. to 11:10 P.M. = ________
16. From 7:20 A.M. to 8:15 A.M. = ________
17. From 11:30 A.M. to 2:25 P.M. = ________
18. From 8:50 A.M. to 7:50 P.M. = ________
19. From 9:15 P.M. to 12:05 A.M. = ________
20. From 8:45 A.M. to 3:25 P.M. = ________

THINK IT THROUGH

Juan started a marathon race at 9:15 A.M. and finished the race 2 hours and 47 minutes later. At what time did Juan finish the race?

POWER BUILDER B

1. From 8:00 P.M. to 11:40 P.M. = ________
2. From 5:30 P.M. to 11:40 P.M. = ________
3. From 4:10 P.M. to 8:30 P.M. = ________
4. From 7:15 A.M. to 10:35 A.M. = ________
5. From 12:25 P.M. to 7:45 P.M. = ________
6. From 11:25 A.M. to 3:45 P.M. = ________
7. From 6:45 A.M. to 11:55 A.M. = ________
8. From 2:05 P.M. to 9:45 P.M. = ________
9. From 2:20 P.M. to 8:40 P.M. = ________
10. From 5:35 P.M. to 11:55 P.M. = ________
11. From 1:40 P.M. to 3:20 P.M. = ________
12. From 5:20 A.M. to 7:45 A.M. = ________
13. From 4:15 A.M. to 8:10 A.M. = ________
14. From 6:25 P.M. to 9:20 P.M. = ________
15. From 4:15 P.M. to 11:10 P.M. = ________
16. From 6:15 P.M. to 8:05 P.M. = ________
17. From 11:40 A.M. to 3:25 P.M. = ________
18. From 7:40 A.M. to 8:35 A.M. = ________
19. From 8:15 A.M. to 12:10 P.M. = ________
20. From 8:25 P.M. to 7:30 A.M. = ________

THINK IT THROUGH

Sarah ran a marathon race in 3 hours and 19 minutes. If the race started at 10:45 A.M., at what time did she finish?

Stay #sharp by reviewing what you learned

LESSON 17 TACK ON TRAILING ZEROS 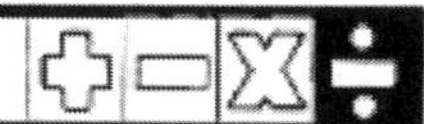

DIVIDE IN YOUR HEAD

1200 ÷ 4

Numbers with trailing zeros are easy to divide in your head.

- Remove the trailing zeros.
- Divide the remaining numbers.
- Tack the trailing zeros onto your answer.

✓4 x 3 00 = 12 00 • Check by multiplying.

TRY THESE IN YOUR HEAD.
Cut off and tack on the trailing zeros.

1. 1200 ÷ 2	**4.** 7) 2800	**7.** 9) 27,000
2. 2400 ÷ 8	**5.** 4) 360	**8.** 3600 ÷ 6
3. 1000 ÷ 5	**6.** 12) 2400	**9.** 3500 ÷ 35
		10. 15) 3000

Power Builder A

1. $2400 \div 6 =$ __________
2. $320 \div 8 =$ __________
3. $7\overline{)420} =$ __________
4. $7\overline{)3500} =$ __________
5. $4\overline{)280} =$ __________
6. $7\overline{)4900} =$ __________
7. $540 \div 6 =$ __________
8. $5600 \div 8 =$ __________
9. $2400 \div 3 =$ __________
10. $5\overline{)3500} =$ __________
11. $1800 \div 2 =$ __________
12. $9\overline{)18{,}000} =$ __________
13. $42{,}000 \div 6 =$ __________
14. $6\overline{)120{,}000} =$ __________
15. $2500 \div 25 =$ __________
16. $48{,}000 \div 6 =$ __________
17. $72{,}000 \div 8 =$ __________
18. $7\overline{)21{,}000} =$ __________
19. $5\overline{)250{,}000} =$ __________
20. $3\overline{)21{,}000} =$ __________

THINK IT THROUGH

How many 5-cent stamps can you buy for $25?

Power Builder B

1. $3200 \div 4 =$ __________
2. $400 \div 8 =$ __________
3. $4\overline{)280} =$ __________
4. $7\overline{)4200} =$ __________
5. $9\overline{)270} =$ __________
6. $8\overline{)4800} =$ __________
7. $540 \div 6 =$ __________
8. $6300 \div 7 =$ __________
9. $2400 \div 3 =$ __________
10. $5\overline{)2500} =$ __________
11. $1600 \div 2 =$ __________
12. $8\overline{)16{,}000} =$ __________
13. $42{,}000 \div 6 =$ __________
14. $4\overline{)160{,}000} =$ __________
15. $1500 \div 15 =$ __________
16. $36{,}000 \div 6 =$ __________
17. $56{,}000 \div 8 =$ __________
18. $7\overline{)21{,}000} =$ __________
19. $5\overline{)45{,}000} =$ __________
20. $3\overline{)27{,}000} =$ __________

THINK IT THROUGH

How many 5-cent stamps can you buy for $100?

Stay ♯sharp by reviewing what you learned

LESSON 18 CANCEL COMMON TRAILING ZEROS

You can divide both numbers in a division problem by the same amount without changing the answer.

Using this idea, it's easy to simplify a problem when both numbers have trailing zeros.

36,000 ÷ 200
÷100
÷100
360 ÷ 2

SHORTCUT:

8000 ÷ 400

Cancel the common trailing zeros.

8000 ÷ 400
80 ÷ 4 = 20

Check by multiplying.

✓2 0 × 4 00 = 8 0 00

TRY THESE IN YOUR HEAD.
Cancel the common trailing zeros.

1. 9000 ÷ 30
2. 900 ÷ 300
3. 9000 ÷ 3000
4. 800 ÷ 20
5. 1000 ÷ 50
6. 2000 ÷ 50
7. 5000 ÷ 50
8. 3600 ÷ 900
9. 10,000 ÷ 100
10. 1,000,000 ÷ 2000

Power Builder A

1. 800 ÷ 40 = ____________
2. 12,000 ÷ 600 = ____________
3. 15,000 ÷ 30 = ____________
4. 2400 ÷ 80 = ____________
5. 60) 3600 = ____________
6. 90) 72,000 = ____________
7. 400) 32,000 = ____________
8. 50) 350 = ____________
9. 800) 4800 = ____________
10. 4900 ÷ 70 = ____________
11. 600) 1200 = ____________
12. 50) 40,000 = ____________
13. 72,000 ÷ 900 = ____________
14. 800) 3200 = ____________
15. 30,000 ÷ 60 = ____________
16. 45,000 ÷ 90 = ____________
17. 500) 20,000 = ____________
18. 70) 4200 = ____________
19. 81,000 ÷ 900 = ____________
20. 45,000 ÷ 50 = ____________

THINK IT THROUGH

The state gets a tax of 10¢ for every dollar of gasoline sold. How many dollars does the state get for gasoline sales of $400,000?

Power Builder A

1. 600 ÷ 30 = ____________
2. 16,000 ÷ 400 = ____________
3. 18,000 ÷ 60 = ____________
4. 3200 ÷ 80 = ____________
5. 50) 2500 = ____________
6. 80) 6400 = ____________
7. 300) 27,000 = ____________
8. 50) 450 = ____________
9. 600) 4800 = ____________
10. 8100 ÷ 90 = ____________
11. 300) 1200 = ____________
12. 50) 30,000 = ____________
13. 56,000 ÷ 700 = ____________
14. 400) 2800 = ____________
15. 40,000 ÷ 80 = ____________
16. 54,000 ÷ 90 = ____________
17. 500) 30,000 = ____________
18. 80) 7200 = ____________
19. 63,000 ÷ 900 = ____________
20. 35,000 ÷ 50 = ____________

THINK IT THROUGH

The state gets a tax of 15¢ for every dollar of gasoline sold. How much money does the state get on gasoline sales of $600,000?

VERY EASY WARMUP – Going beyond 10,000

1. Fill in the blanks.

a) 40,000 + 2,000 + 303 + 70 + 4 = ________.

b) 70,000 +________+ 500 + 40 + 1 = 73,541.

c) ________ + 9,000 + 200 + 8 = 99,208.

2. Circle the **largest** number in each row.

a) 50,665	51,670	54,897
b) 44,431	34,436	43,341
c) 65,613	56,305	65,605
d) 98,093	98,902	89,905

3. Fill in the blanks.

a) In 8**7**,523 the digit **7** stands for ______________.

b) In **1**9,442 the digit **1** stands for ______________.

c) In 86,8**5**8 the digit **5** stands for ______________.

d) In 37,00**2** the digit **2** stands for ______________.

e) In **6**5,111 the digit **6** stands for ______________.

4. Add, and write in words:

a. 30,000 + 2,000 + 700 + 50 + 3 = ______________

b. 40,000 + 1,000 + 200 + 30 + 8 = ______________

5. Write these numbers in words

14,577 ____

85,893 ____

6. Complete the following

a. 72,834 = 70,000 + _________ + 800 + 30 + 4

b. 27,342 = _________ + 7,000 + 300 + _________ + 2

c. 91,348 = 90,000 + 1,000 + _________ + 40 + 8

d. 11,845 = _________ + 800 + 40 + 5

e. 42,803 = _________ + 803

f. 25,115 = _________ + 5,115

g. 72,349 = 72,300 + _________

h. 97,438 = 70,000 + _________

i. 18,455 = _________ + 8,000

j. 67,308 = _________ + 7,300

k. 82,425 = _________ + 2,420

l. 44,935 = _________ + 40,005

7. Fill in the blanks

a) In the number 13,1**4**5 the digit 4 stands for ___________

b) In the number **4**2,219 the digit 4 stands for___________

c) In the number 19,**4**60 the digit 4 stands for ___________

d) In the number 83,00**4** the digit 4 stands for ___________

e) In 30,241, the digit __________ is in the **hundreds place.**

f) In 40,592, the digit _________ is in the **ten thousands place.**

g) In 91,207, the digit _________ is in the **tens place.**

h) In 56,715, the digit _________ is in the **thousands place.**

i) In 19,623, the value of the digit 9 is _______________.

j) In 49,366, the value of the digit 4 is _______________.

k) In 66,721, the value of the digit 2 is _______________.

l) In 80,096, the value of the digit 8 is _______________.

m) In 28,203, the value of the digit 0 is _______________.

8. Circle the smallest number in each row.

a) 43,235 43,325 44,111

b) 71,654 17,566 17,600

c) 33,233 32,333 23,333

d) 13,453 30,452 31,525

9. Start with the number **18,181**, and answer the questions below:

a) If 40,000 were added to this number, the answer would be ___________

b) If 4,000 were added to this number, the answer would be ___________

c) If 400 were added to this number, the answer would be ___________

d) If 40 were added to this number, the answer would be ___________

e) If 4 were added to this number, the answer would be ___________

10. Start with the number **81,818**, and answer the questions below:

a) If 40,000 were removed from this number, the answer would be ________

b) If 4,000 were removed from this number, the answer would be ________

c) If 400 were removed from this number, the answer would be __________

d) If 40 were removed from this number, the answer would be ___________

e) If 4 were removed from this number, the answer would be ___________

A bit of fun:
Which does not belong and why?

11. Fill in the blanks.

a) ________________ is 10,000 more than 34,651

b) ________________ is 12,000 less than 78,155

c) ________________ is 2,000 more than 96,671

d) 65,108 + ____________________ = 69,118

e) 26,108 + ____________________ = 46,108

f) 46,108 + ____________________ = 46,109

g) 60,108 + ____________________ = 64,278

h) 16,108 + ____________________ = 19,278

I) 72,663 – ____________________ = 32,663

j) 47,663 – ____________________ = 17,563

k) 71,663 – ____________________ = 66,663

l) 57,663 – ____________________ = 27,633

m) 77,663 – ____________________ = 55,063

12. Complete these sequences.

a) 25,461, 25,561, 25,661, ________, 25,861

b) 53,450, ________, 55,450, 56,450, 57,450

c) 19,005, 29,005, ________, 49,005, 59,005

d) 99,992, 99,994, 99,996, 99,998, ________

13. Write the BIGGEST; write the smallest.

a) Write the largest 4-digit EVEN number you can make with {1, 2, 5, 8}

__________ Now write the smallest: ___________

b) Write the largest 4-digit ODD number you can make with {1, 2, 5, 8}:

__________ Now write the smallest: ___________

c) Write the largest 5-digit number you can make with {5, 2, 4, 0, 9}:

__________ Now write the smallest: ___________

d) Write the largest 5-digit EVEN number you can make with {5, 2, 4, 0, 9}:

__________ Now write the smallest: ___________

e) Write the largest 5-digit ODD number you can make with {5, 2, 4, 0, 9}:

__________ Now write the smallest: ___________

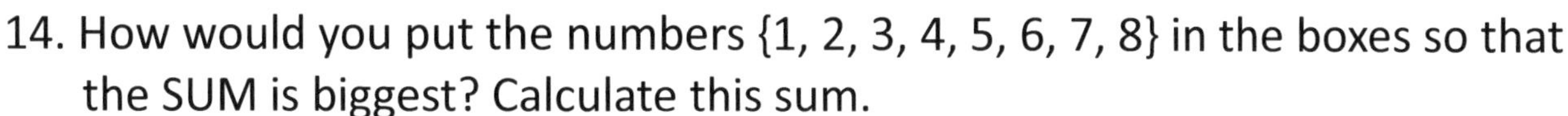

14. How would you put the numbers {1, 2, 3, 4, 5, 6, 7, 8} in the boxes so that the SUM is biggest? Calculate this sum.

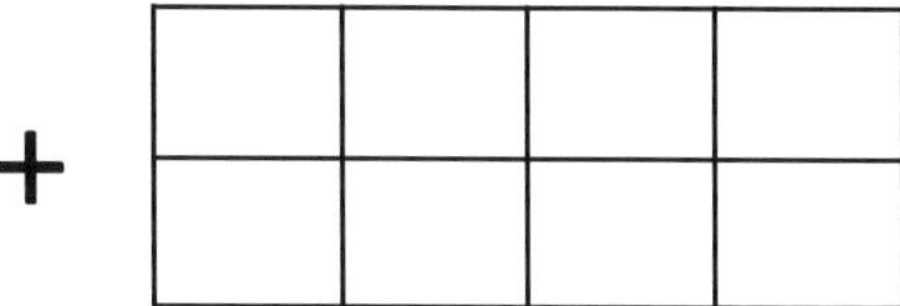

15. How would you put the numbers {1, 2, 3, 4, 5, 6, 7, 8} in the boxes so that the SUM is smallest? Calculate this sum.

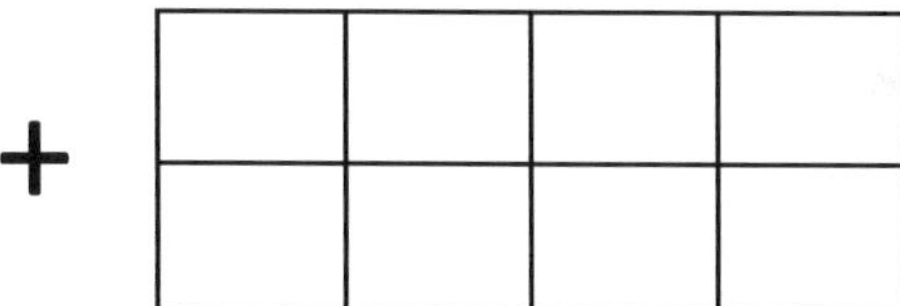

16. How would you put the numbers {1, 2, 3, 4, 5, 6, 7, 8} in the boxes so that the DIFFERENCE is the largest? Calculate this difference.

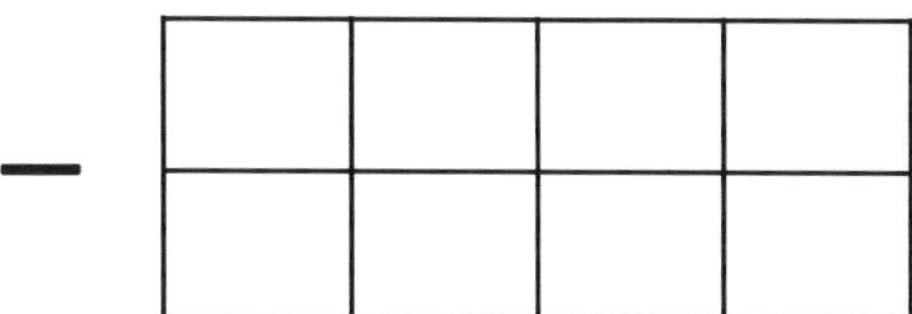

*17. How would you put the numbers {1, 2, 3, 4, 5, 6, 7, 8} in the boxes so that the DIFFERENCE is the smallest? Calculate this difference.

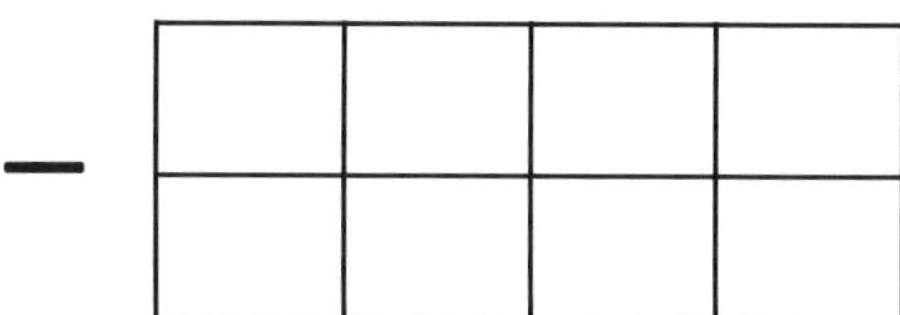

** The star beside a question means it is a little harder. That's all!*

VERY EASY WARMUP - Going beyond 10,000

18. What is the SUM of 11,222 and 22,111?

____

19. What is the DIFFERENCE between 11,222 and 22,111?

____

20. What is the PRODUCT of 11,222 and 3?

____

21. What is the PRODUCT of 11,222 and 7?

____

22. What is the QUOTIENT when 11,222 is divided by 2?

____

23. What is the QUOTIENT when 24,111 is divided by 3?

____

Almost done our VERY EASY WARMUP...

24. A hobby store has 12,124 Pokemon cards in stock, and purchases another 34,695 from one of its customers. How many cards does it have now?

25. Mr. Carlos gets paid $6,400 per month. Every Christmas his employer gives him a bonus of $3,500. How much does he earn in a year?

26. Mr. Carlos pays $2,150 every month in taxes, and in December he pays $3,300 in taxes because of the Christmas bonus he gets. How much tax does he pay during the year?

27. There are 4,645 ducks, 9,530 frogs and 73,450 fish in a lake.
    How many animals are there altogether?

    How many LEGS do all the animals have?

28. David the cat caught 3,460 mice. His brother Benji the cat caught 4 times as many. How many mice did both cats catch together?

29. At the Boston Marathon there are 38,708 men and women.
    There were 6,708 more men than women.

    How many women were running?

    What is the total number of legs of all runners?

The END of the VERY EASY WARMUP

30. Calculate MENTALLY as quickly as you can

28,367 + 9 =	32,335 + 7 =	44,169 + 80 =
28,367 + 90 =	32,335 + 70 =	44,169 + 180 =
28,367 + 900 =	32,335 + 700 =	44,169 + 3,800 =
28,367 + 9,999 =	32,335 + 7,777 =	44,169 + 1,720 =
28,367 + 21,030 =	32,335 + 44,022 =	44,169 + 12,730 =

For the tough ones below you can work with positives and negatives, going from left to right, as in this example:

$$45{,}671 - 38{,}542 = 10{,}000 - 3{,}000 + 100 + 30 - 1 = 7{,}129$$

77,843 – 30 =	32,455 – 6 =	58,934 – 4 =
77,843 – 300 =	32,455 – 60 =	58,934 – 40 =
77,843 – 3,000 =	32,455 – 600 =	58,934 – 400 =
77,843 – 3,333 =	32,455 – 6,000 =	58,934 – 4,000 =
77,843 – 21,700 =	32,455 – 6,666 =	58,934 – 14,924 =
77,843 – 18,040 =	32,455 – 12,322 =	58,934 – 19,320 =
77,843 – 29,900 =	32,455 – 18,450 =	58,934 – 27,395 =

Little mental math to keep us sharp ♯

LESSON 19 TIME AND SPEED MENTAL MATH IN DAILY LIFE

Often, when traveling by car, you may wonder how long it will take to get where you're going.

At 90 Km/h...
How much longer?

CALGARY
360 km

It's easy to figure the time in your head. Just divide the distance by your speed.

Check by multiplying.

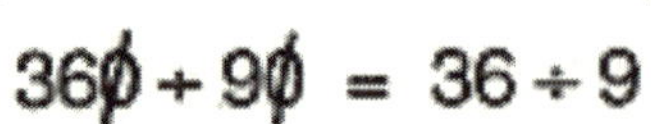

$36\not{0} \div 9\not{0} = 36 \div 9$

$= 4$ hours

✓ $4 \times 90 = 360$

You can use either kilometers or miles to measure distance and speed, as long as you don't mix them in the same problem.

50 60 70
SPEED - MPH

ST. LOUIS
180 miles

$18\not{0} \div 6\not{0} = 3$ hours

✓ $3 \times 60 = 180$

TRY THESE IN YOUR HEAD.
Calculate the travel time.

1. 60 mph, 480 mi
2. 50 mph, 450 mi
3. 60 mph, 180 mi
4. 60 mph, 600 mi
5. 50 mph, 550 mi
6. 90 km/h, 540 km
7. 100 km/h, 900 km
8. 90 km/h, 180 km
9. 100 km/h, 600 km
10. 80 km/h, 720 km

Power Builder A

1. 240 miles at 40 mph = ____________
2. 480 miles at 40 mph = ____________
3. 90 miles at 45 mph = ____________
4. 400 miles at 50 mph = ____________
5. 220 miles at 55 mph = ____________
6. 1000 miles at 50 mph = ____________
7. 700 miles at 350 mph = ____________
8. 900 miles at 450 mph = ____________
9. 2800 miles at 400 mph = ____________
10. 25,000 miles at 500 mph = ____________
11. 450 km at 90 km/h = ____________
12. 320 km at 80 km/h = ____________
13. 350 km at 70 km/h = ____________
14. 240 km at 80 km/h = ____________
15. 360 km at 90 km/h = ____________
16. 4000 km at 800 km/h = ____________
17. 1500 km at 750 km/h = ____________
18. 2700 km at 900 km/h = ____________
19. 4900 km at 700 km/h = ____________
20. 45,000 km at 500 km/h = ____________

THINK IT THROUGH

If you have seven $50 bills, six $20 bills, five $10 bills, and four $1 bills, how much money do you have?

LESSON 19 MENTAL MATH IN DAILY LIFE: TIME AND SPEED

Power Builder A

1. 300 miles at 50 mph = ____________
2. 180 miles at 60 mph = ____________
3. 160 miles at 40 mph = ____________
4. 600 miles at 50 mph = ____________
5. 240 miles at 60 mph = ____________
6. 1500 miles at 50 mph = ____________
7. 450 miles at 150 mph = ____________
8. 1200 miles at 400 mph = ____________
9. 25,000 miles at 500 mph = ____________
10. 26,000 miles at 130 mph = ____________
11. 360 km at 90 km/h = ____________
12. 400 km at 80 km/h = ____________
13. 420 km at 70 km /h = ____________
14. 480 km at 80 km/h = ____________
15. 540 km at 90 km/h = ____________
16. 2400 km at 800 km/h = ____________
17. 2100 km at 700 km/h = ____________
18. 3600 km at 900 km/h = ____________
19. 5600 km at 800 km/h = ____________
20. 35,000 km at 700 km/h = ____________

THINK IT THROUGH

If you have five $50 bills, four $20 bills, three $10 bills, two $5 bills, and one $1 bill, how much money do you have?

We ROUND numbers in order to make them easier to work with. When rounding we give up a little bit of accuracy, but in turn get an estimate for the rounded number that is easier to work with.
Numbers that end in 0, 00, 000, etc., are easier to work with, so we round to them.

For example, in trying to estimate 387 x 21, we may round the 387 to 400, and the 21 to 20, and instead getting the exact answer, we estimate it by calculating 20 x 400 = 8,000, which is pretty close.
ROUNDING and ESTIMATING go hand-in-hand.

Rounding a number to the nearest 10 means selecting the number that is closest to it that is on the "count by 10" list
(a number that ends with AT LEAST one zero).

See examples →

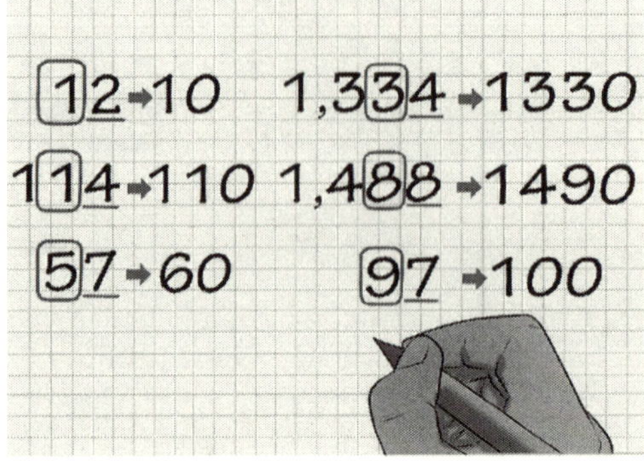

Rounding a number to the nearest 100 means selecting the number that is closest to it that is on the "count by 100" list
(a number that ends with AT LEAST two zeros).

See examples →

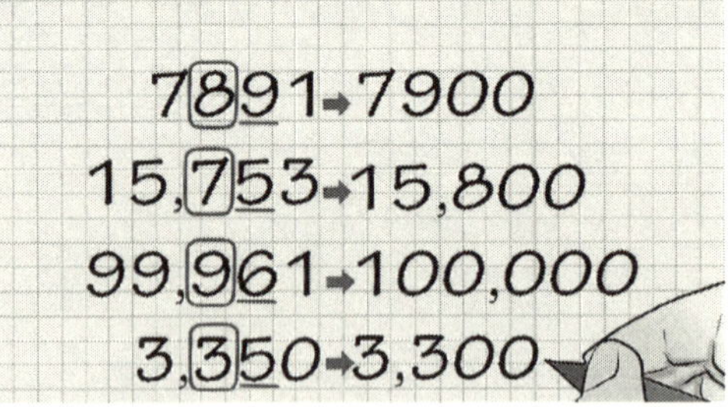

Rounding a number to the nearest 1000 means selecting the number that is closest to it that is on the "count by 1000" list
(a number that ends with AT LEAST three zeros).

See examples →

8,800 → 9,000
1,015 → 1,000
12,450 → 12,000
333,878 → 334,000

There are two small mistakes on this page. Can you find them?

Rounding

And now that we have seen so many examples, let us do some ourselves. REMEMBER that the "5" is always rounded UP. For example, 65 rounded to the nearest 10 is 70, and not 60, even though it is exactly between the 60 and the 70.

Round to the nearest	10	100	1,000	10,000
Example 1: 12,347	12,350	12,300	12,000	10,000
Example 2: 39,855	39,860	39,900	40,000	40,000
Now you do the rounding				
23,456				
75,555				
7,789				
14,241				
81,188				
96,919				
22,222				
34,567				
182				
35,000				
1,617				
19,995				
44,444				
55,555				
99,999				

1) Round 314 to the nearest hundred.
2) Round 4,843 to the nearest hundred.
3) Round 67,545 to the nearest ten.
4) Round 43,050 to the nearest ten.
5) Round 7,888 to the nearest thousand.
6) Round 524,548 to the nearest thousand.
7) Round 256,804 to the nearest hundred thousand.
8) Round 9,984 to the nearest hundred.
9) Round 404,869 to the nearest ten.
10) Round 215,328 to the nearest thousand.
11) Round 83,295 to the nearest ten thousand.
12) Round 422 to the nearest ten.
13) Round 88,257 to the nearest thousand.
14) Round 2,796 to the nearest ten.
15) Round 637,900 to the nearest thousand.
16) Round 753 to the nearest ten.
17) Round 4,706 to the nearest hundred.
18) Round 770 to the nearest hundred.
19) Round 212 to the nearest ten.
20) Round 92,240 to the nearest ten thousand.

1. ________
2. ________
3. ________
4. ________
5. ________
6. ________
7. ________
8. ________
9. ________
10. ________
11. ________
12. ________
13. ________
14. ________
15. ________
16. ________
17. ________
18. ________
19. ________
20. ________

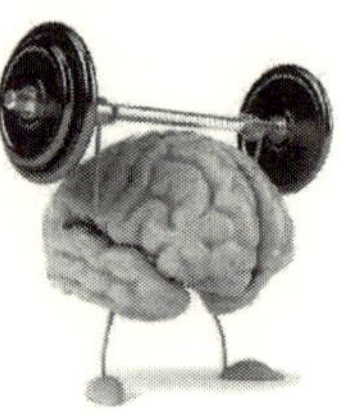

Use any of the four basic operations mathematical signs (+,×,÷,−, and brackets) between the digits to get 100.

1 2 7 5 4 2

1) Which choice(s) when rounded to the nearest ten will result in 40?

A. 27
B. 41
C. 35
D. 33

2) Which choice(s) when rounded to the nearest ten will result in 650?

A. 661
B. 638
C. 653
D. 655

3) Which choice(s) when rounded to the nearest ten thousand will result in 40,000?

A. 42,000
B. 33,000
C. 32,000
D. 48,000

4) Which choice(s) when rounded to the nearest thousand will result in 4,000?

A. 4,160
B. 3,623
C. 3,171
D. 2,744

5) Which choice(s) when rounded to the nearest thousand will result in 46,000?

A. 46,200
B. 45,200
C. 45,300
D. 46,900

6) Which choice(s) when rounded to the nearest hundred thousand will result in 7,400,000?

A. 7,462,414
B. 7,425,436
C. 7,374,322
D. 7,436,655

7) Which choice(s) when rounded to the nearest hundred thousand will result in 7,700,000?

A. 7,734,418
B. 7,784,489
C. 7,616,483
D. 7,667,914

8) Which choice(s) when rounded to the nearest hundred will result in 97,800?

A. 97,820
B. 97,914
C. 97,683
D. 97,726

9) Which choice(s) when rounded to the nearest ten thousand will result in 60,000?

A. 62,287
B. 68,499
C. 52,119
D. 50,772

10) Which choice(s) when rounded to the nearest thousand will result in 35,000?

A. 36,197
B. 35,149
C. 34,625
D. 35,297

11) Which choice(s) when rounded to the nearest hundred will result in 900?

A. 766
B. 955
C. 1,026
D. 917

12) Which choice(s) when rounded to the nearest hundred will result in 26,700?

A. 26,790
B. 26,710
C. 26,560
D. 26,650

A. Use reasonable rounding and estimate

Example: 84,367 ÷ 5,038 ≅ 85,000 ÷ 5,000 = 85 ÷ 5 = 17

1. 2,836 ÷ 991 ≅ ____________________
2. 26,367 + 9,089 ≅ ____________________
3. 8,359 × 7 ≅ ____________________
4. 28,367 − 9,766 ≅ ____________________
5. 28,367 ÷ 3,038 ≅ ____________________
6. 32,935 + 17,888 ≅ ____________________
7. 1,335 × 69 ≅ ____________________
8. 32,335 − 17,800 ≅ ____________________
9. 2,335 × 32 ≅ ____________________
10. 32,335 ÷ 1,536 ≅ ____________________

B. What number am I?

1. I am the **smallest** number that when rounded to the nearest 10, you get 160. What number am I? ____________
2. I am the **biggest** number that when rounded to the nearest 10, you get 160. What number am I? ____________
3. When you round me to the nearest 10 or to the nearest 100, you get the same answer. What number could I be? ____________
4. When you round me to the nearest 10 or to the nearest 1000, you get the same answer. What number could I be? ____________

A little mental math to keep us sharp ♯

LESSON 14 TACK ON TRAILING ZEROS

Notice what happens when one factor is multiplied by 10 . . . The product is also multiplied by 10.

$$5 \times 3 = 15 \quad \xrightarrow{\times 10} \quad 50 \times 3 = 150$$

You can use that idea to multiply numbers with trailing zeros.

For each time that a factor is multiplied by 10, tack another trailing zero onto the product.

5 × 3	50 × 3	50 × 30	500 × 30	500 × 300
15	150	1500	15000	150000

Remember these steps:

- Remove the trailing zeros.
- Multiply the remaining numbers.
- Tack on **ALL** the zeros.

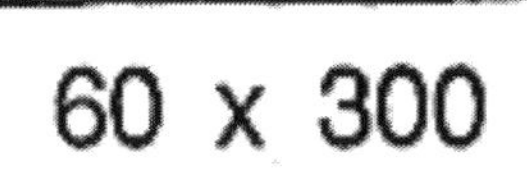

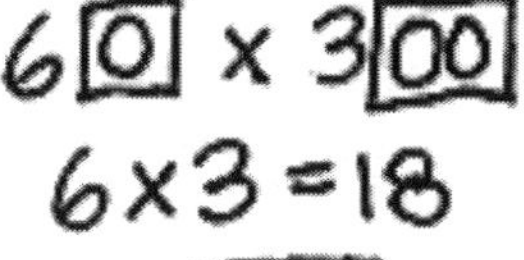

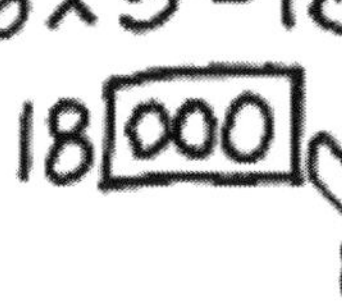

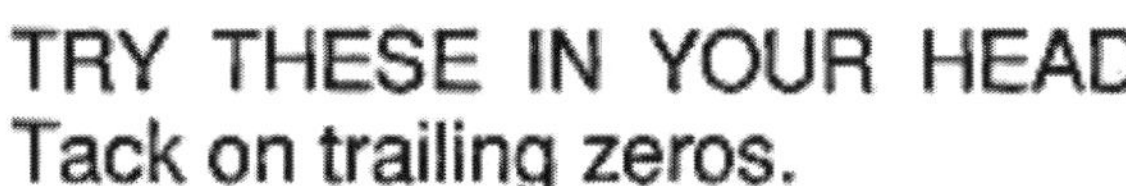

TRY THESE IN YOUR HEAD.
Tack on trailing zeros.

1. 4 x 20
2. 4 x 50
3. 50 x 20
4. 50 x 50
5. 300 x 9
6. 7 x 800
7. 90 x 30
8. 5 x 8000
9. 30 x 500
10. 200 x 300

POWER BUILDER A

1. 7 x 30 = ______
2. 8 x 60 = ______
3. 9 x 20 = ______
4. 5 x 40 = ______
5. 500 x 9 = ______
6. 300 x 8 = ______
7. 5 x 800 = ______
8. 30 x 200 = ______
9. 400 x 60 = ______
10. 70 x 500 = ______
11. 50 x 600 = ______
12. 300 x 50 = ______
13. 90 x 200 = ______
14. 7 x 8000 = ______
15. 50 x 6000 = ______
16. 800 x 700 = ______
17. 900 x 500 = ______
18. 7000 x 60 = ______
19. 300 x 700 = ______
20. 50 x 8000 = ______

THINK IT THROUGH

List all the different products that can be formed by multiplying any two numbers on this card.

40	30
60	20

MENTAL MATH IN JUNIOR HIGH — LESSON 14 TACK ON TRAILING ZEROS

POWER BUILDER B

1. 6 x 40 = ______
2. 7 x 50 = ______
3. 8 x 30 = ______
4. 5 x 60 = ______
5. 500 x 7 = ______
6. 300 x 6 = ______
7. 5 x 400 = ______
8. 20 x 400 = ______
9. 600 x 40 = ______
10. 500 x 90 = ______
11. 50 x 200 = ______
12. 500 x 50 = ______
13. 70 x 400 = ______
14. 3 x 600 = ______
15. 50 x 8000 = ______
16. 600 x 300 = ______
17. 800 x 500 = ______
18. 8000 x 60 = ______
19. 200 x 600 = ______
20. 50 x 4000 = ______

THINK IT THROUGH

List all the different products that can be formed by multiplying any two numbers on this card.

800	30
600	40

LESSON 15 FRONT-END MULTIPLICATION

$$\begin{array}{r} 524 \\ \times\ 3 \\ \hline \end{array}$$

Multiplying in your head is easier if you break a number into parts and multiply the front-end numbers first.

- Break up 524.
- Multiply from the front to the back . . .
- Add as you go along.

500 + 20 + 4

MENTAL MATH TIP

Focus on the left (front-end) digits by covering the others.

TRY THESE IN YOUR HEAD.
Multiply from the front.

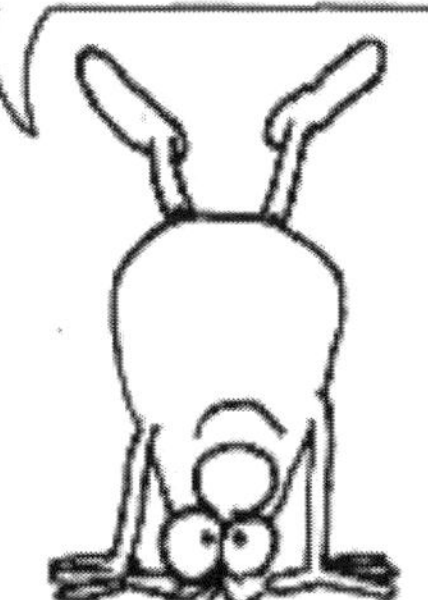

1. 4 x 55
2. 4 x 76
3. 45 x 6
4. 8 x 25
5. 4 x 625
6. 405 x 3
7. 2 x 545
8. 8 x 625
9. 450 x 5
10. 3 x 235

POWER BUILDER A

1. 6 x 28 = ______
2. 5 x 82 = ______
3. 7 x 36 = ______
4. 5 x 66 = ______
5. 4 x 84 = ______
6. 6 x 45 = ______
7. 8 x 53 = ______
8. 9 x 72 = ______
9. 4 x 126 = ______
10. 4 x 325 = ______
11. 5 x 218 = ______
12. 2 x 849 = ______
13. 6 x 55 = ______
14. 3 x 428 = ______
15. 7 x 450 = ______
16. 4 x 825 = ______
17. 5 x 315 = ______
18. 3 x 675 = ______
19. 4 x 925 = ______
20. 6 x 215 = ______

THINK IT THROUGH

Look at the number sentences in the box. Find a pattern and use it to mentally calculate 15 x 37 and 21 x 37.

3 x 37 = 111
6 x 37 = 222
9 x 37 = 333
12 x 37 = 444

MENTAL MATH IN JUNIOR HIGH

POWER BUILDER B

1. 7 x 27 = ______
2. 5 x 62 = ______
3. 8 x 46 = ______
4. 10 × 33 = ______
5. 8 × 42 = ______
6. 15 × 18 = ______
7. 4 × 106 = ______
8. 6 × 108 = ______
9. 3 x 126 = ______
10. 4 x 625 = ______
11. 5 x 219 = ______
12. 6 × 283 = ______
13. 10 × 26 = ______
14. 6 × 214 = ______
15. 9 × 350 = ______
16. 5 × 660 = ______
17. 9 × 175 = ______
18. 9 × 225 = ______
19. 8 x 525 = ______
20. 5 x 319 = ______

THINK IT THROUGH

Look at the number sentences in the box. Find a pattern and use it to mentally calculate 28 x 15,873 and 42 x 15,873.

7 x 15,873 = 111,111
14 x 15,873 = 222,222
21 x 15,873 = 333,333

Practicing LONG Multiplication: 4 by 1
First write down your ESTIMATE, and only then solve.

Example:

My estimate is 4000x4=16,000

	4	1	0	2
			×	4
1	6	4	0	8

Row	Problem 1	Problem 2	Problem 3	Problem 4
1	4102 × 4 = 16408	4813 × 7	6412 × 3	7555 × 2
2	8867 × 7	5954 × 4	4658 × 2	2337 × 8
3	9037 × 3	3705 × 3	4779 × 8	5922 × 2
4	8554 × 4	5918 × 6	2773 × 2	8011 × 8
5	5955 × 8	2261 × 2	4208 × 9	6864 × 6
6	6963 × 9	7150 × 6	7905 × 2	2478 × 8

Practicing LONG Multiplication: 3 by 2

First write down your ESTIMATE, and only then solve.

Example:

My estimate is 15x140=2100

		1		
		1	4	1
		×	1	4
		5	6	4
	1	4	1	0
	1	9	7	4

Problems:

- 188 × 10
- 466 × 27
- 874 × 67
- 169 × 52
- 660 × 11
- 547 × 15
- 874 × 35
- 431 × 26
- 897 × 24
- 710 × 17
- 335 × 15
- 801 × 62
- 811 × 44
- 156 × 27
- 706 × 78

Practicing LONG Multiplication: 3 by 3
First write down your ESTIMATE, and only then solve.

Example:

My estimate is 550x300=165,000

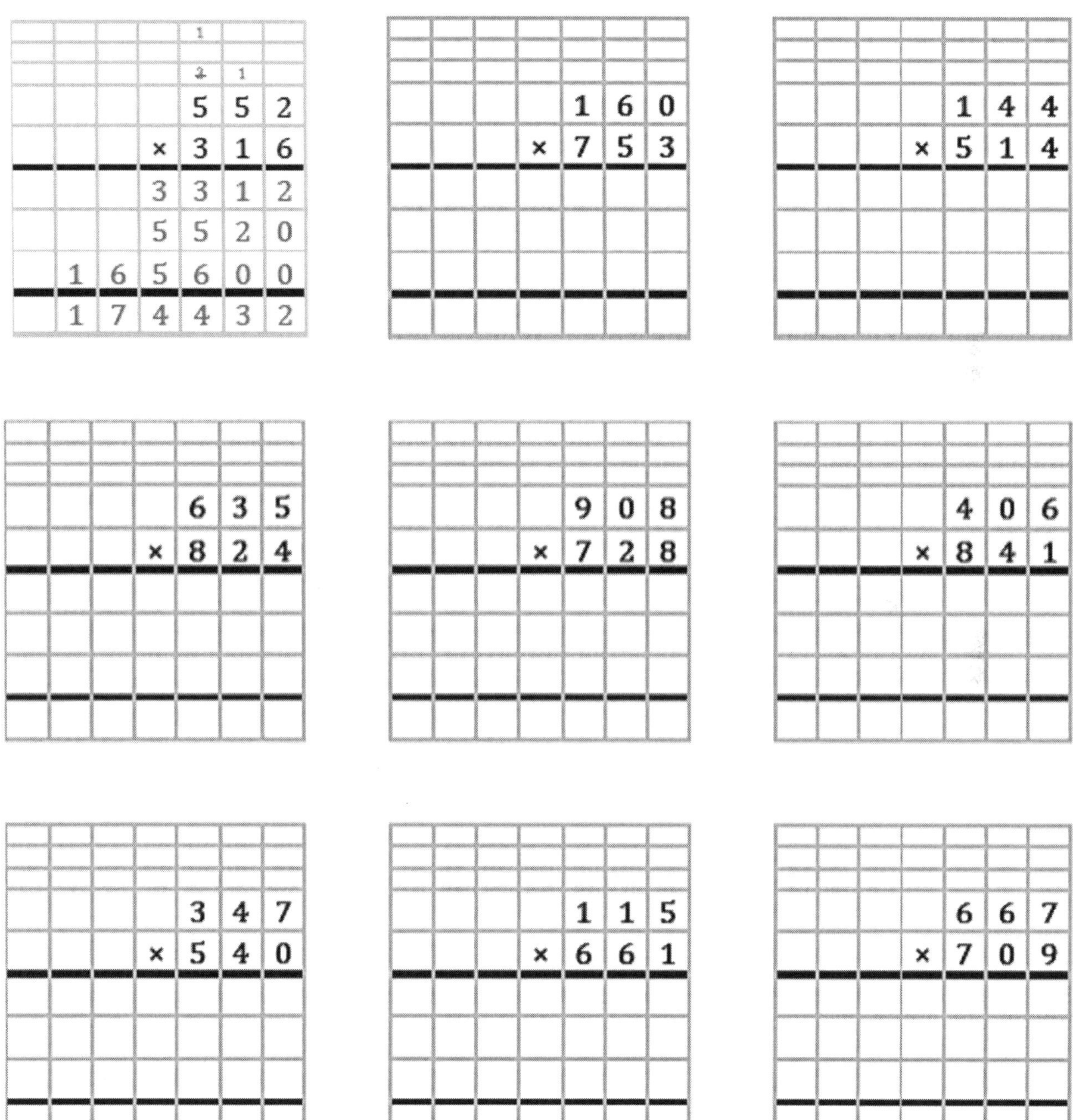

We have practiced division both by breaking the big number into pieces, dividing piece by piece, and also by using LONG DIVISION. Let us do 4038 divided by 6 as an example.

If we do it piece by piece, we may break the 4038 to 3600+420+18, because all three pieces are easy to divide by 6. Then we would say "6 goes 600 times into 3600, 70 times into 420, and 3 times into 18, so the final answer is 673".

LONG division looks like this →

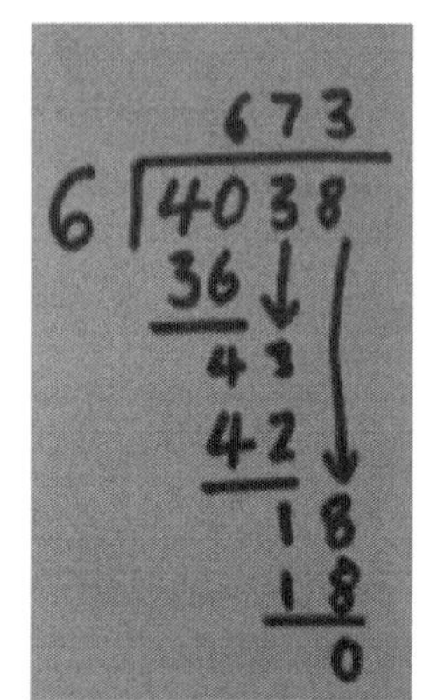

We all know it is quite LONG, and has many steps.
It can be shortened greatly by eliminating all the subtractions and carrying the remainder instead. For instance, we first ask "how many 6s go into 40?" The answer is 6 with remainder 4.
Instead of subtracting 36 from 40, we can carry the remainder and attach it to the next digit. We keep doing it as we go along.

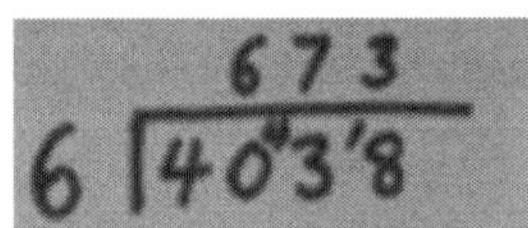

← SHORT division takes a lot less writing

Here we would start by saying: 6 goes into 40 six times with remainder 4, so we write the 6 above the 0 of the 40, and attach the remainder to the next digit to get 43, which is exactly what we got when we did long division. Then we ask how many 6s go into 43. The answer is 7R1, so we write down the 7 above the 3 of the 43, and carry the remainder to the next digit to get 18. Finally we ask how many 6s go into 18. The answer is 3 remainder 0, so we write down the 3 above the 8 and we are done.

It is important to understand that **LONG division and SHORT division are the exact same thing.** The only difference is that in short division we skip the subtraction step for calculating the remainders. We instead calculate them in our heads.

Look at this next example of short division→
5 goes into 8 once, remainder 3, so write the 1 and carry the 3.
5 goes into 34 six times with remainder 4, so write down the 6 and carry the 4. Finally 5 goes into 47 9R2 times, so write the 9, and keep the 2 as the final remainder. The answer is 169 remainder 2.

Practice SHORT Division
First write down your ESTIMATE, and only then solve.

$5\overline{)642}$	$4\overline{)3441}$	$3\overline{)1081}$	$5\overline{)862}$
$9\overline{)5197}$	$6\overline{)4917}$	$9\overline{)3831}$	$4\overline{)2839}$
$2\overline{)347}$	$5\overline{)2298}$	$8\overline{)4836}$	$4\overline{)571}$
$6\overline{)5396}$	$3\overline{)2444}$	$2\overline{)751}$	$2\overline{)1973}$
$8\overline{)1619}$	$7\overline{)3295}$	$8\overline{)1621}$	$9\overline{)4469}$

Use SHORT Division for all the EVEN questions
Use LONG Division for all the ODD questions
Which method do you like more?

(1)
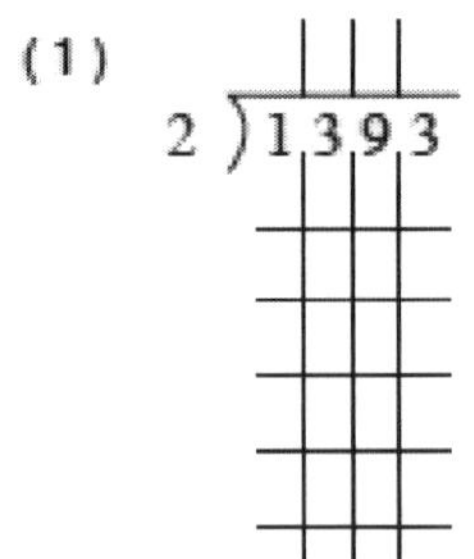

(2)
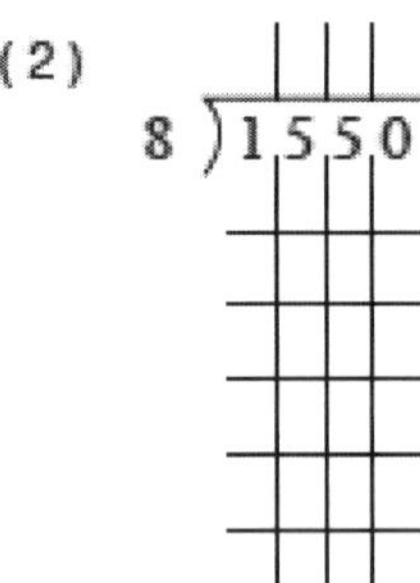

(3)
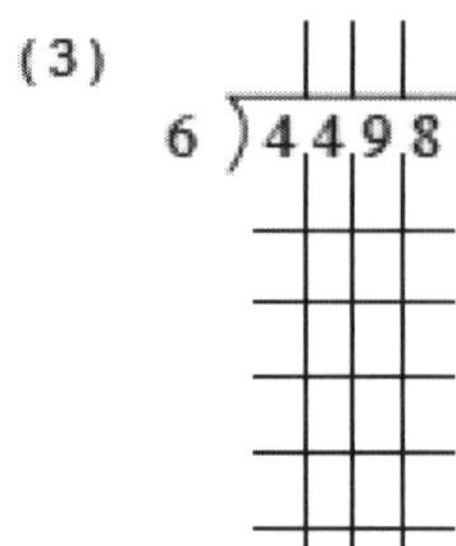

(4) 9) 2,5,9,0

(5) 7) 2,8,8,6

(6) 3) 2,9,9,5

(7) 4) 2,9,5,0

(8)
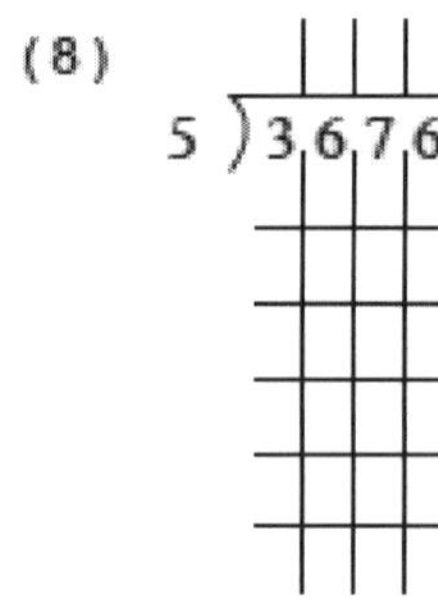

(9) 2) 1,5,7,9

(10) 9) 6,8,1,7

(11) 8) 7,6,6,9

(12) 3) 1,8,3,4

(13) 4) 3,4,1,8

(14) 7) 1,9,0,0

(15) 5) 2,6,2,7

(16) 6) 2,3,7,7

For each question use either SHORT or LONG Division.
Your choice.

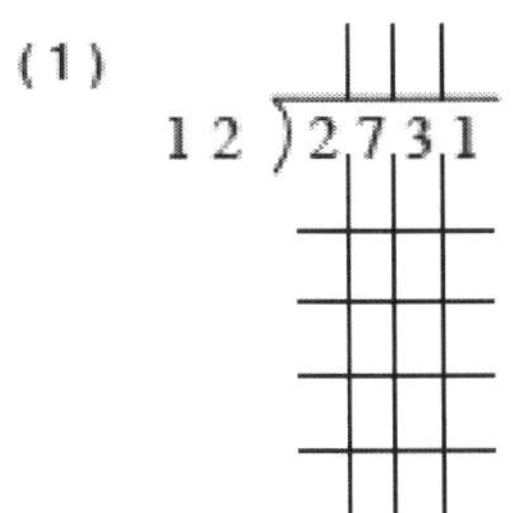

(1) 12) 2731

(2) 13) 3247

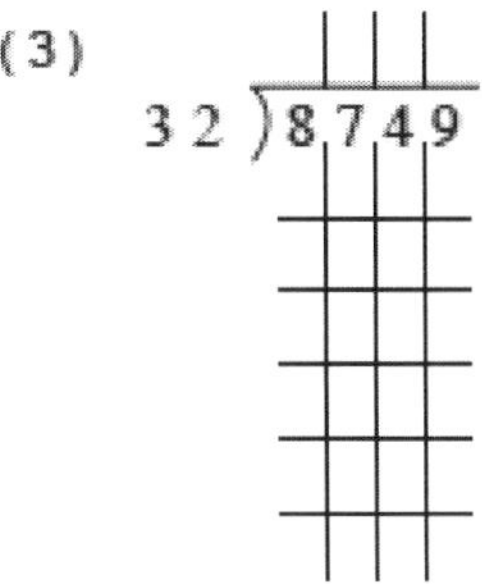

(3) 32) 8749

(4) 11) 6128

(5) 41) 6279

(6) 21) 4680

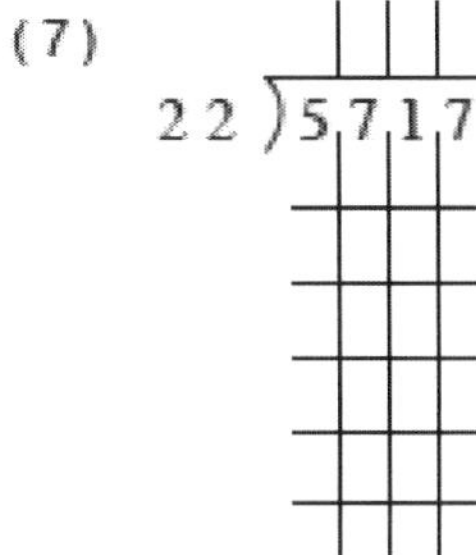

(7) 22) 5717

(8) 33) 5672

(9) 42) 5926

(10) 43) 9601

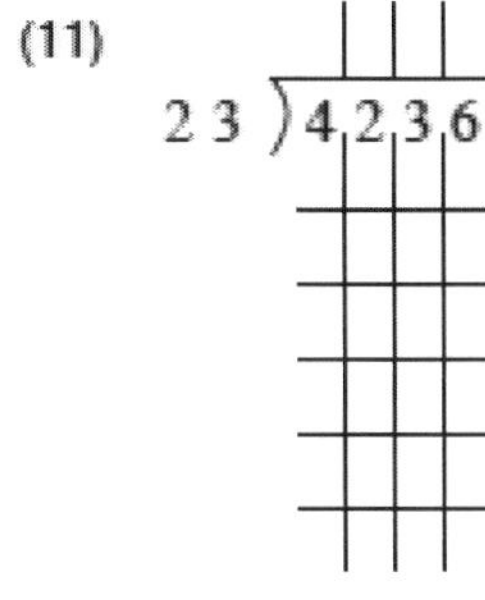

(11) 23) 4236

(12) 31) 5147

(13) 22) 3919

(14) 32) 6913

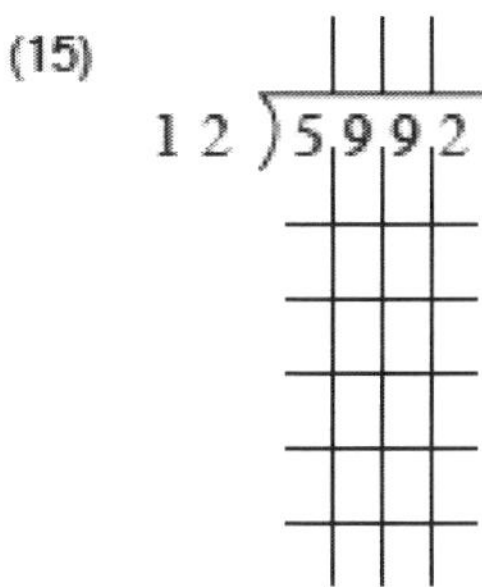

(15) 12) 5992

(16) 33) 5492

DIVISIBILITY

We say that "A is **DIVISIBLE** by B" if B divides A without a remainder. In other words, if A÷B is a whole number, then A is divisible by B.

Examples:

- 6 is divisible by 2 because $6 \div 2 = 3$ without any remainder.
- 7 is NOT divisible by 2 because $7 \div 2 = 3$ with a remainder of 1.
- 15 is NOT divisible by 4, but 16 and 20 are.
- 2 is NOT divisible by 6 because 6 does not go into 2.

If A is divisible by B, then we say that B is a FACTOR, or a DIVISOR of A.

Examples:

- 10 is divisible by 1, 2, 5 and 10, so 10 has 4 factors (or 4 divisors)
- 3 is a divisor (or factor) of 15, but 15 is NOT a divisor of 3 (common mistake)
- The number 1 is a divisor (or factor) of any number
- Any number is divisor (or factor) of itself: for instance, 6 is a factor of 6

TRUE OR FALSE?

- 2 is a factor of 10 ____________________
- 3 is a factor of 20 ____________________
- 1 is a factor of 15 ____________________
- 6 is a divisor of 3 ____________________
- 70 is divisible by 7 ____________________
- The smallest factor of every number is 1 ____________________
- 24 is divisible by 8 ____________________
- The largest factor of every number is itself ____________________
- 44 is divisible by 12 ____________________
- A number cannot have an odd number of factors ____________________

Prime Numbers and Snakes

Let's try making all rectangles with an area of 6.

Here is the first one, the 1×6 "snake":

The next one is of course a 2×3 rectangle:

NOTE: We do not consider a rotation of a rectangle to be a new one. For example, we say that "two rows of three" and "three rows of two" are the same rectangle.

Now try to find all different rectangles we can build with an area of 16:

We start with the 1×16 "snake":

but there is also the 2×8 rectangle:

and the 4×4 square:

Remember that a square is a rectangle as well. It is a rectangle with 4 equal sides.

Next we will find all rectangles with an area of 7:

The first one, and the ONLY one, is the 1×7 "snake":

This is because 7 is a **PRIME NUMBER.** A prime number is a number that can only be drawn as a snake. There are no other rectangles for 7 because the only numbers that divide nicely into 7 are 1 and 7. **You can think of prime numbers as numbers that have exactly 2 divisors: 1 and themselves.**

- Can you find all the primes that are less than 10? ______________________
- Is 17 a prime number? How do you know? ____________________

____

- Is 30 a prime number? How do you know? ____________________

____

Looking for Primes

Example: Draw all rectangles with area of 12:

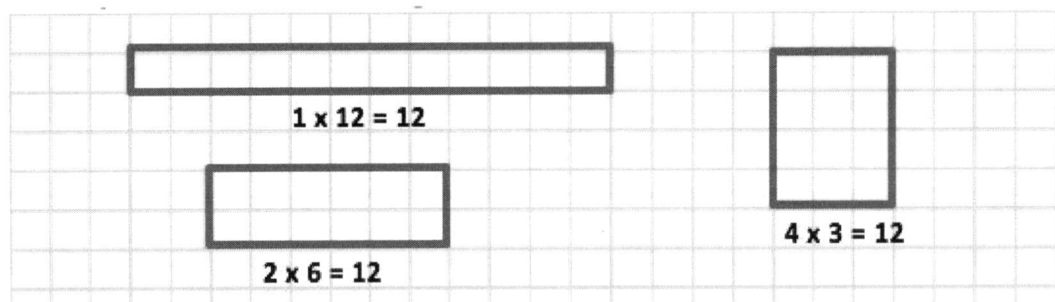

So 12 is clearly NOT a prime, because it can be divided by 1, 2, 3, 4, 6 and 12.

Exercise 1: Draw and colour all rectangles with areas of 2 (Red), 3 (Blue), 4 (Green), 5 (Yellow) and 8 (Orange). Write the area inside each shape. Put a * beside each snake number.

Exercise 2: Draw and colour all rectangles with areas of 9 (Red), 10 (Blue), and 11 (Green). Write the area inside each shape. Put a * beside each snake number.

Looking for Primes

Exercise 3: Draw and colour all rectangles with areas of 13 (Red), 14 (Blue) and 15 (Green). Write the area inside each shape. Put a * beside each snake number.

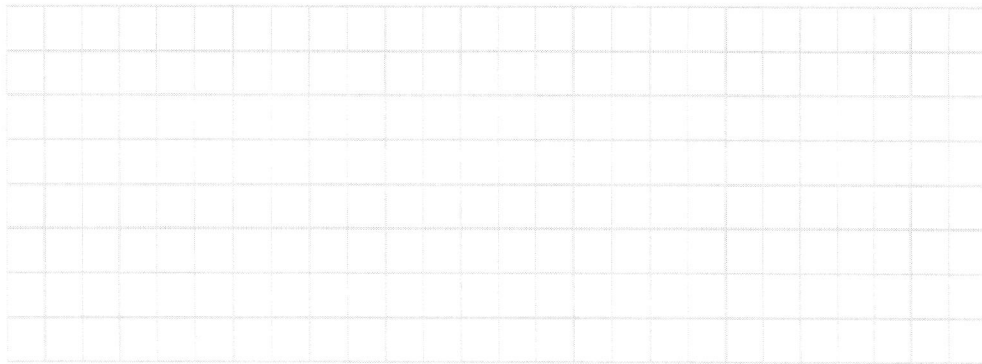

Exercise 4: Draw and colour all rectangles with areas of 17 (Red) and 18 (Blue). Write the area inside each shape. Put a * beside each snake number.

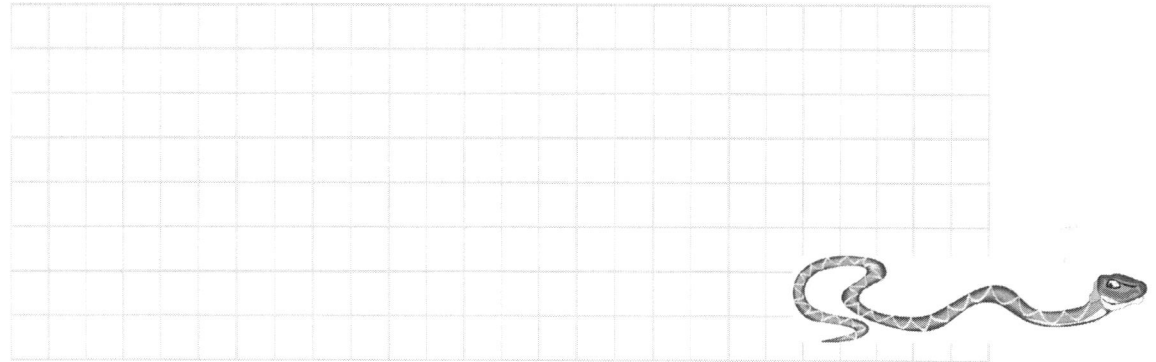

Exercise 5: Draw and colour all rectangles with areas of 19 (Yellow) and 20 (Green). Write the area inside each shape. Put a * beside each snake number.

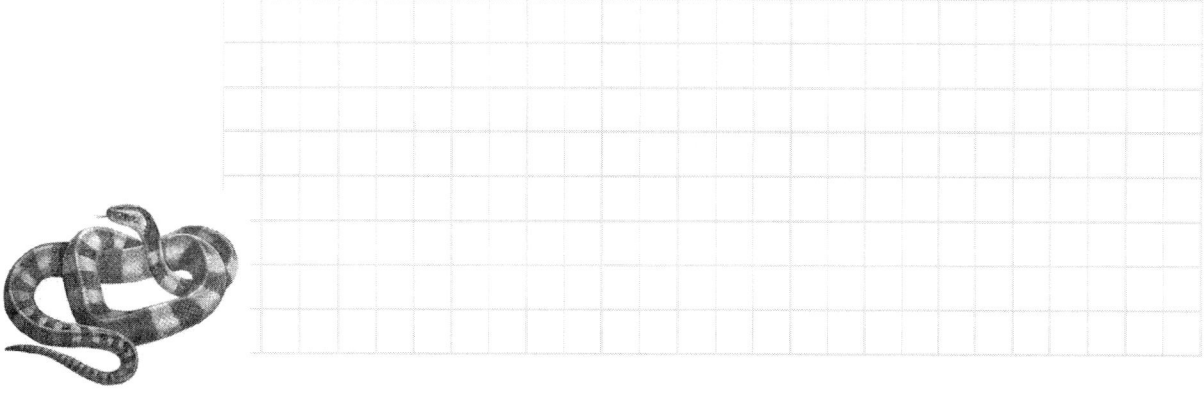

PRIME NUMBERS from 1-20

A PRIME NUMBER is a number that has EXACTLY TWO divisors: 1 and itself.
The number 1 is NOT a prime (think why!) The smallest prime number is 2.
2 is also the ONLY EVEN prime; all other prime numbers are odd (think why!)

Number	Divisors	How many?	Prime?	Prime factorization
1	1	1	✗	
2	1,2	2	✓	
3	1,3	2	✓	
4	1,2,4	3	✗	2×2
5				
6				
7				
8				
9				
10				
11				
12	1,2,3,4,6,12	6	✗	2×2×3
13				
14				
15				
16				
17				
18				
19				
20				

KNOW BY HEART the prime factorization of the numbers from 2 to 20, and most importantly: KNOW which ones are PRIMES. Prime numbers are incredibly important. They are the building blocks, the "atoms" of our number system. Every whole number greater than 1 is either a prime, or can be written as a product of primes. Here is the prime factorization from 2 to 20:

2, 3, 2x2, **5,** 2x3, **7,** 2x2x2, 3x3, 2x5, **11,** 2x2x3, **13,** 2x7, 3x5, 2x2x2x2, **17,** 2x3x3, **19,** 2x2x5

THINK: 1. Can you think of 2 prime numbers that add up to 24? Find all pairs.

____

2. Can you think of 2 prime numbers that add up to 25? Find all pairs.

____

PRIME NUMBERS from 21-40

Let's keep going and discover PRIMES that are a little bigger than 20

Number	Divisors	How many?	Prime?	Prime factorization
21				
22				
23				
24				
25				
26				
27				
28				
29				
30				
31				
32	1,2,4,8,16,32	6	✗	2×2×2×2×2
33				
34				
35				
36				
37				
38				
39				
40				

A number that is not a prime is called a **COMPOSITE** number.
Each of the counting numbers 1, 2, 3... is either a prime or a composite except the number 1.
The number 1 is a little strange: it is not a prime and not a composite.

INVESTIGATION: 1. What numbers between 1 and 40 have an ODD number of factors?

___

2. Do you observe a pattern? Can you explain it?

___

___

3. How many numbers between 1 and 100 have an odd number of divisors?

___

PRIME NUMBERS from 41-60

Let's keep going and discover PRIMES that are a little bigger than 40.
In order to make your life easier as you get into bigger numbers, observe that:
FACTORS COME IN PAIRS!

Example: The Factors of 60.

The smallest factor of 60 is 1, which means that 1 times *something* is 60, that *something* is of course 60, so we have our first pair: 1 and 60. The next factor is 2. Ask 2 × ? =60. The answer is 30, so we get our next pair: 2 and 30. The best way to get them all is to use this "Rainbow Method": first and last, second and second last and so on, until you get them all. This way we do not miss out on any of them.

Number	Divisors	How many?	Prime?	Prime factorization
41				
42				
43				
44				
45				
46				
47				
48				
49				
50				
51				
52	1,2,4,13,26,52	6	✗	2×2×13
53				
54				
55				
56				
57				
58				
59				
60				

Brainteaser

What comes NEXT? **5, 6, 10, 19, 35, ?**

FACTORING TREES

Factoring trees are excellent for finding the prime factorization of larger numbers.

Example 1: Prime factorization of 42

These are two possible factoring trees for factoring the number 42. The tree helps us keep track of the factors as we go along. NOTE that there is more than one way to create the tree, but no matter if you start with 2 × 21 or with 6 × 7, the final result will be the same: 42 = **2 × 3 × 7**

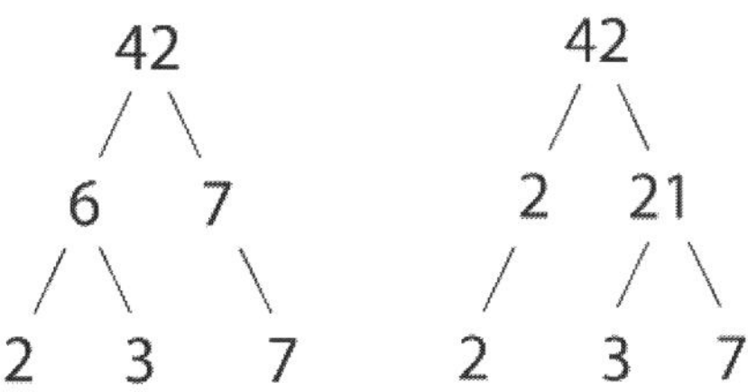

Example 2: Prime factorization of 108

Here are three possible factoring trees for factoring the number 108. All of them will, at the end, give the same answer: 108 = **2 × 2 × 3 × 3 × 3.** As you make up the tree, it is a good habit to circle the primes as you go, so you can find them easily when you write the prime factored form.

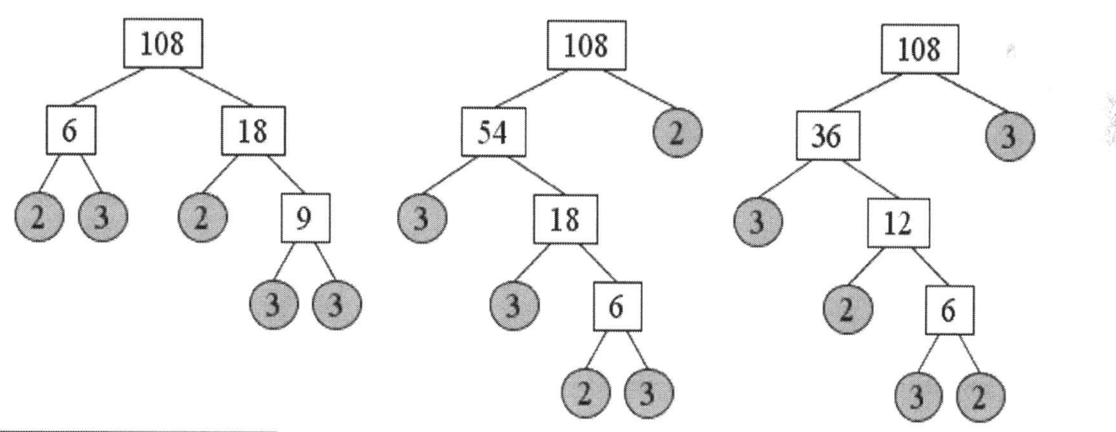

Another Brainteaser (with TREES)

When Donald Duck died, he left his 4 daughters the plot of land on the left and the 4 trees. He told them they must divide it in a way that all 4 pieces have the same shape, and each daughter gets a tree. How can they do it?

FACTORING TREES

A. Now do a few on your own. Under each tree write the prime factored form of the number on top of the tree.

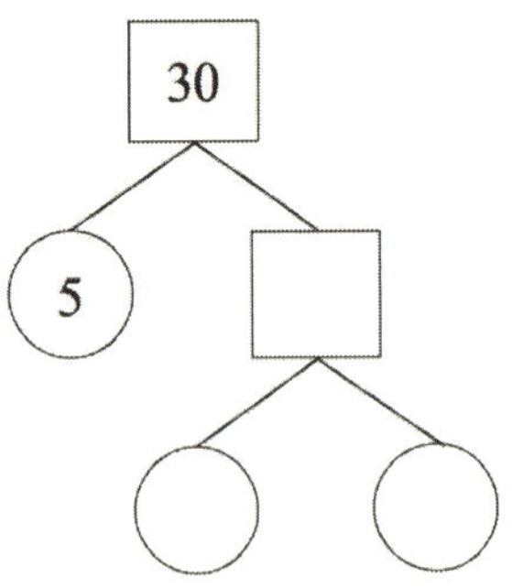

81

9

Factored form: 30 = __________ 81 = __________

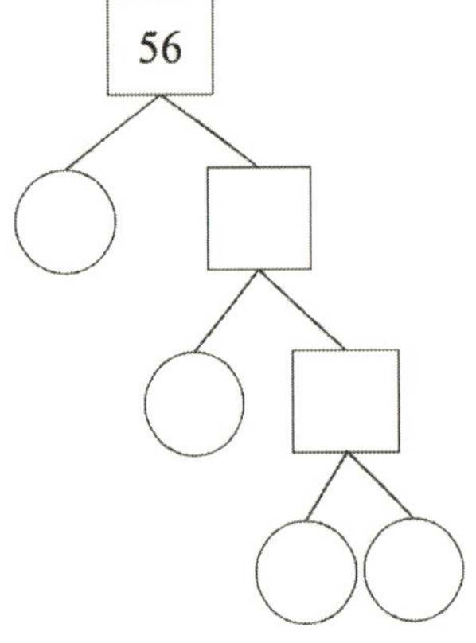

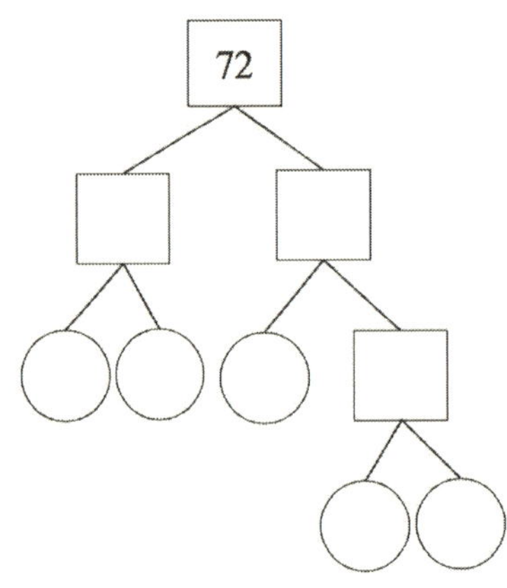

Factored form: 56 = __________ 72 = __________

Another Brainteaser with TREES

How many animals can you spot hiding in the trees? Do not factor them...

FACTORING TREES

B. Construct factoring trees for the following numbers, and write under each tree the factored form of each number.

1. **280**
2. **216**
3. **1,000**

C. Complete these factoring trees and write beside or under each tree the correct prime factorized form.

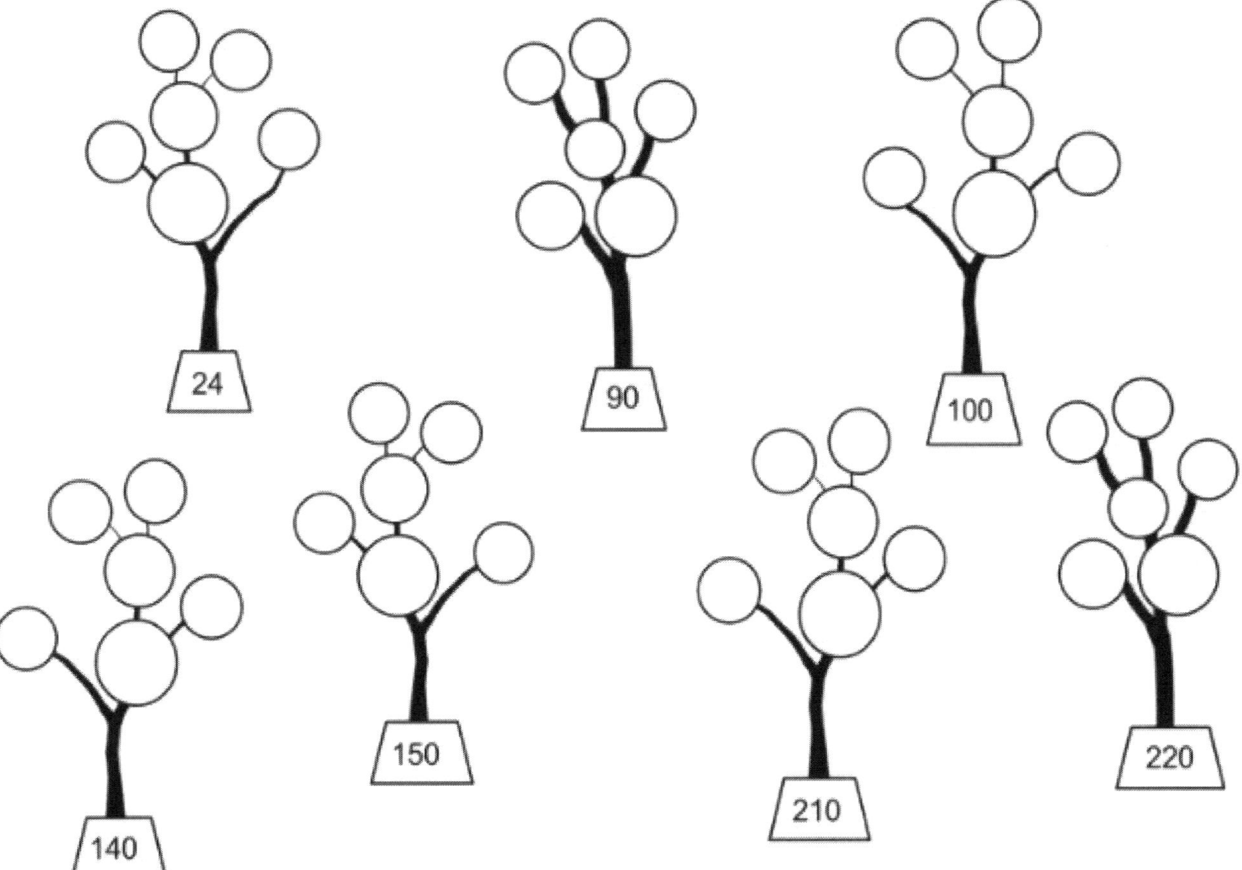

FACTORING TREES

D. Give the prime factored form of each of these numbers. You can use scrap paper if you need to construct factoring trees. Make sure to list the primes from small to big. [See HINT at bottom the of this page].

Example: **156** = 2 × 78 = 2 × 2 × 39 = **2 × 2 × 3 × 13**

26	______________	325	______________
90	______________	139	______________
35	______________	126	______________
96	______________	118	______________
99	______________	142	______________
85	______________	122	______________
65	______________	155	______________
94	______________	134	______________
128	______________	48	______________
156	______________	150	______________

Hint

1 2 3 5 7
11 13 17 19
23 29
31 37
41 43 47
53 59
61 67
71 73 79
83 89
97

A little mental math to keep us sharp

LESSON 4 SUBTRACTING FROM THE LEFT 

There are two types of subtraction problems.

THOSE THAT **NEED** REGROUPING	456−28 5247−149

THOSE THAT **DON'T NEED** REGROUPING	547−131 4287−122

$$\begin{array}{r} 4358 \\ -\,2142 \\ \hline \end{array}$$

No regrouping!

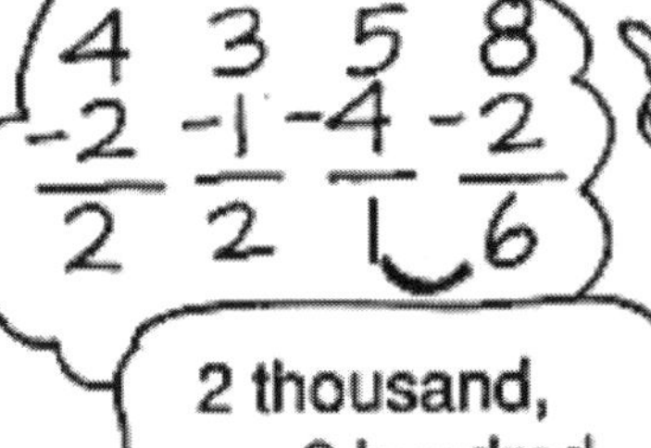

2 thousand, 2 hundred, 16.

If no regrouping is needed, you can subtract quickly in your head.

Start at the left and say the answer one part at a time.

It works with decimals, too. Try it with these problems:

$$\begin{array}{r} 4.27 \\ -\,1.13 \\ \hline \end{array} \qquad \begin{array}{r} 8.94 \\ -\,5.72 \\ \hline \end{array}$$

TRY THESE IN YOUR HEAD. Subtract from the left.

1. 375 − 232
2. 987 − 723
3. 486 − 425
4. 5206 − 2104
5. 8345 − 6340
6. 9154 − 5014
7. 4.75 − 1.32
8. 9.87 − 7.23
9. 45.6 − 31.6
10. 8.45 − 6.15

POWER BUILDER A

1. 427 − 315 = ____________
2. 876 − 550 = ____________
3. 736 − 524 = ____________
4. 945 − 540 = ____________
5. 697 − 346 = ____________
6. 8275 − 4160 = ____________
7. 5260 − 4160 = ____________
8. 9854 − 3421 = ____________
9. 8547 − 5034 = ____________
10. 95,476 − 82,153 = ____________
11. 4.95 − 1.23 = ____________
12. 6.04 − 4.02 = ____________
13. 9.57 − 3.54 = ____________
14. 6.24 − 2.13 = ____________
15. 7.54 − 5.04 = ____________
16. 11.27 − 1.15 = ____________
17. 19.88 − 8.77 = ____________
18. 51.47 − 30.25 = ____________
19. 83.59 − 43.56 = ____________
20. 75.75 − 25.20 = ____________

THINK IT THROUGH

The difference between the squares of two consecutive even numbers is 36. What are the numbers?

MENTAL MATH IN JUNIOR HIGH — LESSON 4 SUBTRACTING FROM THE LEFT

POWER BUILDER B

1. 359 − 224 = ____________
2. 668 − 330 = ____________
3. 845 − 223 = ____________
4. 835 − 230 = ____________
5. 786 − 135 = ____________
6. 6484 − 2150 = ____________
7. 4480 − 2180 = ____________
8. 7654 − 2533 = ____________
9. 7458 − 4247 = ____________
10. 89,753 − 57,412 = ____________
11. 6.84 − 2.63 = ____________
12. 5.07 − 3.05 = ____________
13. 7.84 − 5.82 = ____________
14. 8.07 − 7.04 = ____________
15. 8.87 − 5.66 = ____________
16. 12.57 − 2.54 = ____________
17. 19.89 − 9.77 = ____________
18. 27.56 − 12.34 = ____________
19. 51.37 − 41.36 = ____________
20. 89.67 − 35.40 = ____________

THINK IT THROUGH

The difference between the squares of two consecutive even numbers is 44. What are the numbers?

48

Tests for Divisibility

Divisibility by 2

A number is divisible by 2 the last digit is 0, 2, 4, 6, or 8. If it is divisible by 2, the number is EVEN, otherwise it is ODD.

TEST: If the last digit is even, the whole number is divisible by 2.

Examples:

- 24,918 is divisible by 2 because the last digit (8) is even.
- 5,781 is NOT divisible by 2 because the last digit (1) is odd.

Exercise: Circle all the numbers that are divisible by 2:

12,019	4,333	5,204	13,999	3,000	65,652
0	151	16,001	4,896	50	8,657

Divisibility by 3

A number is divisible by 3 if the SUM OF ITS DIGITS is divisible by 3. For instance, 13,455 is divisible by 3 because 1+3+4+5+5=18. Since 18 is divisible by 3, so is the whole number.

TEST: If the sum of the digits is divisible by 3, so is the whole number.

Examples:

- 23,928 is divisible by 3 because the sum of the digits is 24.
- 5,780 is NOT divisible by 3 because the sum of its digits is 20..

Exercise: Circle all the numbers that are divisible by 3:

12,219	4,333	5,204	13,999	3,101	65,652
0	251	16,002	4,896	507	8,657

Tests for Divisibility

Divisibility by 4

A number is divisible by 4 if the two digit number at the end of it is divisible by 4. For instance, in order to decide if 52,742 is divisible by 4, we only need to look at the 42 at the end and ignore all the rest. Since 42 in not divisible by 4, then 52,742 is not divisible by 4 either.

TEST: If the two-digit number at the end is divisible by 4, so is the whole number.

Examples:

- 24,918 is NOT divisible by 4 because 18 is not divisible by 4.
- 5,760 is divisible by 4 because 60 is divisible by 4.

Exercise: Circle all the numbers that are divisible by 4:

12,020	4,333	5,204	13,988	3,000	65,652
0	154	16,001	4,894	50	8,656

Divisibility by 6

Since 6 = 2 × 3, for a number to be divisible by 6, it must be divisible by 2 and by 3. You must check BOTH.

TEST: If the last digit is even AND the sum of the digits is divisible by 3, then the number is divisible by 6.

Examples:

- 23,924 is divisible by 6 because it is even, and is also divisible by 3.
- 5,788 is NOT divisible by 6 because it is not divisible by 3.

Exercise: Circle all the numbers that are divisible by 6:

12,218	4,333	5,204	13,999	3,101	65,652
0	251	16,002	4,896	506	8,656

Divisibility

Check each number for divisibility by 2, 3, 4 and 6.
Put ✗ or ✓ as necessary.

128	
By 2	✓
By 3	✗
By 4	✓
By 6	✗

345	
By 2	
By 3	
By 4	
By 6	

1,250	
By 2	
By 3	
By 4	
By 6	

750	
By 2	
By 3	
By 4	
By 6	

663	
By 2	
By 3	
By 4	
By 6	

734	
By 2	
By 3	
By 4	
By 6	

132	
By 2	
By 3	
By 4	
By 6	

500	
By 2	
By 3	
By 4	
By 6	

950	
By 2	
By 3	
By 4	
By 6	

380	
By 2	
By 3	
By 4	
By 6	

2,500	
By 2	
By 3	
By 4	
By 6	

Another Brainteaser (without trees this time.)

What number should replace the question mark?

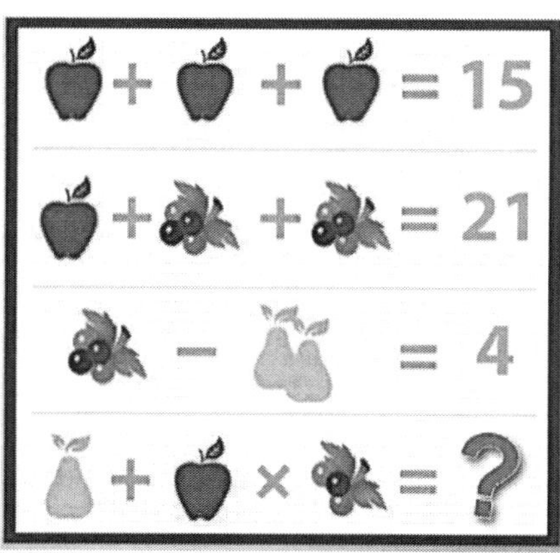

Tests for Divisibility

Divisibility by 7

There is NO good test for divisibility by 7. That's TOO BAD!

Divisibility by 8

A number is divisible by 8 if the 3-digit number at the end of it is divisible by 8. For instance, in order to decide if 52,742 is divisible by 8, we only need to look at the 742 at the end and ignore all the rest. Since 742=720+**22** in not divisible by 8, then 52,742 is not divisible by 8 either.

TEST: If the 3-digit number at the end is divisible by 8, so is the whole number.

Examples:

- 23,928 is divisible by 8 because 928=800+80+48 is divisible by 8.
- 5,180 is NOT divisible by 8 because 180=160+**20** is not divisible by 8.

Exercise: Circle all the numbers that are divisible by 8:

12,218	4,333	5,204	13,999	3,104	65,652
0	252	16,002	4,896	508	8,657

Divisibility by 5 or 10

A number is divisible by 5 if it ends with a 0 or a 5. A number is divisible by 10 if it ends with a 0. Both tests are very easy to apply.

TESTS: If the last digit is 0 or 5, the number is divisible by 5.
If the last digit is 0, the number is divisible by 10.

Examples:

- 23,925 is divisible by 5 because it ends with a 5.
- 5,780 is divisible by BOTH 5 and 10 because it ends with a 0.

Divisibility

Check each number for divisibility by 3, 5, 6 and 8.
Put ✗ or ✓ as necessary.

308	
By 3	
By 5	
By 6	
By 8	

866	
By 3	
By 5	
By 6	
By 8	

222	
By 3	
By 5	
By 6	
By 8	

3,050	
By 3	
By 5	
By 6	
By 8	

650	
By 3	
By 5	
By 6	
By 8	

900	
By 3	
By 5	
By 6	
By 8	

548	
By 3	
By 5	
By 6	
By 8	

176	
By 3	
By 5	
By 6	
By 8	

1,700	
By 3	
By 5	
By 6	
By 8	

325	
By 3	
By 5	
By 6	
By 8	

365	
By 3	
By 5	
By 6	
By 8	

Challenger

Can you make up a 2-digit number that is divisible by 2, 3, 4, 5 and 6?
Your answer: ________________

**Can you make up a 3-digit number that is divisible by 2, 3, 4, 5, 6 and 7?*
Your answer: ________________

Divisibility by 9

A number is divisible by 9 if the SUM OF ITS DIGITS is divisible by 9. This test is very similar to the test for divisibility by 3. For instance, 13,455 is divisible by 9 because 1+3+4+5+5=18. Since 18 is divisible by 9, so is the whole number.

TEST: If the sum of the digits is divisible by 9, so is the whole number.

Examples:

- 23,928 is NOT divisible by 9 because the sum of the digits is 24, which is not divisible by 9.
- 5,787 is is divisible by 9 because the sum of its digits is 27, and 9 divides 27.

Exercise: Circle all the numbers that are divisible by 9:

12,219	4,333	5,202	13,999	3,141	65,652
0	851	16,002	4,896	507	8,657

Divisibility

Check each number for divisibility by 4, 6, 7 and 9. Put ✗ or ✓ as necessary.

385	
By 4	
By 6	
By 7	
By 9	

284	
By 4	
By 6	
By 7	
By 9	

440	
By 4	
By 6	
By 7	
By 9	

264	
By 4	
By 6	
By 7	
By 9	

3,424	
By 4	
By 6	
By 7	
By 9	

999	
By 4	
By 6	
By 7	
By 9	

642	
By 4	
By 6	
By 7	
By 9	

450	
By 4	
By 6	
By 7	
By 9	

738	
By 4	
By 6	
By 7	
By 9	

256	
By 4	
By 6	
By 7	
By 9	

9,448	
By 4	
By 6	
By 7	
By 9	

Greatest Common Factor

The **Greatest Common Factor** of two numbers A and B is the **largest** number that divides them both. It is also called the **Greatest Common Divisor** (GCD). For example, the GCD of 6 and 8 is 2, and the GCD of 20 and 35 is 5.

The GCD of two numbers may equal to the smaller of the the two. For instance, the GCD of 7 and 21 is equal to 7 because this is the largest number that is a divisor of both.

Example: Find the GCD of 20 and 32

The divisors of 20 are: 1, 2, 4, 5, 10, 20

The divisors of 32 are: 1, 2, 4, 8, 16, 32

Looking at both lists we see that the largest common divisor is **4.**

For each pair write down the Greatest Common Factor

16 and 64=_____	12 and 30=____	21 and 33=_____
12 and 20=_____	13 and 65=_____	11 and 78=_____
35 and 18=_____	12 and 21=_____	18 and 28=_____
24 and 96=_____	15 and 75=_____	14 and 84=_____
12 and 56=_____	14 and 77=_____	24 and 64 = ____
12 and 28=_____	17 and 68=_____	30 and 45=_____
19 and 95=_____	12 and 23=_____	15 and 90=_____
12 and 66=_____	19 and 48=_____	24 and 30=_____
14 and 87=_____	12 and 26=_____	15 and 95=_____

1. Write all the numbers **from 1 to 30** in the Venn Diagram. Make sure you place each number in its right place: common factors should be placed in the middle, where the two circles intersect.

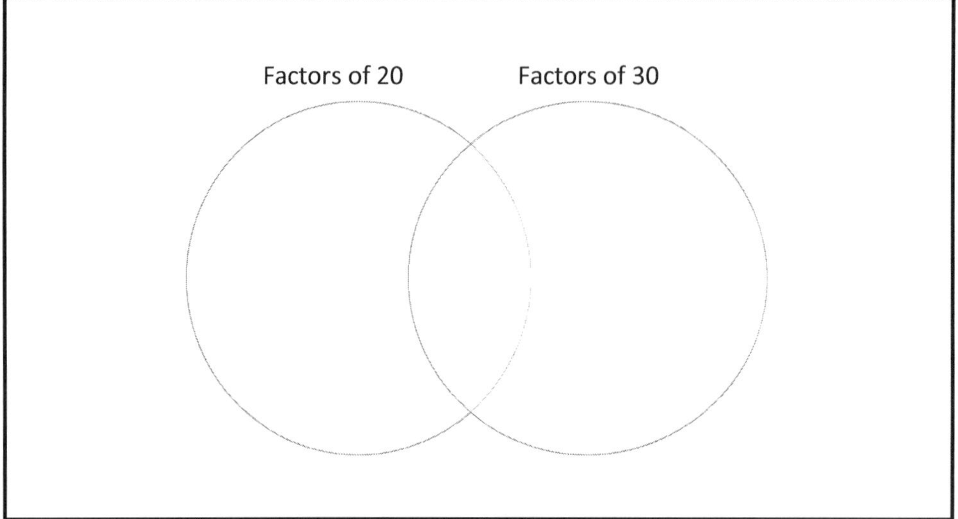

The common factors of 20 and 30 are: ________________

The greatest common factor of 20 and 30 is: ______________

2. Write all the numbers **from 1 to 45** in the Venn Diagram. Make sure you place each number in its right place: common factors should be placed in the middle, where the two circles intersect.

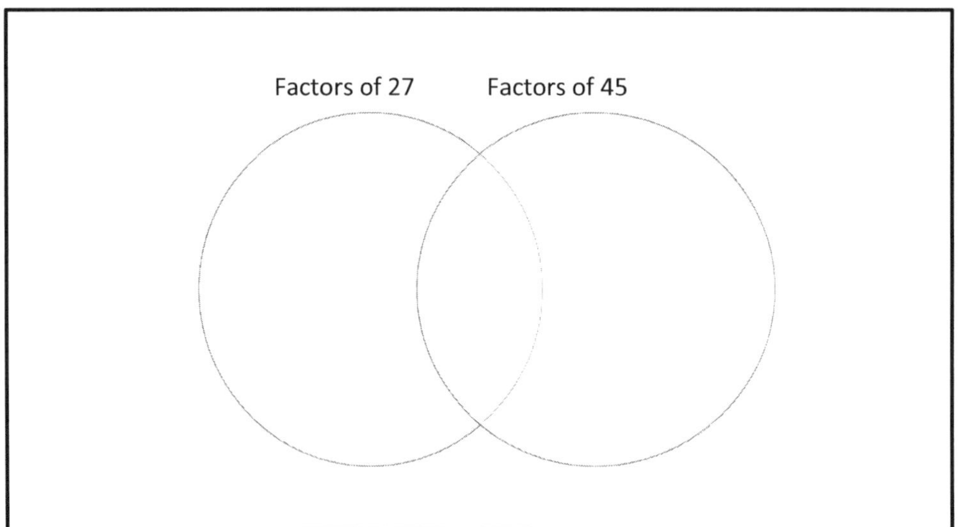

The common factors of 27 and 45 are: ________________

The greatest common factor of 27 and 45 is: ______________

GREATEST COMMON FACTOR

The **Greatest Common Factor (or Divisor)** of three numbers A and B and C is the **largest** number that divides them all.

Example:
In order to find the GCD of 10, 12 and 28, we could list the divisors of all three of them, and then look for the **largest** divisor that is on all three lists:

Divisors of 10: 1, **2**, 5, 10
Divisors of 12: 1, **2**, 3, 4, 6, 12
Divisors of 28: 1, **2**, 4, 7, 14, 28

The largest number that is common to all three lists is 2, so GCD(10,12,28)=2

Find the greatest common factors of the following sets of numbers.

14, 16 and 20 =_____

35, 25 and 15 =_____

24, 18 and 96 =_____ 24, 18 and 78 =_____

12, 16 and 56 =_____ 18, 24 and 66 = _____

16, 24 and 28 =_____ 12, 24 and 28 =_____

19, 38 and 95 =_____ 18, 36 and 72 =_____

12, 36 and 60 =_____ 12, 30 and 60 =_____

14, 21 and 87 =_____ 15, 21 and 81 =_____

20, 25 and 75 =_____ 21, 25 and 33 =_____

16, 24 and 64 =_____ 14, 24 and 64 =_____

Multiples

*X is a **multiple** of Y if Y divides X nicely without leaving a remainder.*

Examples:

- *6 is a multiple of 2 because 2 is a factor of 6*
- *17 is not a multiple of 5 because 5 is not a factor of 17*
- *40 is a multiple of 10 because 10 is a divisor of 40*

1) Which choice is a multiple of 2?
A. 35
B. 25
C. 32
D. 33

2) Which choice is a multiple of 9?
A. 162
B. 179
C. 113
D. 143

3) Which choice is a multiple of 3?
A. 37
B. 51
C. 35
D. 41

4) Which choice is a multiple of 5?
A. 93
B. 63
C. 65
D. 84

5) Which choice is a multiple of 10?
A. 112
B. 190
C. 128
D. 186

6) Which choice is a multiple of 9?
A. 141
B. 163
C. 180
D. 155

7) Which choice is a multiple of 2?
A. 37
B. 36
C. 23
D. 39

8) Which choice is a multiple of 10?
A. 195
B. 186
C. 190
D. 113

9) Which choice is a multiple of 3?
A. 58
B. 39
C. 49
D. 40

10) Which choice is a multiple of 10?
A. 120
B. 163
C. 121
D. 161

11) Which choice is a multiple of 6?
A. 75
B. 121
C. 90
D. 82

12) Which choice is a multiple of 5?
A. 100
B. 72
C. 91
D. 92

13) Which choice is a multiple of 9?
A. 172
B. 166
C. 135
D. 161

14) Which choice is a multiple of 2?
A. 39
B. 33
C. 30
D. 29

15) Which choice is a multiple of 5?
A. 82
B. 62
C. 60
D. 72

A little mental math to keep us sharp ♯

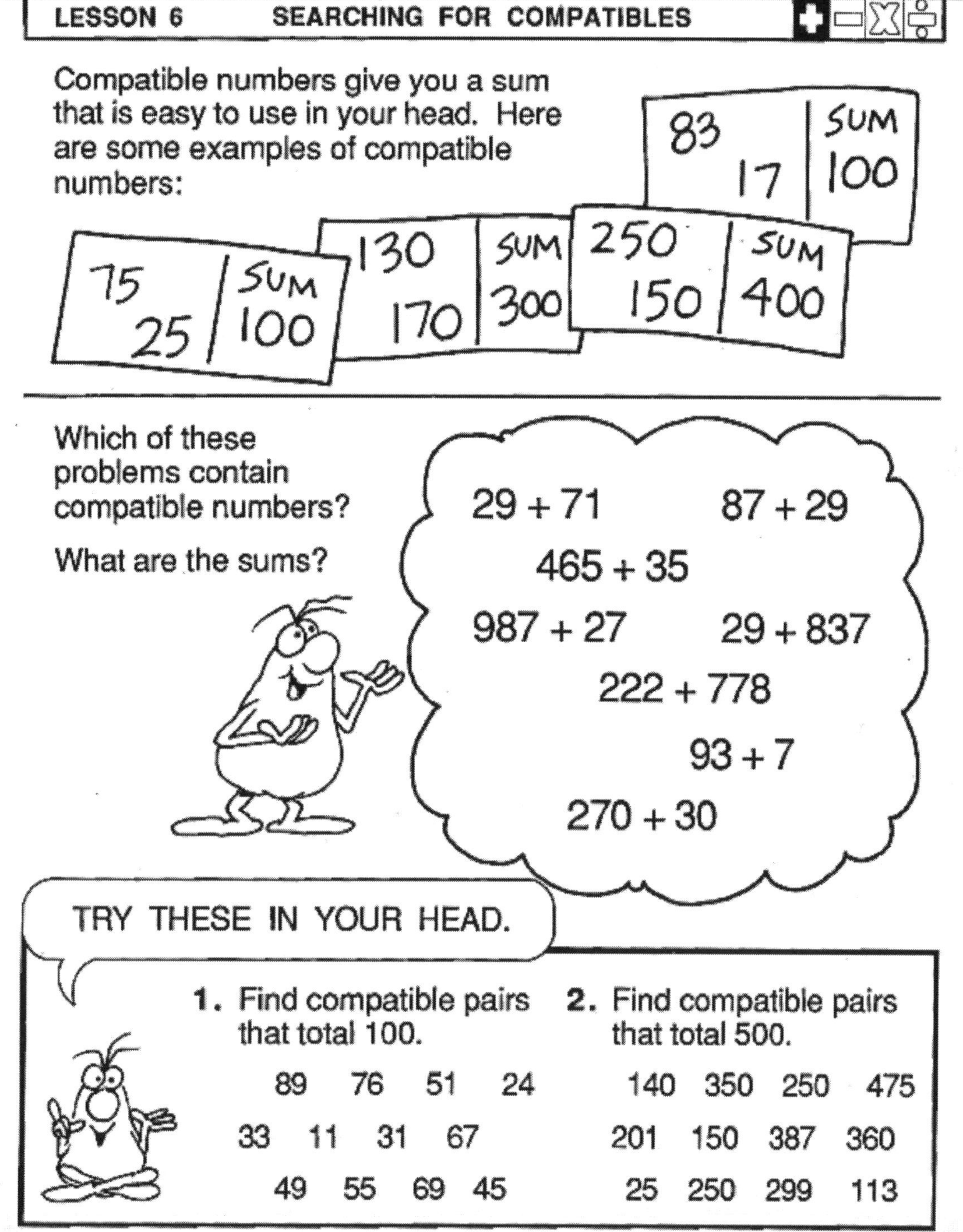

LESSON 6 SEARCHING FOR COMPATIBLES
Compatible numbers give you a sum that is easy to use in your head. Here are some examples of compatible numbers:
83 17 SUM 100
75 25 SUM 100
130 170 SUM 300
250 150 SUM 400
Which of these problems contain compatible numbers?
What are the sums?
29 + 71
87 + 29
465 + 35
987 + 27
29 + 837
222 + 778
93 + 7
270 + 30
TRY THESE IN YOUR HEAD.
1. Find compatible pairs that total 100.
89 76 51 24
33 11 31 67
49 55 69 45
2. Find compatible pairs that total 500.
140 350 250 475
201 150 387 360
25 250 299 113

POWER BUILDER A

1. 45 + ______ ______ = 100	11. 125 + ______ ______ = 400
2. 73 + ______ ______ = 100	12. 239 + ______ ______ = 300
3. 19 + ______ ______ = 100	13. 544 + ______ ______ = 700
4. 58 + ______ ______ = 100	14. 199 + ______ ______ = 500
5. 37 + ______ ______ = 100	15. 436 + ______ ______ = 800
6. 350 + ______ ______ = 1000	16. 275 + ______ ______ = 500
7. 275 + ______ ______ = 1000	17. 143 + ______ ______ = 300
8. 635 + ______ ______ = 1000	18. 333 + ______ ______ = 600
9. 876 + ______ ______ = 1000	19. 45 + ______ ______ = 200
10. 444 + ______ ______ = 1000	20. 685 + ______ ______ = 900

THINK IT THROUGH

A 10-m tape breaks at the 565 mm mark.
How much of the tape is left?

POWER BUILDER B

1. 55 + ______ ______ = 100	11. 275 + ______ ______ = 400
2. 76 + ______ ______ = 100	12. 149 + ______ ______ = 300
3. 29 + ______ ______ = 100	13. 233 + ______ ______ = 700
4. 43 + ______ ______ = 100	14. 299 + ______ ______ = 500
5. 68 + ______ ______ = 100	15. 634 + ______ ______ = 800
6. 250 + ______ ______ = 1000	16. 175 + ______ ______ = 500
7. 375 + ______ ______ = 1000	17. 134 + ______ ______ = 300
8. 445 + ______ ______ = 1000	18. 444 + ______ ______ = 600
9. 759 + ______ ______ = 1000	19. 35 + ______ ______ = 200
10. 666 + ______ ______ = 1000	20. 258 + ______ ______ = 900

In a 10-km run, Jack quit after 2500 m.
What distance was he from the finish?

52

Adding & Subtracting Like Fractions

Like Fractions are fractions with the same denominators. They "speak the same language" and therefore can be added and subtracted with each other easily.

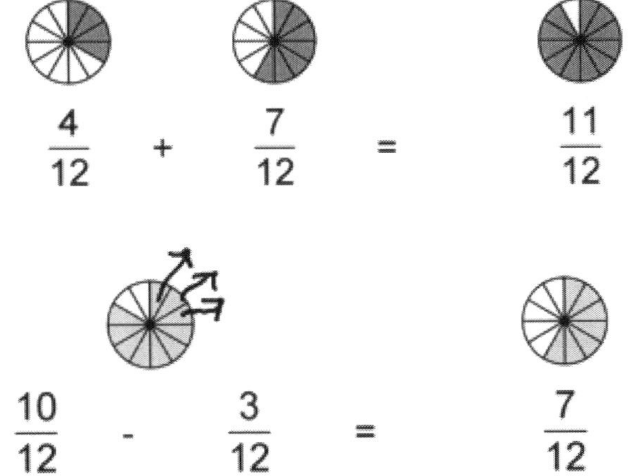

Knowing how many parts make up a whole helps. The denominator tells you how many parts the whole is divided into. For example, here we are dividing the whole into 9 parts, each of them is one ninth. What fraction do you need to add to $\frac{5}{9}$ in order to make up a whole?

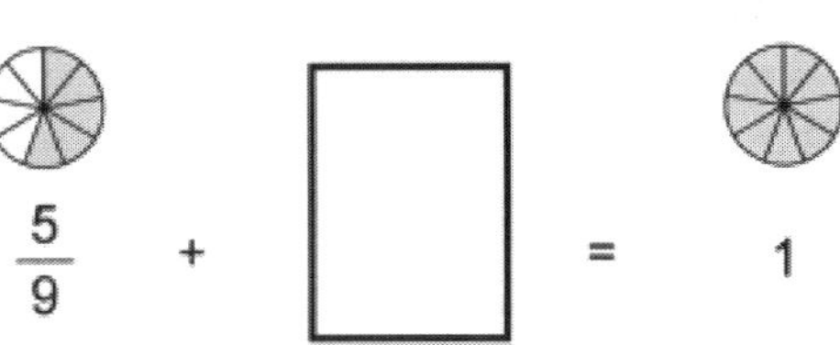

When adding mixed numbers, add the wholes and fractions parts separately, then regroup.

For example:

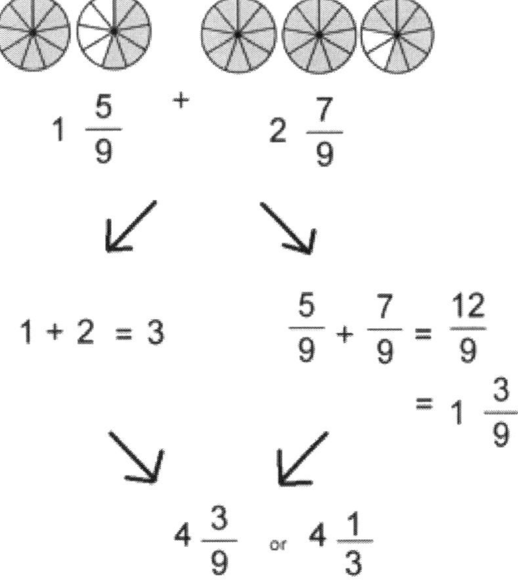

Adding fractions with same denominator

Add the following fractions by shading and write the equation

Ex)

$\frac{3}{7}+\frac{2}{7}=\frac{5}{7}$ ______________________

1)

____

2)

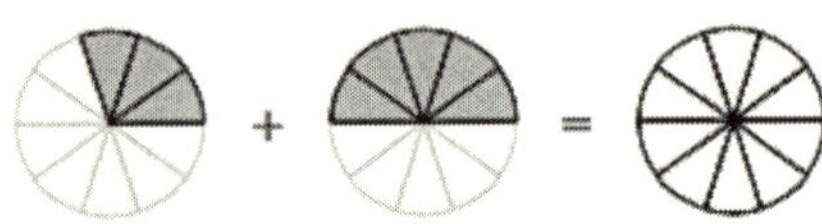

____

3)

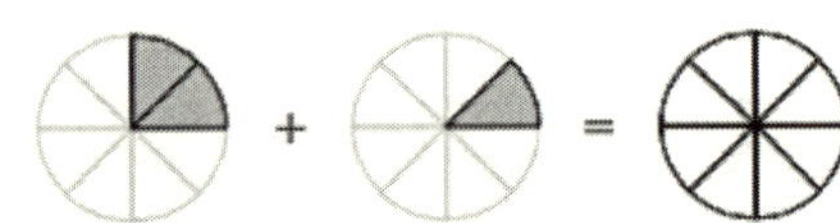

____

4)

____

5)

____

6)

____

7)

____

8)

____

9)

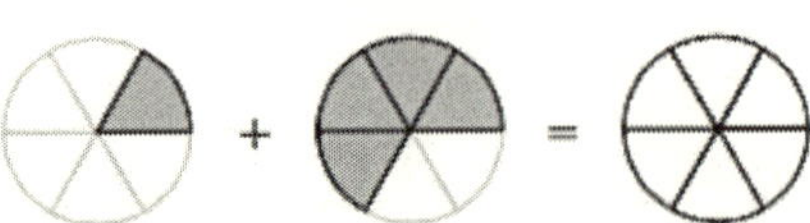

____

10)

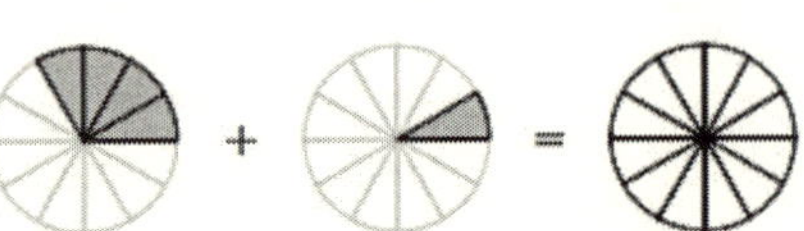

____

$1\ ^3/_5 + 2\ ^4/_5 = ?$

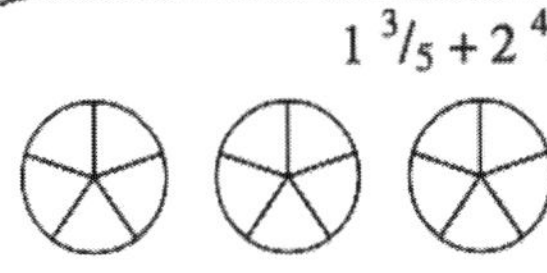

To solve a fraction addition problem one strategy is to shade in the whole amounts first (1 & 2).

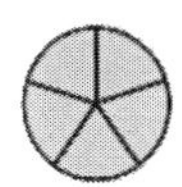 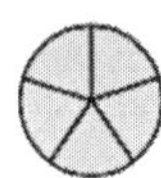 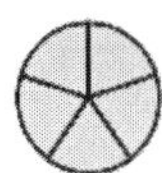  

Next fill in the fraction amounts ($^3/_5$ & $^4/_5$).

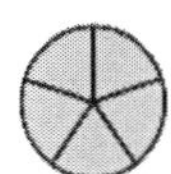  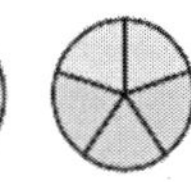 

When all of the pieces are filled in we can see that $1\ ^3/_5 + 2\ ^4/_5 = 4\ ^2/_5$

1) $3\ ^9/_{10} + 1\ ^2/_{10} =$ ________________

2) $2\ ^4/_5 + 2\ ^1/_5 =$ ________________

3) $2\ ^9/_{10} + 2\ ^1/_{10} =$ ________________

4) $2\ ^2/_3 + 3\ ^1/_3 =$ ________________

5) $2\ ^9/_{12} + 3\ ^4/_{12} =$ ________________

6) $2\ ^7/_{10} + 2\ ^5/_{10} =$ ________________

7) $3\ ^2/_4 + 2\ ^1/_4 =$ ________________

8) $1\ ^2/_4 + 2\ ^3/_4 =$ ________________

9) $3\ ^1/_5 + 2\ ^2/_5 =$ ________________

10) $1\ ^2/_4 + 2\ ^2/_4 =$ ________________

11) $2\ ^2/_5 + 1\ ^2/_5 =$ ________________

12) $3\ ^1/_{12} + 2\ ^{10}/_{12} =$ ________________

Adding fractions with same denominator

Give your final answer as a MIXED NUMBER in simplest form

Example: $7\frac{3}{8}+4\frac{5}{8}=11+\left(\frac{3}{8}+\frac{5}{8}\right)=11+\frac{8}{8}=11+1=12$

1. $\frac{4}{5}+\frac{4}{5}=$ ____________________

2. $4\frac{3}{5}+\frac{12}{5}=$ ____________________

3. $\frac{13}{5}+7\frac{24}{5}=$ ____________________

4. $2\frac{2}{3}+\frac{5}{3}=$ ____________________

5. $\frac{5}{18}+\frac{7}{18}=$ ____________________

6. $6\frac{8}{9}+2\frac{4}{9}=$ ____________________

7. $9\frac{3}{4}+1\frac{3}{4}=$ ____________________

8. $8\frac{7}{8}+1\frac{3}{8}=$ ____________________

9. $4\frac{1}{7}+1\frac{3}{7}=$ ____________________

10. $\frac{33}{5}+\frac{17}{5}=$ ____________________

11. $3\frac{2}{5}+3\frac{4}{5}=$ ____________________

12. $31\frac{1}{6}+3\frac{5}{6}=$ ____________________

Adding fractions with same denominator

Give your final answer as a MIXED NUMBER in simplest form

Example: $3\frac{2}{5}+4\frac{4}{5}=7+\left(\frac{2}{5}+\frac{4}{5}\right)=7+\frac{6}{5}=7+1\frac{1}{5}=8\frac{1}{5}$

1. $\frac{1}{9}+\frac{7}{9}=$ ________________________

2. $\frac{13}{5}+\frac{4}{5}=$ ________________________

3. $3\frac{3}{5}+\frac{24}{5}=$ ________________________

4. $2\frac{6}{7}+\frac{4}{7}=$ ________________________

5. $\frac{20}{3}+\frac{8}{3}=$ ________________________

6. $4\frac{3}{4}+\frac{30}{4}=$ ________________________

7. $\frac{7}{3}+\frac{14}{3}=$ ________________________

8. $\frac{7}{8}+1\frac{4}{8}=$ ________________________

9. $4\frac{7}{9}+1\frac{4}{9}=$ ________________________

10. $\frac{23}{9}+\frac{7}{9}=$ ________________________

11. $5\frac{2}{11}+3\frac{4}{11}=$ ________________________

12. $2\frac{5}{6}+6\frac{5}{6}=$ ________________________

Mixed Numbers and Improper Fractions – Quick review

An **IMPROPER FRACTION** is a fraction in which the numerator is bigger than the denominator **(Top>Bottom)**. Such fractions are bigger than a whole. These are all examples of improper fractions: $\frac{5}{2}$, $\frac{14}{5}$, $\frac{7}{4}$, $\frac{101}{23}$

A **MIXED NUMBER** is a number that has a whole number part and a fraction part. These are all examples of mixed numbers: $3\frac{5}{2}$, $7\frac{4}{5}$, $20\frac{1}{4}$, $6\frac{21}{23}$

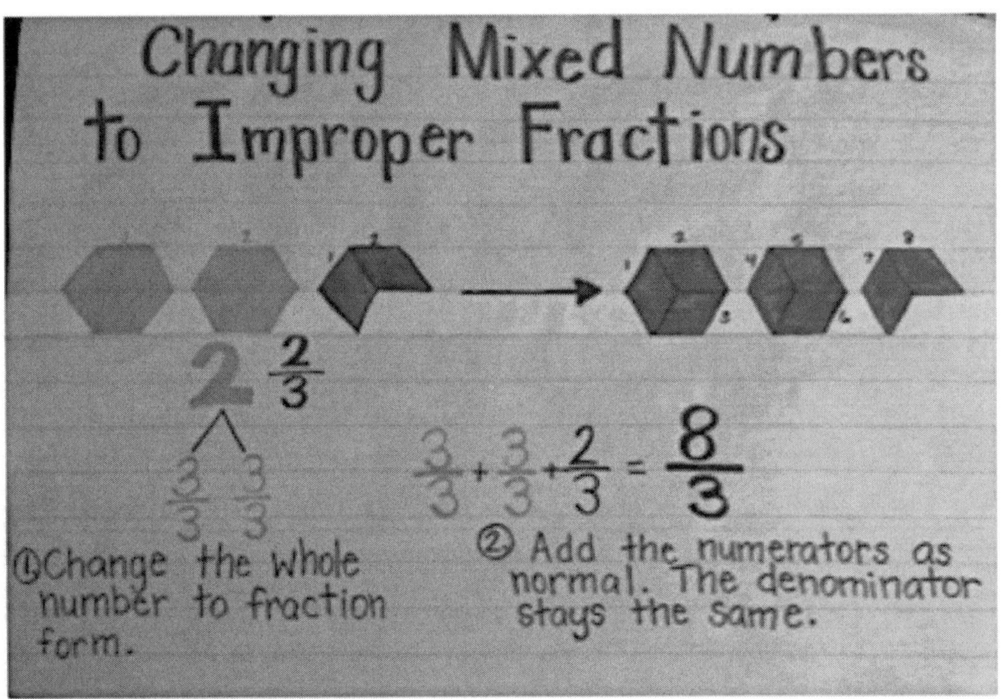

Changing Improper Fractions to Mixed Numbers

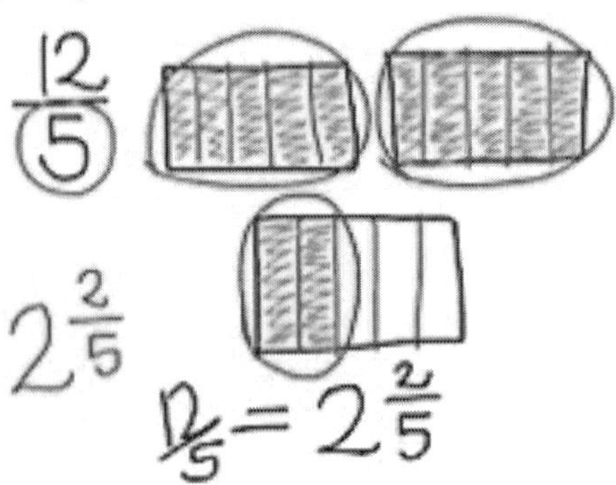

From Improper Fractions to Mixed Number – Quick Review

Follow the example and convert each to a mixed number in simplest form.

Ex) $\frac{24}{7} = 3\frac{3}{7}$

1) $\frac{55}{8} =$

2) $\frac{17}{8} =$

3) $\frac{43}{7} =$

4) $\frac{17}{2} =$

5) $\frac{5}{3} =$

6) $\frac{46}{6} =$

7) $\frac{50}{7} =$

8) $\frac{20}{3} =$

9) $\frac{22}{4} =$

10) $\frac{32}{3} =$

11) $\frac{43}{4} =$

12) $\frac{91}{9} =$

13) $\frac{38}{4} =$

14) $\frac{22}{9} =$

15) $\frac{19}{2} =$

16) $\frac{42}{10} =$

17) $\frac{31}{4} =$

18) $\frac{7}{2} =$

19) $\frac{24}{9} =$

20) $\frac{80}{9} =$

From Mixed Number to Improper Fractions – Quick Review

Follow the example and convert each to an improper fraction in simplest form.

Ex) $4\frac{3}{4} = \frac{19}{4}$

1) $5\frac{6}{8} =$

2) $8\frac{2}{3} =$

3) $8\frac{7}{8} =$

4) $5\frac{1}{2} =$

5) $3\frac{2}{4} =$

6) $3\frac{6}{9} =$

7) $9\frac{2}{10} =$

8) $10\frac{1}{2} =$

9) $1\frac{5}{6} =$

10) $3\frac{1}{7} =$

11) $9\frac{2}{7} =$

12) $10\frac{1}{3} =$

13) $9\frac{3}{4} =$

14) $8\frac{3}{6} =$

15) $9\frac{9}{10} =$

16) $7\frac{6}{7} =$

17) $7\frac{2}{5} =$

18) $9\frac{4}{9} =$

19) $4\frac{3}{7} =$

20) $1\frac{1}{6} =$

Equivalent Fractions – Quick Review

Write the correct equivalent fractions in the circles.

Remember: to get an equivalent fraction we multiply (or divide) the numerator and the denominator by the same number: $\frac{A}{B} = \frac{Ax}{Bx}$

1.

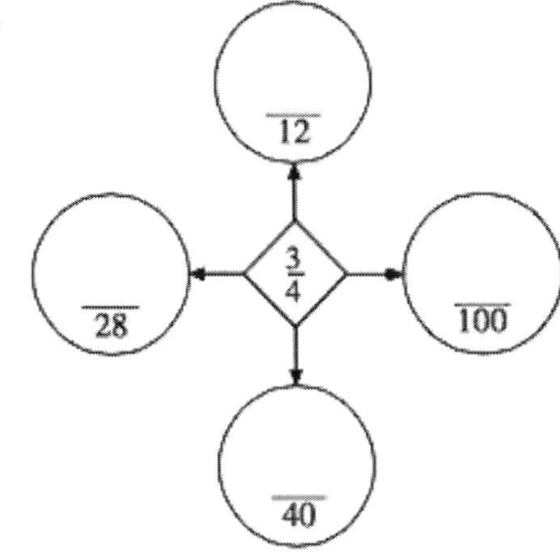

2.

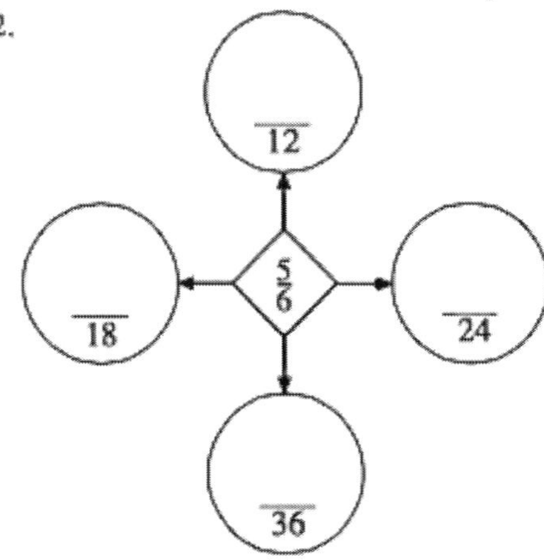

3.

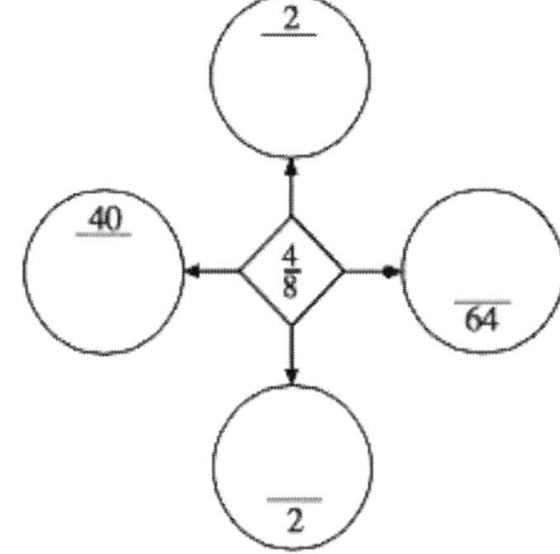

4.

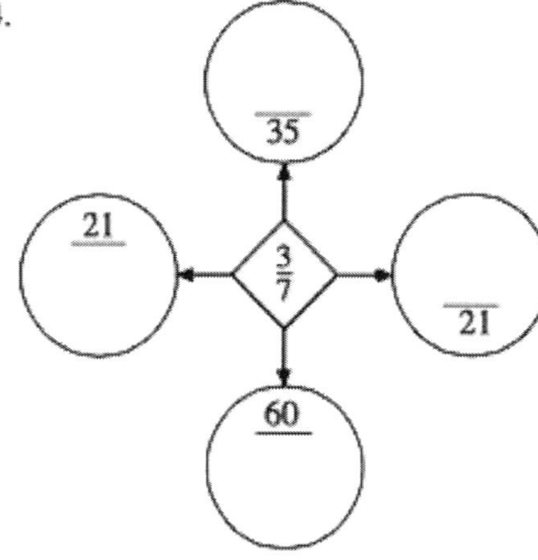

5.

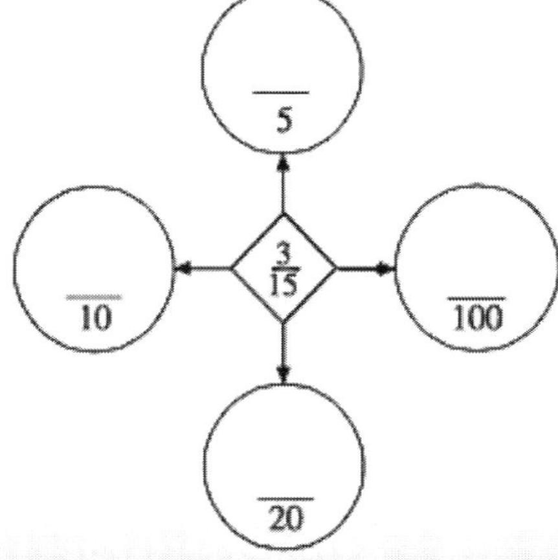

6.

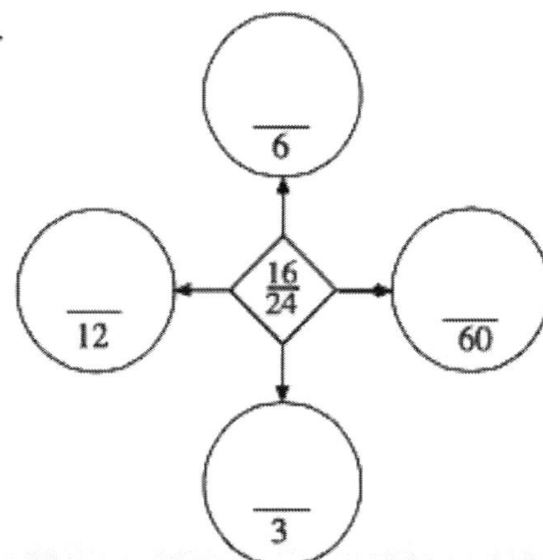

Reducing Fractions to Simplest Form – Quick Review

Reduce each fraction to an equivalent fraction in simplest form.
The key is to divide numerator and denominator by the same number.

Ex) $\frac{12}{18} = \frac{2}{3}$ **1)** $\frac{35}{40} = \_\_$ **2)** $\frac{30}{48} = \_\_$

3) $\frac{2}{4} = \_\_$ **4)** $\frac{9}{54} = \_\_$ **5)** $\frac{5}{20} = \_\_$

6) $\frac{4}{32} = \_\_$ **7)** $\frac{7}{42} = \_\_$ **8)** $\frac{14}{16} = \_\_$

9) $\frac{20}{32} = \_\_$ **10)** $\frac{3}{12} = \_\_$ **11)** $\frac{9}{24} = \_\_$

12) $\frac{6}{9} = \_\_$ **13)** $\frac{4}{24} = \_\_$ **14)** $\frac{9}{18} = \_\_$

15) $\frac{10}{30} = \_\_$ **16)** $\frac{63}{72} = \_\_$ **17)** $\frac{28}{32} = \_\_$

18) $\frac{7}{21} = \_\_$ **19)** $\frac{10}{12} = \_\_$ **20)** $\frac{10}{80} = \_\_$

What makes up 1 WHOLE – Quick review

1) $\frac{7}{8} + ? = 1$

2) $? + \frac{5}{7} = 1$

3) $\frac{1}{10} + ? = 1$

4) $\frac{1}{3} + ? = 1$

5) $\frac{3}{4} + ? = 1$

6) $? + \frac{4}{5} = 1$

7) $? + \frac{1}{2} = 1$

8) $\frac{6}{7} + ? = 1$

9) $\frac{3}{9} + ? = 1$

10) $? + \frac{2}{5} = 1$

11) $\frac{4}{6} + ? = 1$

12) $? + \frac{2}{7} = 1$

13) $? + \frac{8}{9} = 1$

14) $\frac{1}{8} + ? = 1$

15) $? + \frac{5}{6} = 1$

16) $? + \frac{2}{3} = 1$

17) $? + \frac{6}{9} = 1$

18) $? + \frac{5}{9} = 1$

19) $\frac{3}{5} + ? = 1$

20) $\frac{2}{4} + ? = 1$

1. ____________
2. ____________
3. ____________
4. ____________
5. ____________
6. ____________
7. ____________
8. ____________
9. ____________
10. ____________
11. ____________
12. ____________
13. ____________
14. ____________
15. ____________
16. ____________
17. ____________
18. ____________
19. ____________
20. ____________

Subtracting fractions with the same denominator

Solve the subtraction questions; you may use the picture to assist you

1) $6\frac{4}{5} - 4\frac{2}{5} =$ 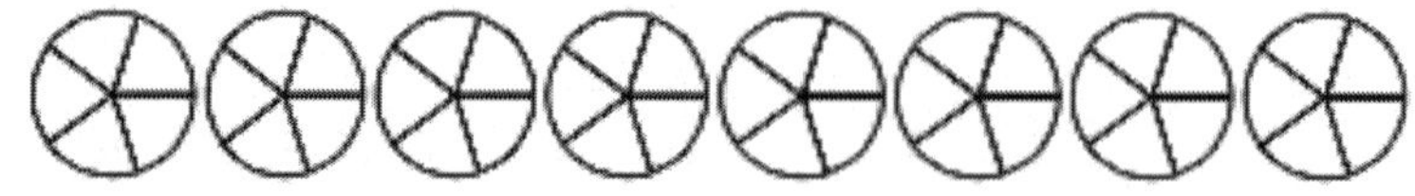 ______

2) $6\frac{4}{5} - 2\frac{1}{5} =$ 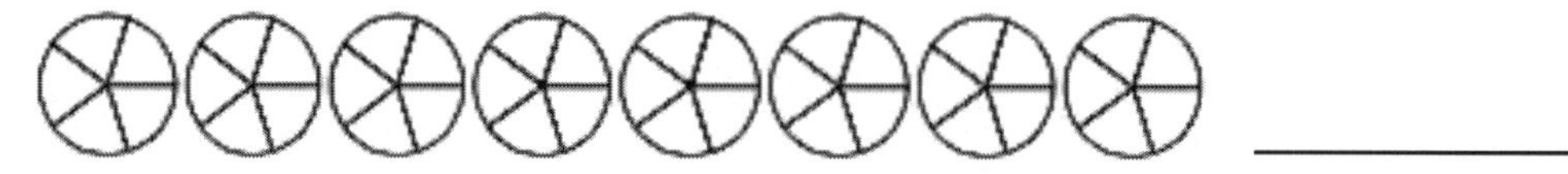 ______

3) $3\frac{1}{4} - 1\frac{2}{4} =$ 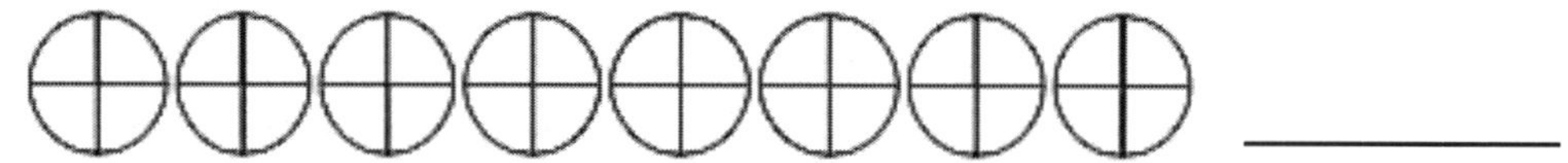 ______

4) $4\frac{2}{10} - 2\frac{8}{10} =$ 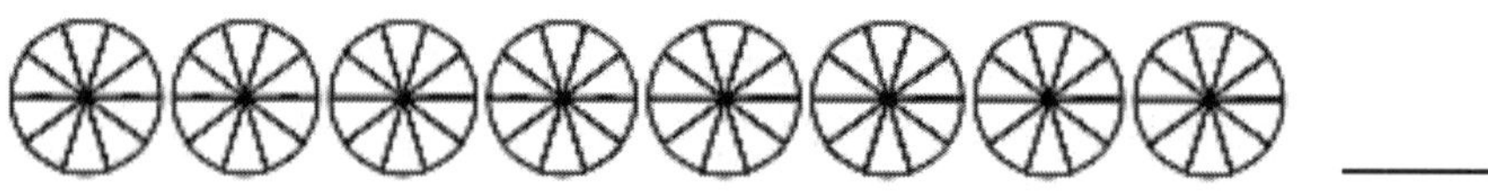 ______

5) $4\frac{2}{3} - 1\frac{2}{3} =$ 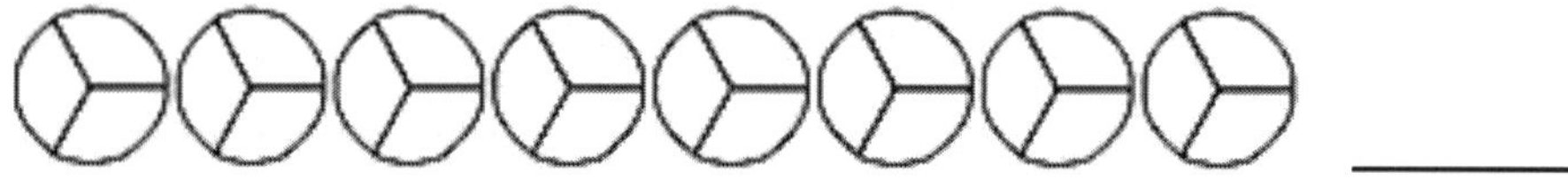 ______

6) $5\frac{3}{10} - 3\frac{1}{10} =$ 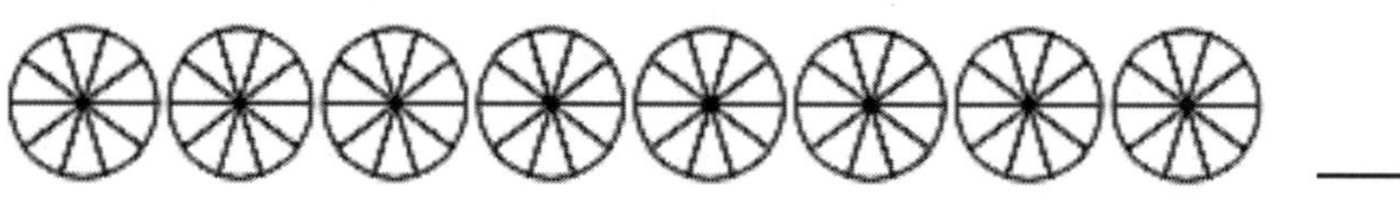 ______

7) $3\frac{5}{6} - 1\frac{2}{6} =$ 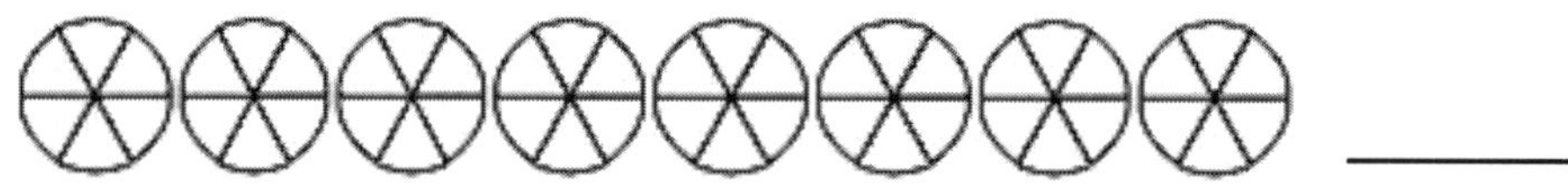 ______

8) $6\frac{2}{4} - 4\frac{1}{4} =$ 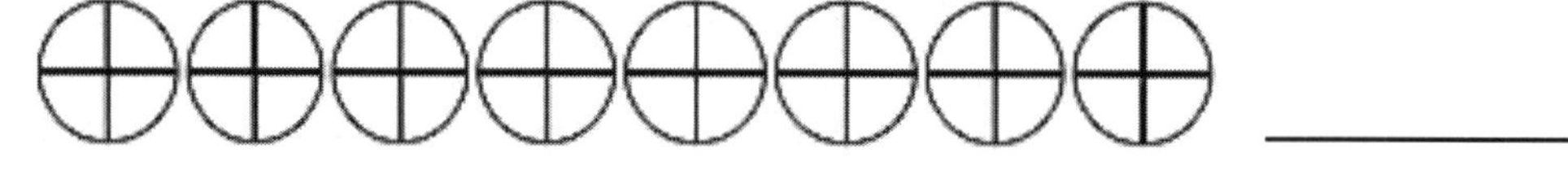 ______

9) $7\frac{3}{8} - 3\frac{5}{8} =$ 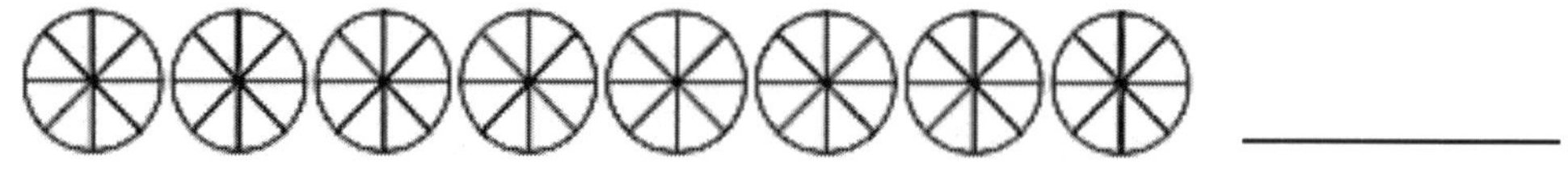 ______

10) $7\frac{4}{12} - 2\frac{5}{12} =$ 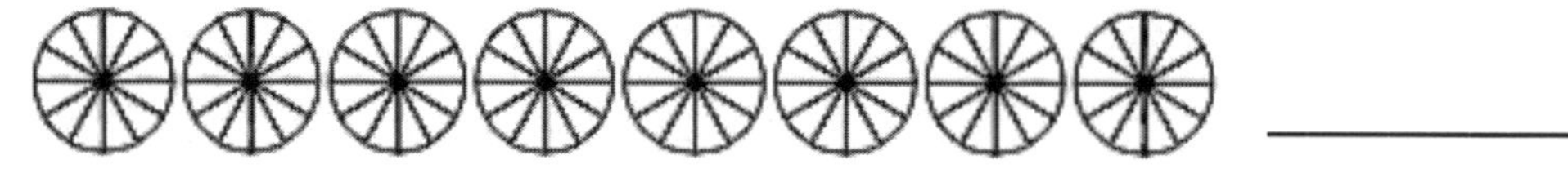 ______

11) $7\frac{3}{5} - 1\frac{3}{5} =$ 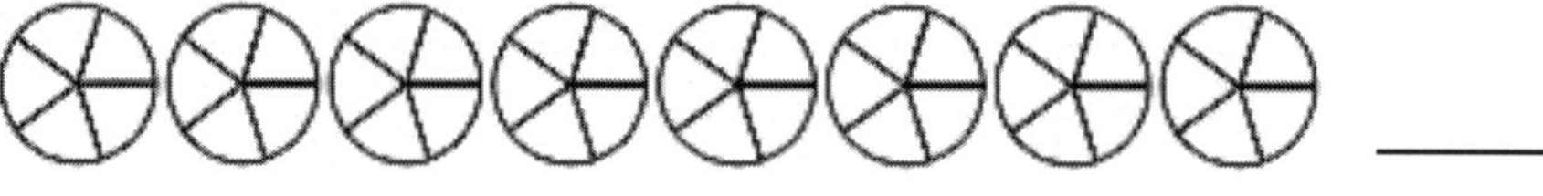 ______

12) $4\frac{2}{8} - 2\frac{7}{8} =$ 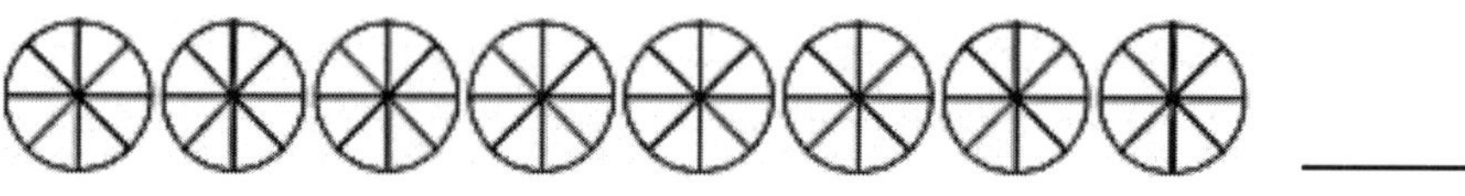 ______

POSITIVES AND NEGATIVES

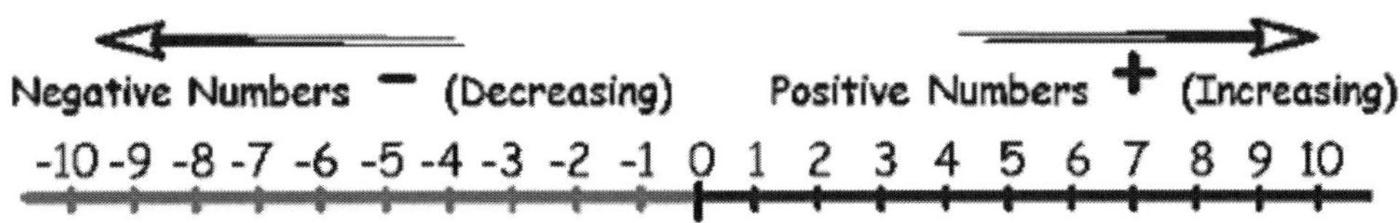

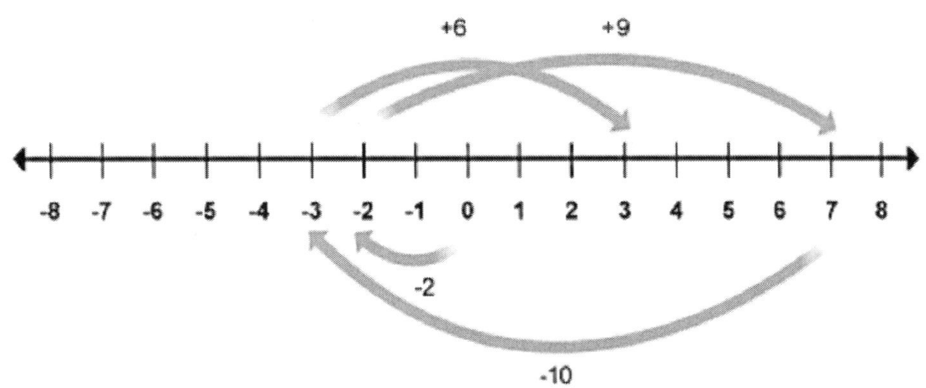

Solve the following (visualize a number line):

$7 - 6 =$	$8 - 3 =$	$20 - 4 =$
$6 - 7 =$	$3 - 8 =$	$4 - 20 =$

What is the relationship between $(\boldsymbol{A} - \boldsymbol{B})$ and $(\boldsymbol{B} - \boldsymbol{A})$?

Now try with simple fractions:

$\frac{7}{11} - \frac{6}{11} =$	$\frac{11}{15} - \frac{4}{15} =$	$\frac{20}{21} - \frac{4}{21} =$
$\frac{6}{11} - \frac{7}{11} =$	$\frac{4}{15} - \frac{11}{15} =$	$\frac{4}{21} - \frac{20}{21} =$

Consider the following strategy for subtraction:

$$2\frac{1}{7} - \frac{4}{7}$$

$$\swarrow \quad \searrow$$

$$2 \quad \frac{1}{7} - \frac{4}{7}$$

Not enough!
I can only take away 1/7 for now, and still need to take another 3/7 away...

$$\searrow \quad \swarrow$$

$$2 - \frac{3}{7} = 1\frac{4}{7}$$

We can use this strategy to subtract mixed numbers with like-fractions (same denominators). Subtract whole numbers first, fractions next, and then combine the two results to get the final answer. Look at these examples:

Examples:

a. $3\frac{7}{11} - 1\frac{6}{11} = (3-1) + \left(\frac{7}{11} - \frac{6}{11}\right) = 2\frac{1}{11}$

b. $5\frac{6}{11} - 1\frac{7}{11} = (5-1) + \left(\frac{6}{11} - \frac{7}{11}\right) = 4 - \frac{1}{11} = 3\frac{10}{11}$

c. $13\frac{2}{7} - 4\frac{6}{7} = (13-4) + \left(\frac{2}{7} - \frac{6}{7}\right) = 9 - \frac{4}{7} = 8\frac{3}{7}$

Try these on your own following the above examples:

e. $12\frac{4}{7} - 10\frac{5}{7} =$ ______________________________

f. $7\frac{4}{11} - 1\frac{9}{11} =$ ______________________________

g. $5\frac{2}{5} - 1\frac{4}{5} =$ ______________________________

h. $14\frac{8}{11} - 10\frac{4}{11} =$ ______________________________

Subtracting fractions with same denominators

Give your final answer in simplest form

Example: $7\frac{3}{8} - 4\frac{5}{8} = 3 + \left(\frac{3}{8} - \frac{5}{8}\right) = 3 - \frac{2}{8} = 2\frac{6}{8} = 2\frac{3}{4}$

1. $5\frac{1}{7} - 2\frac{3}{7} =$ ____________________

2. $4\frac{3}{5} - 1\frac{2}{5} =$ ____________________

3. $7\frac{3}{11} - 1\frac{4}{11} =$ ____________________

4. $8\frac{2}{3} - 1\frac{1}{3} =$ ____________________

5. $6\frac{3}{18} - \frac{11}{18} =$ ____________________

6. $6\frac{8}{9} - 2\frac{4}{9} =$ ____________________

7. $9\frac{1}{4} - 1\frac{3}{4} =$ ____________________

8. $8\frac{3}{8} + 6\frac{7}{8} =$ ____________________ (did you notice it is addition?)

9. $4\frac{1}{7} - 1\frac{3}{7} =$ ____________________

10. $\frac{33}{5} - \frac{18}{5} =$ ____________________

11. $13\frac{2}{5} - 3\frac{4}{5} =$ ____________________

12. $35\frac{1}{6} - 6\frac{5}{6} =$ ____________________

13. $14\frac{1}{7} + 1\frac{6}{7} =$ ____________________

14. $25\frac{3}{5} - \frac{14}{5} =$ ____________________

Brainteaser
*Circle all the ones where exactly **one quarter** is shaded.*

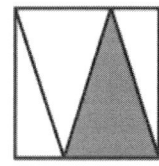

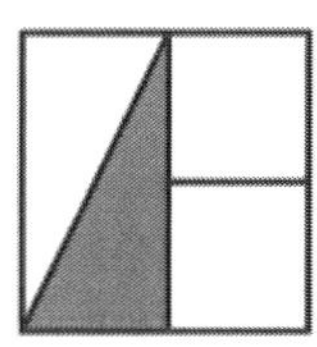

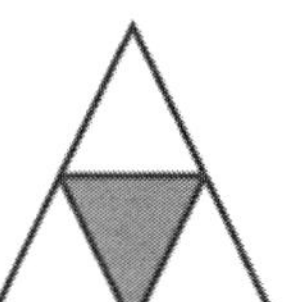

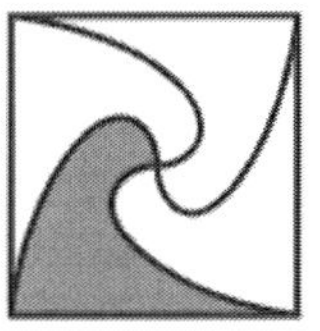

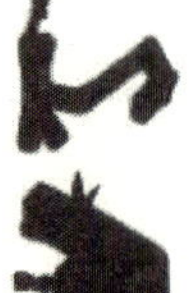

Subtracting fractions with same denominator

Give your final answer as a MIXED NUMBER in simplest form

Example: $13\frac{1}{5} - 4\frac{4}{5} = 9 + \left(\frac{1}{5} - \frac{4}{5}\right) = 9 - \frac{3}{5} = 8\frac{2}{5}$

1. $\frac{19}{9} - \frac{7}{9} =$ ____________________

2. $\frac{13}{6} - \frac{9}{6} =$ ____________________

3. $13\frac{3}{5} - \frac{24}{5} =$ ____________________

4. $2\frac{6}{7} - \frac{9}{7} =$ ____________________

5. $5\frac{2}{3} - 1\frac{1}{3} =$ ____________________

6. $4\frac{1}{4} - 1\frac{3}{4} =$ ____________________

7. $14\frac{1}{3} - 2\frac{2}{3} =$ ____________________

8. $8\frac{1}{8} - 1\frac{5}{8} =$ ____________________

9. $4\frac{7}{9} - 1\frac{4}{9} =$ ____________________

10. $3\frac{3}{10} - \frac{7}{10} =$ ____________________

11. $5\frac{2}{11} - 3\frac{4}{11} =$ ____________________

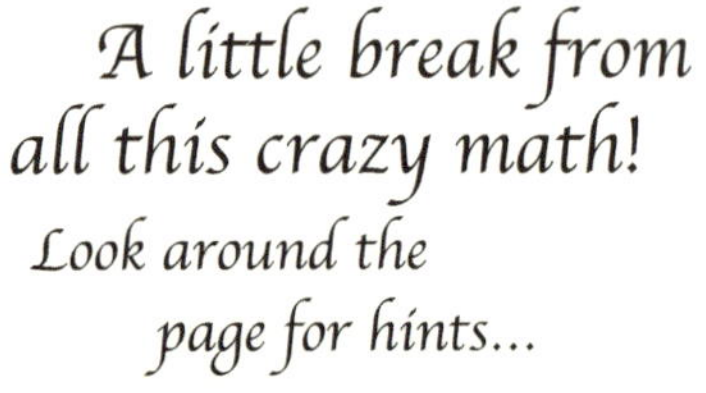

A little break from
all this crazy math!
Look around the
page for hints...

1 It has a tail, likes catching mice and sounds like 'hat'. ....
2 It lives in the sea and sounds like 'park'. ....
3 It's green, jumps very well and sounds like 'dog'. ....
4 It sings, sometimes lives in a cage, and sounds like 'word'. ....
5 It eats grass and sounds like 'now'. ....
6 It doesn't have legs and sounds like 'cake'. ....
7 It's always hungry, has a little beard and sounds like 'boat'. ....
8 It flies at night and sounds like 'Pat'. ....
9 It's very big, swims in the sea, and sounds like 'tail'. ....
10 It's very small, eats cheese and sounds like 'house'. ....

Area and Perimeter: Review II

What is AREA?
Area tells us the size of a shape or figure: how much SPACE it occupies. We measure it in little squares (squared units). Essentially, calculating area is asking ourselves: how many 1x1 tiles do I need to cover the whole shape.

Remember: Area is measured in **SQUARED UNITS** (cm^2, m^2, etc.)

The area of a square that has a side-length of 1cm is 1 squared centimeter ($1cm^2$), which looks like this: [square] 1 cm, 1 cm

To find the area of a square that has side-length of 4cm, for instance, we can divide the square into squared centimeters as in the picture.

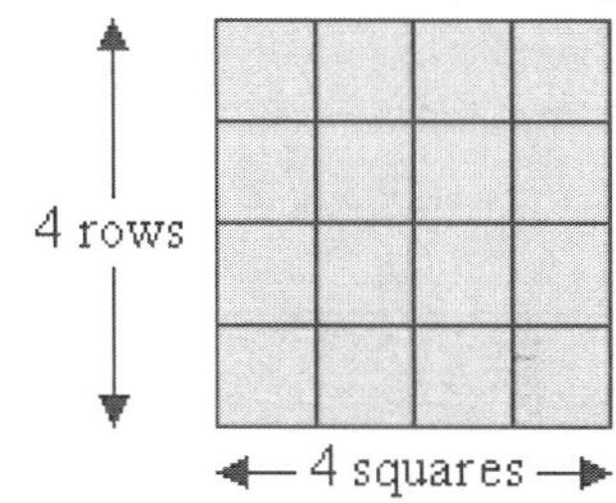

Using the method of counting squares, we find that the area of the square is 16 cm^2. Similarly, the area of a square that has side-length of 5cm will be $25cm^2$, etc.

What is PERIMETER?
The perimeter of a shape is an easier concept than area. All that it means is the DISTANCE around the shape. In other words, if we were to walk along all edges of the shape once, what distance would we be covering?

Remember: Perimeter is measured in **LINEAR UNITS** (cm, m, etc.)

To find the perimeter of the shape on the right, you just need to decide on a starting point (one of the vertices) and then go around the shape, keeping track of the distances that you walk.
In this case P=3+3+2+1+1+2=12cm

The area of this shape is the number of little squares needed to form the shape, which is $8cm^2$.

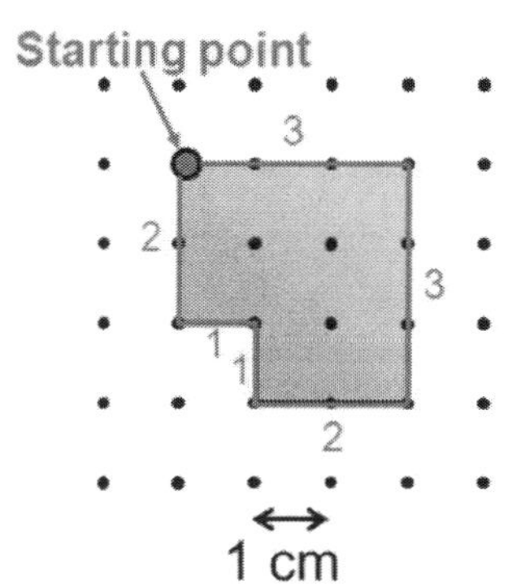

Area of a Rectangle

The area of a RECTANGLE is easily obtained by multiplying the length by the width. For example, if the length is 5cm and the width is 2cm, we get two rows of 5 (1 cm × 1 cm) squares in each, so the area is $2 \times 5 = 10\text{cm}^2$, just like you see in the picture:

5 cm, 2 cm

1	2	3	4	5
10	9	8	7	6

So the area of a rectangle with width of W units and length of L units is give by the formula **Area = L × W** squared units:

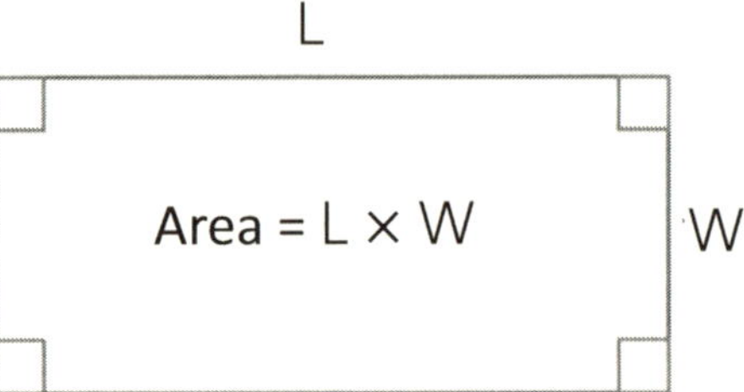

The PERIMETER, of course, is calculated by adding up the side lengths:

Perimeter = L+L+W+W = 2L+2W

Exercise: Find the **AREA** of each of the following rectangles:

1. Length=8cm, Width=3cm Area= ______________cm^2
2. Length=11m, Width=7m Area= ______________m^2
3. Length=18cm, Width=15cm Area= ______________cm^2
4. Length=14m, Width=3m Area= ______________m^2
5. Length=7in, Width=20in Area= ______________in^2

Find the **PERIMETER** of each of the following rectangles:

1. Length=8cm, Width=3cm Perimeter= ______________cm
2. Length=11m, Width=7m Perimeter = ______________m
3. Length=18cm, Width=15cm Perimeter = ______________cm
4. Length=14m, Width=3m Perimeter = ______________m
5. Length=17in, Width=29in Perimeter = ______________in

Calculate the Area and the Perimeter of each rectangle

Write your answers inside or beside each rectangle. Make sure to use the right units.

(a) 8 cm, 3 cm

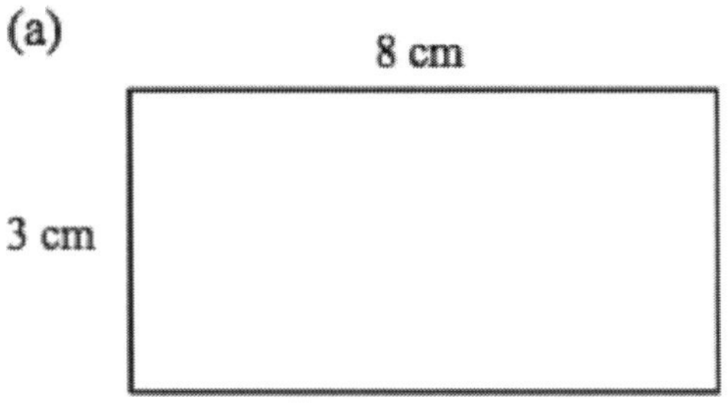

(b) 2 cm, 4 cm

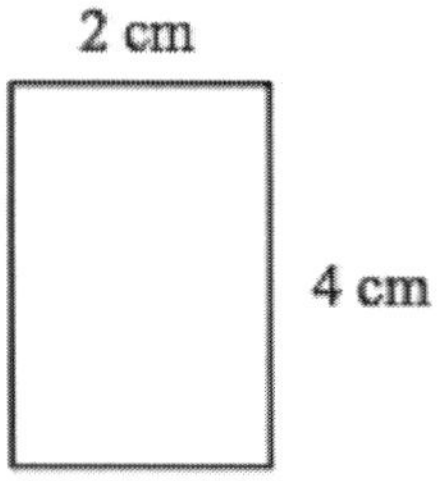

(c) 4 cm, 9 cm

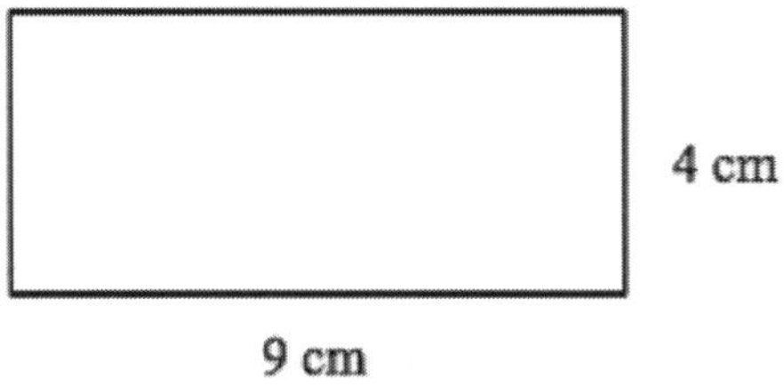

(d) 1 mm, 11 mm

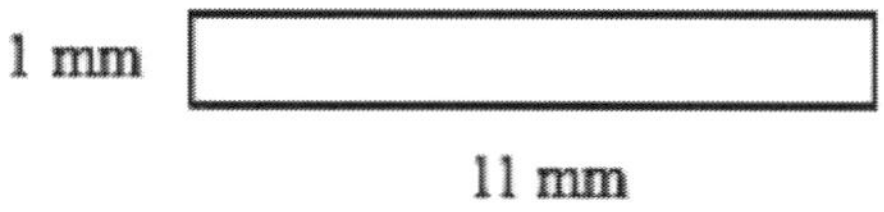

(e) 7 cm, 6 cm

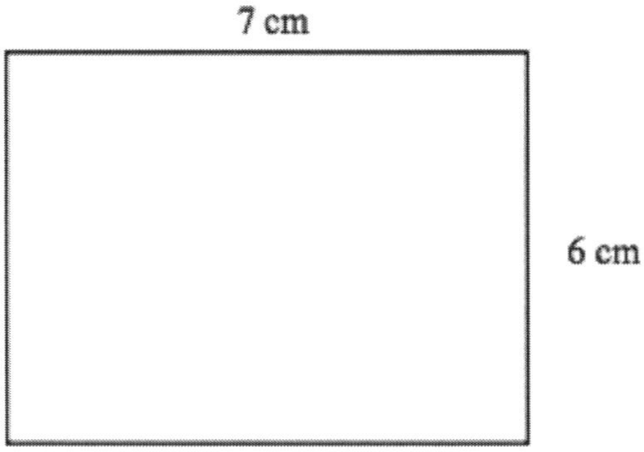

(f) 9 mm, 3 mm

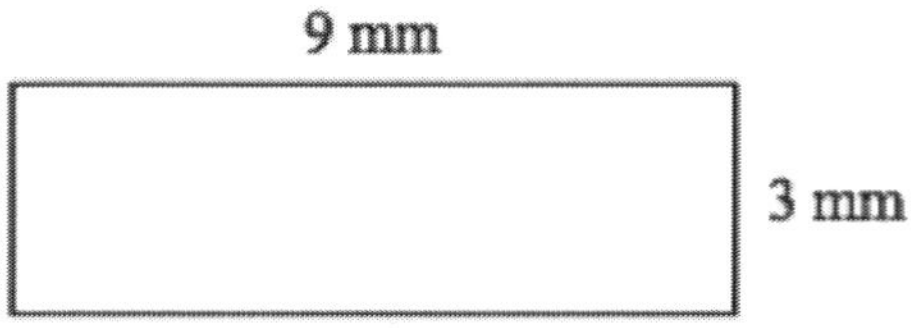

CRAZY Difficult Brainteaser

What is greater than God,
more evil than the devil,
poor people have it,
rich people need it,
and if you eat it—you die?

Answer: ____________________

Area of a COMPOSITE shape made of rectangles

A COMPOSITE shape is one that is made of few shapes "glued" together. For example, look at this L-shape figure, and notice that it is made up of two rectangles. In order to find its area, we can use one of two strategies:

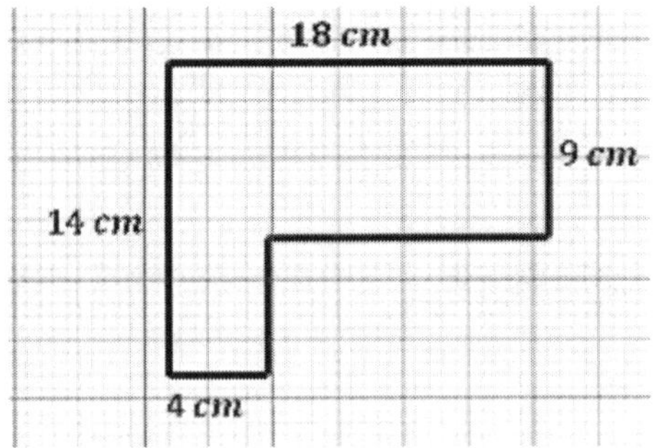

STRATEGY 1: Cut it into 2 rectangles and add up their areas.

Here we can cut it into 2 rectangles in 2 different ways:

Way 1

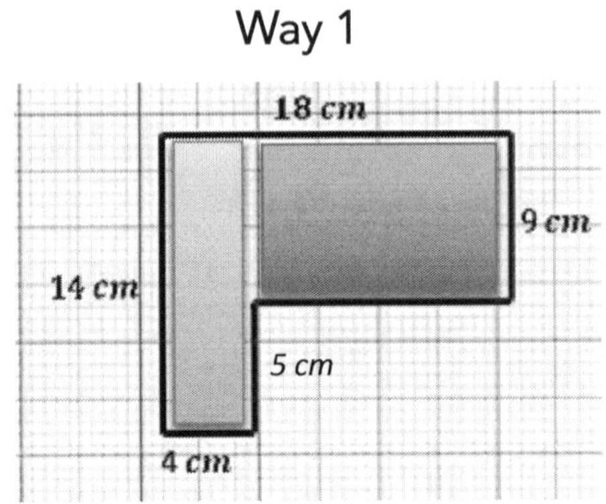

Area = $(4\times14)+(14\times9)=182\text{cm}^2$

Way 2

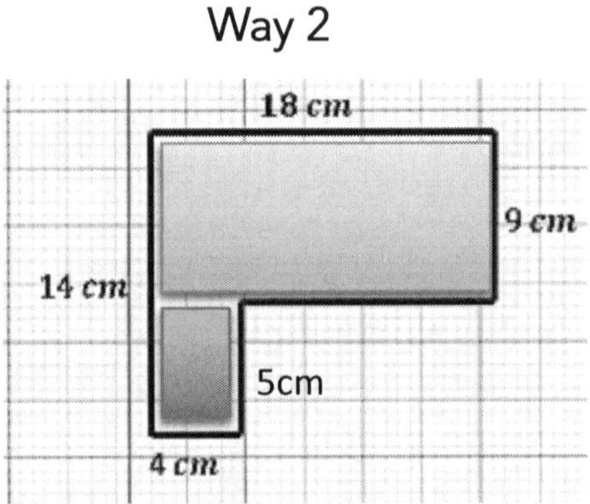

Area = $(4\times5)+(18\times9)=182\text{cm}^2$

STRATEGY 2: Calculate the area of the whole 18×14 rectangle and subtract the "missing piece":

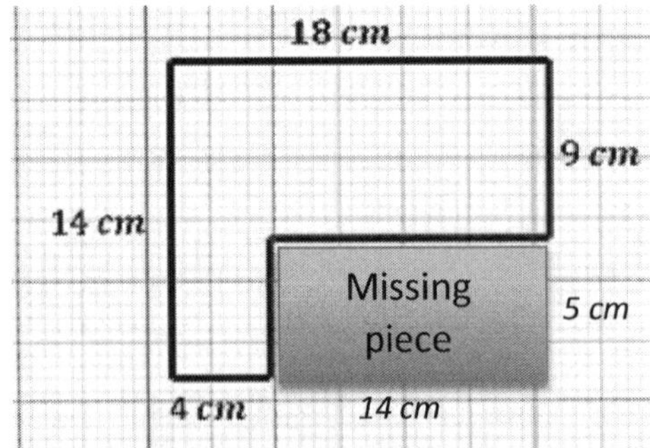

The calculation here will be: Area= $(18\times14)-(14\times5)=182\text{cm}^2$

Both strategies obviously give the same result, because both are correct. Choose the one that you like the most and that makes sense to you.

Calculate the Area and the Perimeter of each composite shape

(a)

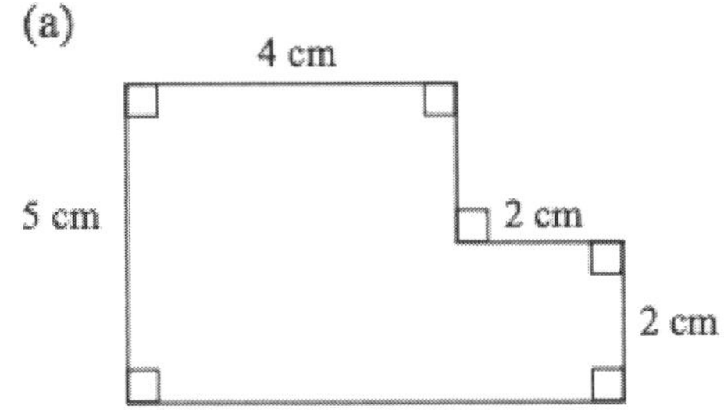

(b)

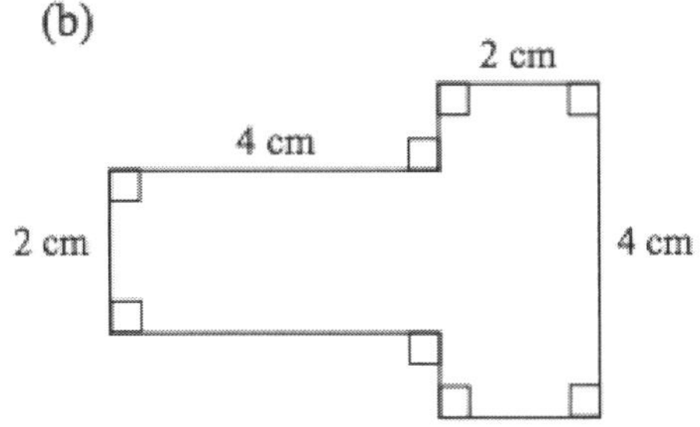

(c)

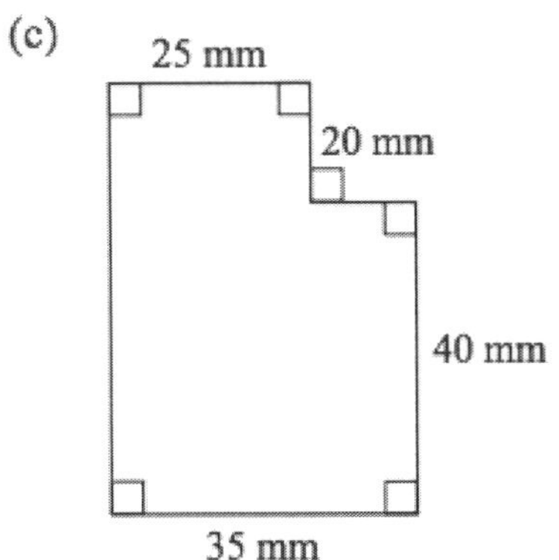

(d)

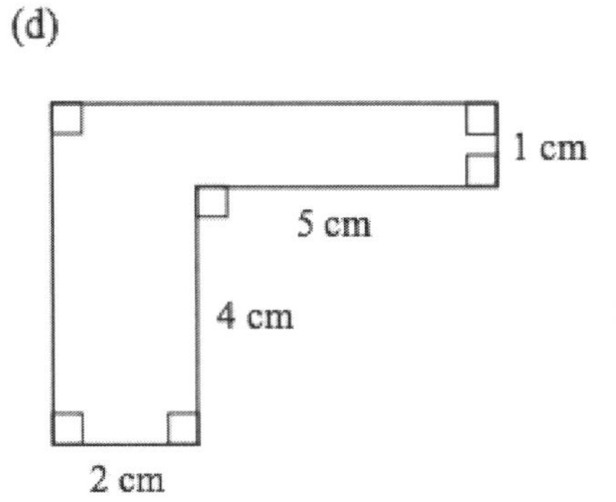

(e)

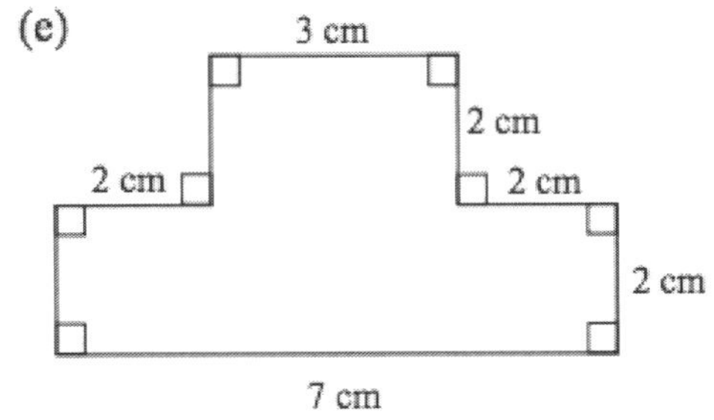

(f)

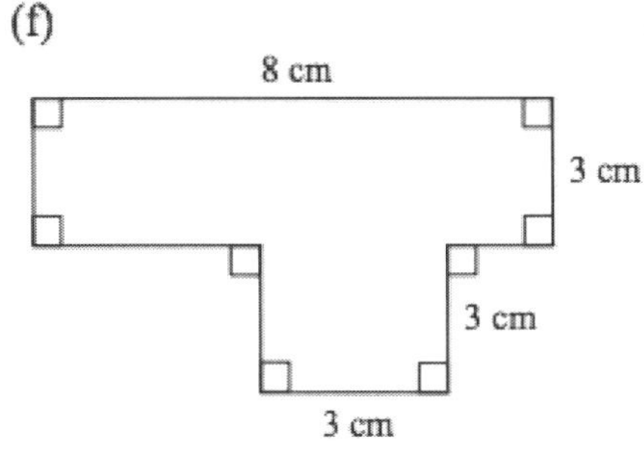

Explain how this can be if nobody is lying:

THREE DOCTORS SAID THAT ROBERT WAS THEIR BROTHER.
ROBERT SAID HE HAD NO BROTHERS.

Calculate the shaded AREA of each composite shape

HINT: Frequently, the easiest way is to do it by SUBTRACTION: subtract the area you do not need from the area of the big rectangle.

(a)

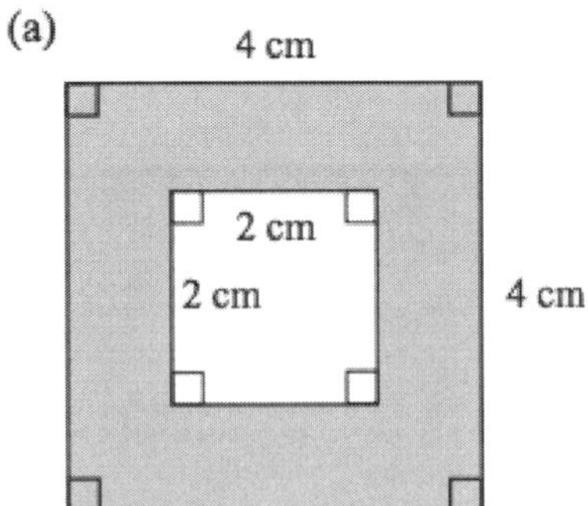

(b)

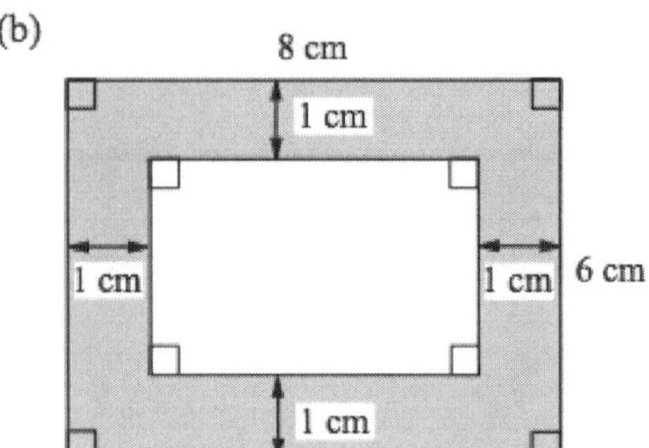

(c)

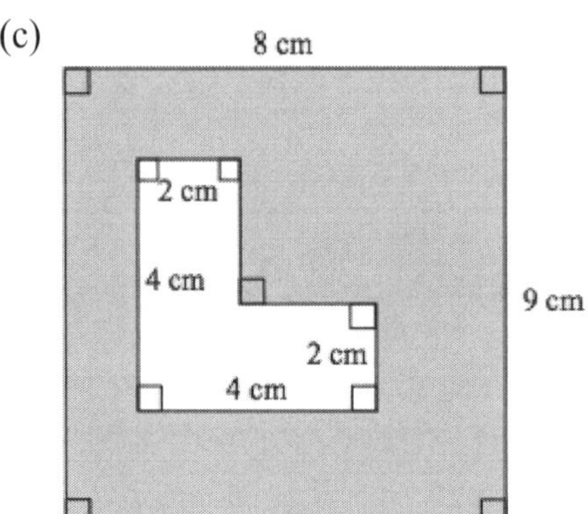

And how about this crazy question?

This is so hard that I put a hint on p.2 once you give up.

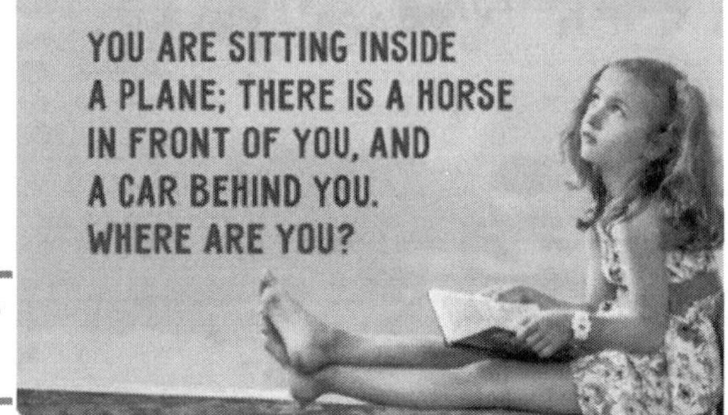

YOU ARE SITTING INSIDE
A PLANE; THERE IS A HORSE
IN FRONT OF YOU, AND
A CAR BEHIND YOU.
WHERE ARE YOU?

Calculate the AREA and PERIMETER of each composite shape

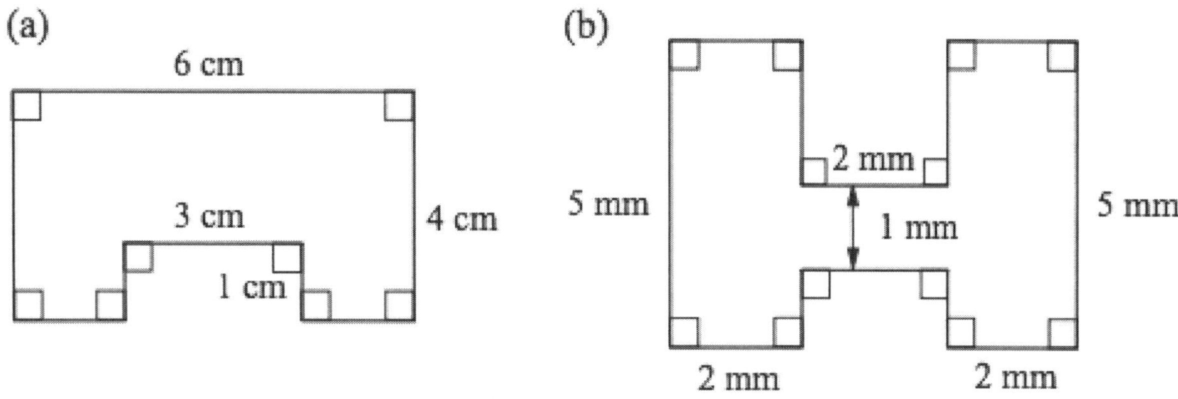

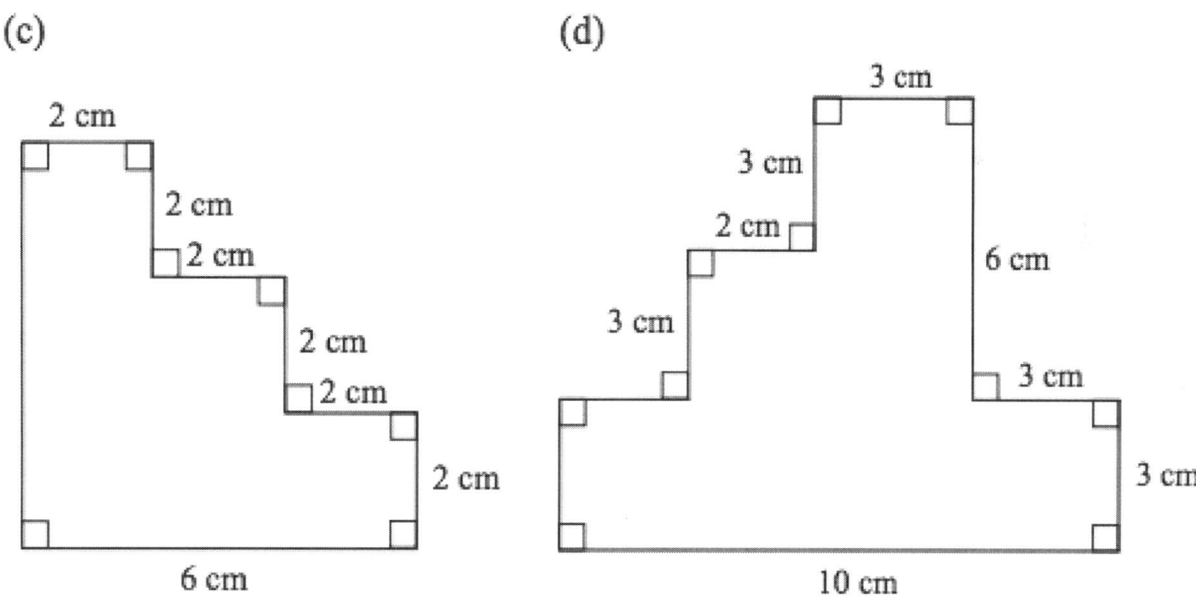

A little mental math to keep us sharp

LESSON 7 MAKE YOUR OWN COMPATIBLES 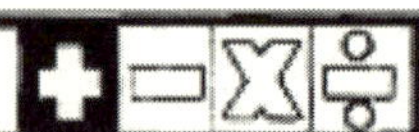

Adding in your head is easier when you make your own compatible pairs, then adjust.

Like this . . .

Make your own compatibles. Adjust the answer.

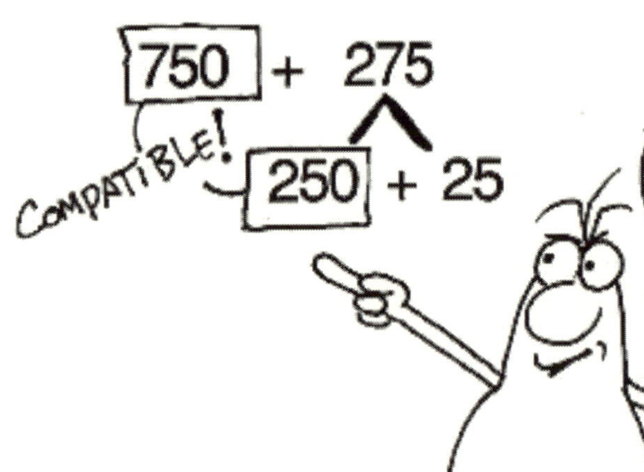

750 + 250 = 1000,
plus 25 → 1025.
So, 750 + 275 = 1025.

TRY THESE IN YOUR HEAD.
Make compatibles and adjust.

1. 75 + 28
2. 69 + 35
3. 188 + 213
4. 427 + 75
5. 450 + 65
6. 580 + 423
7. 795 + 206
8. 253 + 752
9. 1150 + 356
10. 1250 + 757

POWER BUILDER A

1. 25 + 79 = ______
2. 45 + 57 = ______
3. 18 + 85 = ______
4. 75 + 28 = ______
5. 68 + 33 = ______
6. 159 + 42 = ______
7. 125 + 277 = ______
8. 468 + 35 = ______
9. 109 + 393 = ______
10. 254 + 349 = ______
11. 435 + 568 = ______
12. 295 + 706 = ______
13. 455 + 456 = ______
14. 263 + 738 = ______
15. 375 + 526 = ______
16. 276 + 727 = ______
17. 459 + 544 = ______
18. 2500 + 501 = ______
19. 425 + 176 = ______
20. 725 + 277 = ______

THINK IT THROUGH

If 867 + 133 = 1000, what is 867 + 135? 868 + 132? 8.67 + 1.33?

POWER BUILDER B

1. 75 + 26 = ______
2. 35 + 67 = ______
3. 19 + 82 = ______
4. 27 + 75 = ______
5. 65 + 38 = ______
6. 143 + 58 = ______
7. 275 + 127 = ______
8. 235 + 67 = ______
9. 362 + 139 = ______
10. 155 + 249 = ______
11. 345 + 659 = ______
12. 307 + 695 = ______
13. 285 + 717 = ______
14. 155 + 846 = ______
15. 518 + 485 = ______
16. 475 + 426 = ______
17. 365 + 337 = ______
18. 4246 + 555 = ______
19. 425 + 376 = ______
20. 525 + 478 = ______

THINK IT THROUGH

If 655 + 1345 = 2000, what is 655 + 1355? 645 + 1355? 6.55 + 13.45?

Types of Lines

Characteristics	What You Draw	What You Say	What You Write
Parallel lines never cross and stay the same distance apart. They are coplanar. They have 0 points in common.		Line AB is parallel to line CD or line l is parallel to line j	$\overleftrightarrow{AB} \parallel \overleftrightarrow{CD}$ or line $l \parallel$ line j
Intersecting lines pass through the same point. They have one point in common.		Lines HG and EF intersect at point I.	$\overleftrightarrow{HG}$ intersects $\overleftrightarrow{EF}$. (There is no symbol for intersection of lines.)
Perpendicular lines intersect at right angles. They have one point in common.		Line LM is perpendicular to line JK.	$\overleftrightarrow{LM} \perp \overleftrightarrow{JK}$.
Coincident lines are the same line. They have an infinite number of points in common.		Line NO and line OP are coincident lines.	(There is no symbol for coincident lines.)

Parallel lines

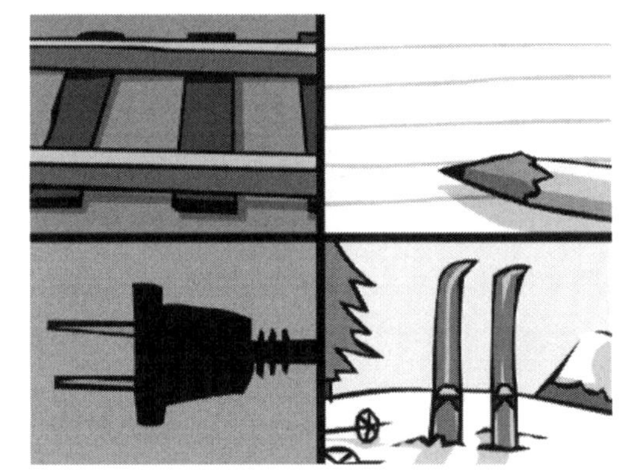

We see them everywhere: train-tracks, parking lot markings, the lines in our notebook, the top and the bottom edges of the window. **Parallel lines have the same direction, and they never intersect.** The symbol we use to indicate that two lines are parallel is || (which makes sense).

Perpendicular lines

We see them everywhere: in the corners of windows and doors, the angle between the wall and the floor, parking lot markings, the lines in our graph paper notebook. **Perpendicular lines intersect at a right (90^0) angle.** The symbol we use to indicate that two lines are parallel is $\perp$ (which makes sense).

For each pair of lines, indicate parallel, perpendicular or neither.

1) 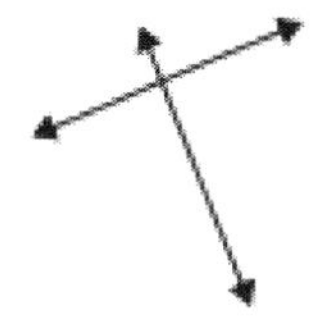

2) 

3) 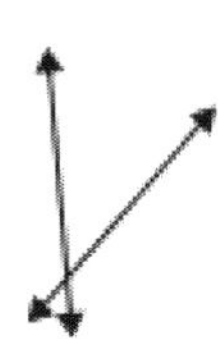

4) 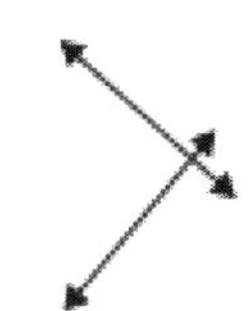

5) 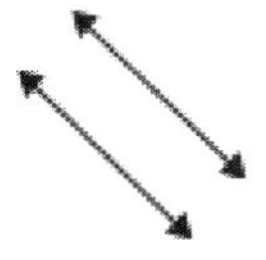

6) 

7) 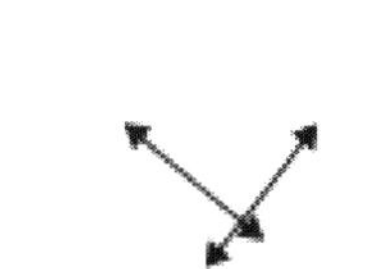

8) 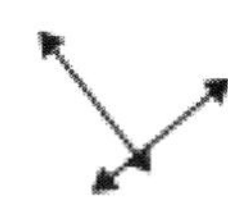

9) 

10) 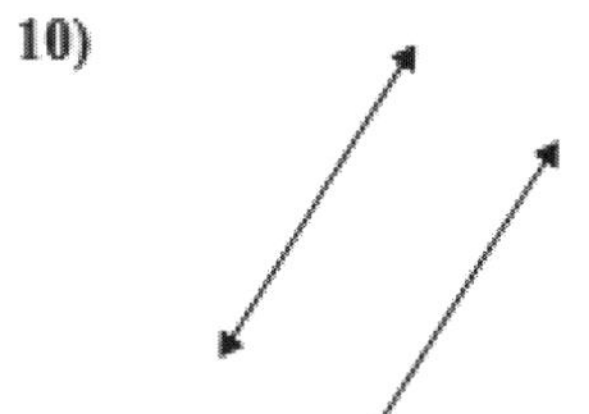

11) 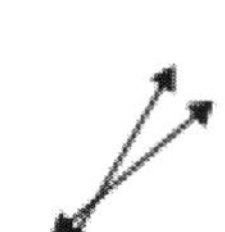

12) 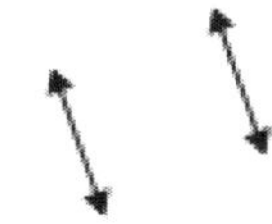

13) 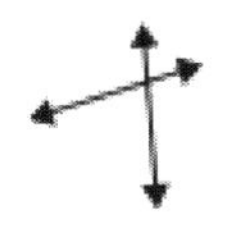

14) 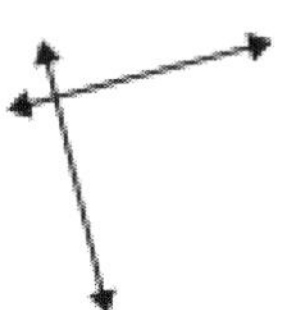

15) 

1. ____________
2. ____________
3. ____________
4. ____________
5. ____________
6. ____________
7. ____________
8. ____________
9. ____________
10. ____________
11. ____________
12. ____________
13. ____________
14. ____________
15. ____________

Look carefully at the picture and answer the questions below.

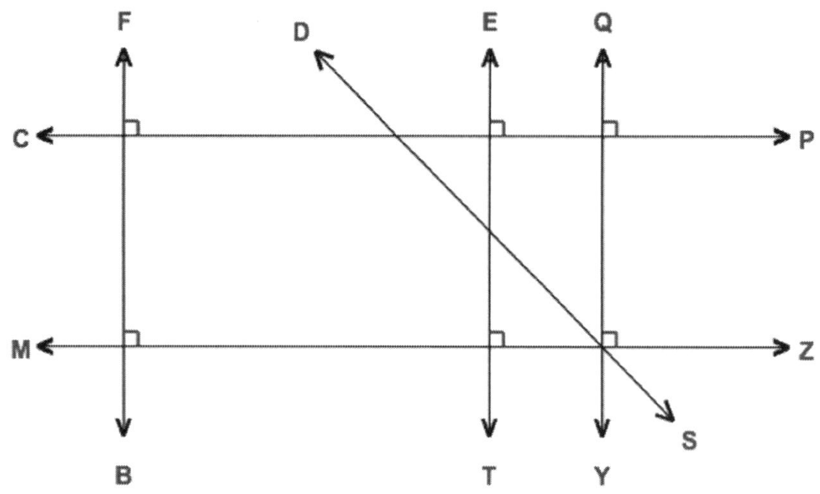

1)	Line QY and Line ET are ______________ lines.	6)	Line DS and Line ET are ______________ lines.
2)	Line MZ and Line ET are ______________ lines.	7)	Line FB and Line DS are ______________ lines.
3)	Line CP and Line MZ are ______________ lines.	8)	Line CP and Line ET are ______________ lines.
4)	Line MZ and Line FB are ______________ lines.	9)	Line FB and Line ET are ______________ lines.
5)	Line QY and Line DS are ______________ lines.	10)	Line MZ and Line DS are ______________ lines.

How many sticks? 8 or 7?

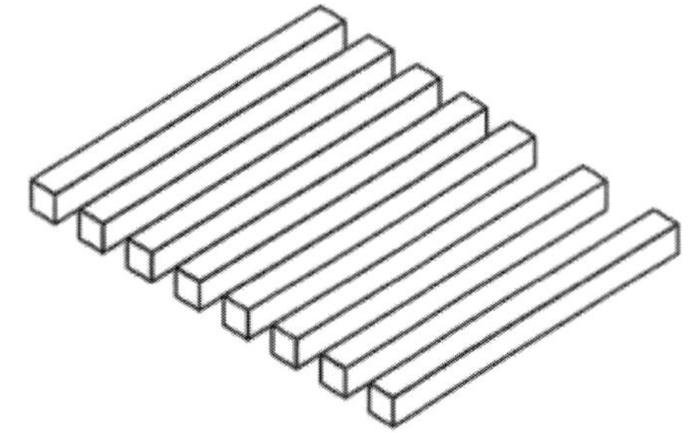

How many legs does the elephant have?

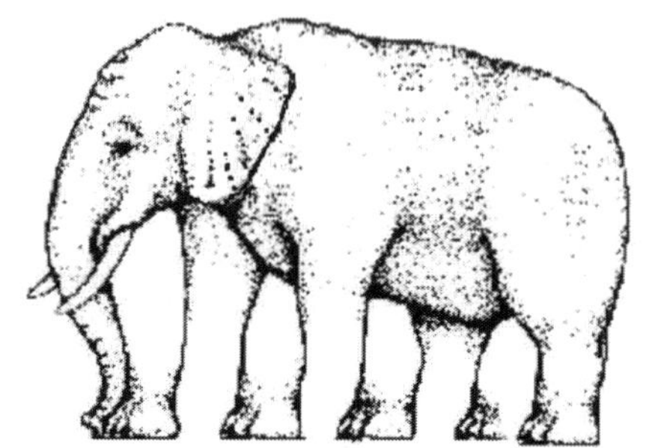

In each box, indicate all lines that are **parallel or perpendicular**

Use proper notation, as in the example

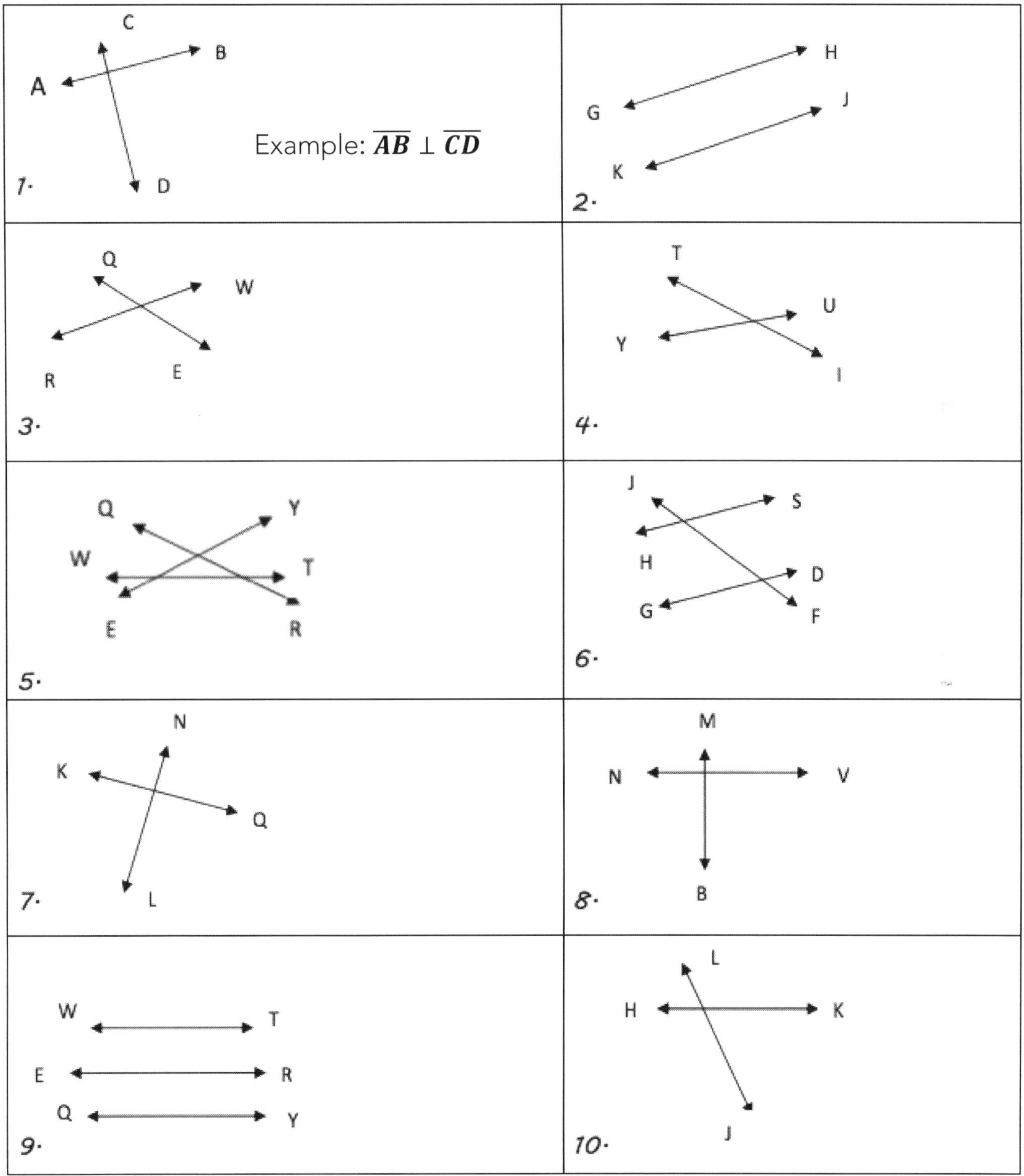

1. Find all pairs of parallel lines and all pairs of perpendicular lines in this picture. List them all and make sure to use proper notation!

   Example: *line BC* $\perp$ *line AG*

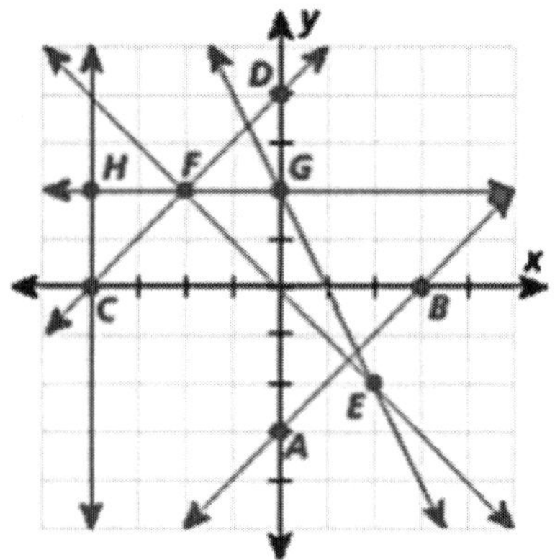

2. There are 3 pairs of parallel spaghettis in this picture. Find them and colour them using a different colour for each pair.

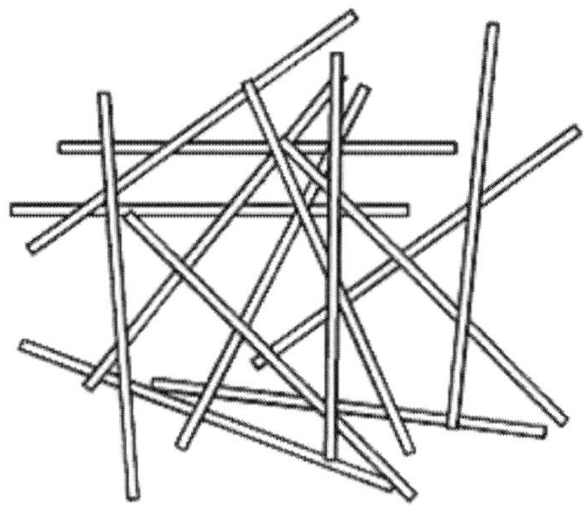

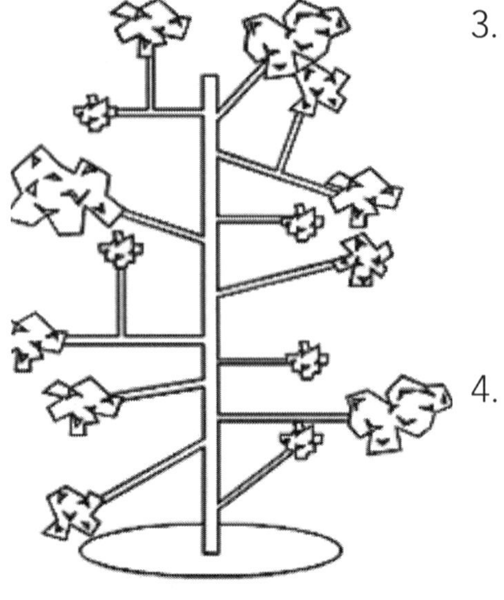

3. Circle all intersections where the two lines are perpendicular to each other. Can you find all 8?

4. Colour all lines that are parallel to each other the same colour. How many colours will you need to use?

Drawing parallel and perpendicular lines

1. Draw a line parallel to line $\overline{PQ}$ that passes through point S. Call it *Line1*.
Hint: an easy way to draw parallel lines is by using both sides of the ruler.

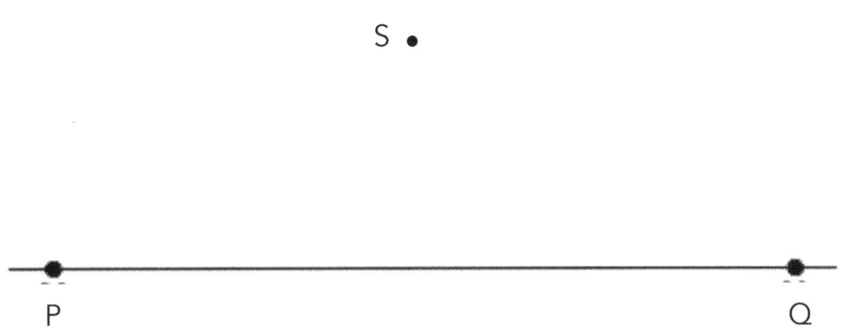

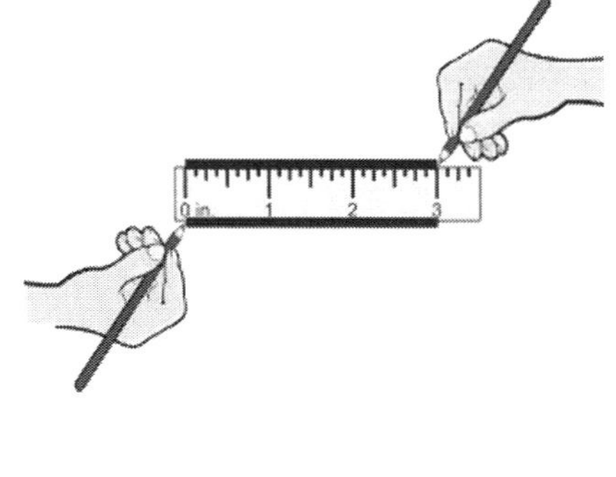

2. Draw two lines that are perpendicular to line $\overline{XY}$.
Call them *Line2* and *Line3*.

Hint: an easy way to draw perpendicular lines is by sliding a **set square** (fancy way of saying a triangular ruler) along a regular ruler→

Make sure they intersect at a 90^0 angle.

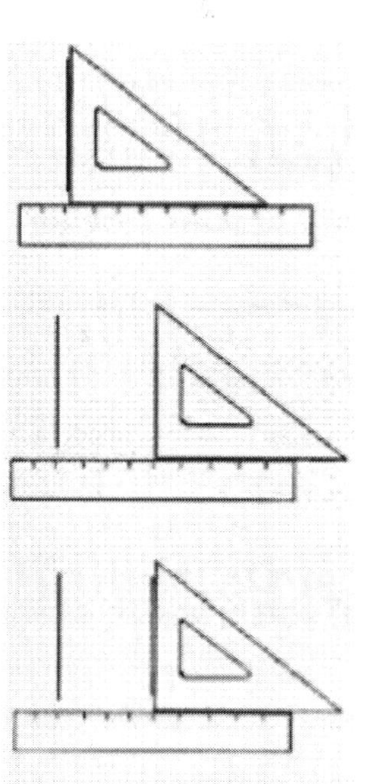

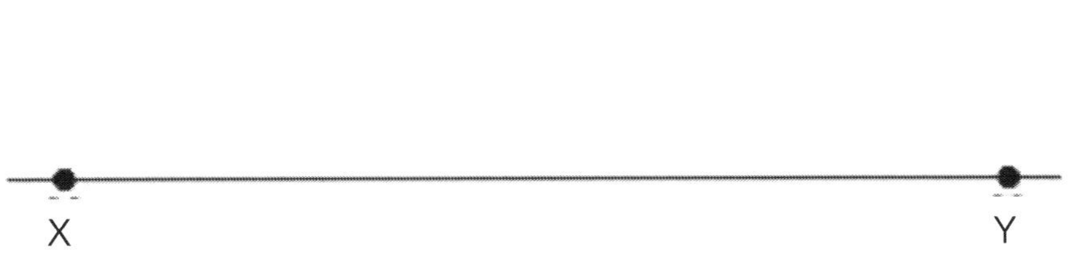

3. What do you observe about the 2 lines you drew?

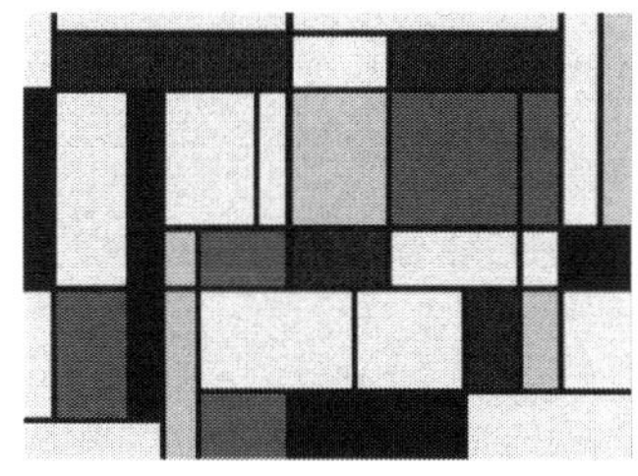

Drawing parallel and perpendicular lines

4. Draw a line perpendicular to line $\overline{PQ}$, that passes through point S. Call it *Line1*. Make sure to **use a protractor**, and follow the method in the picture

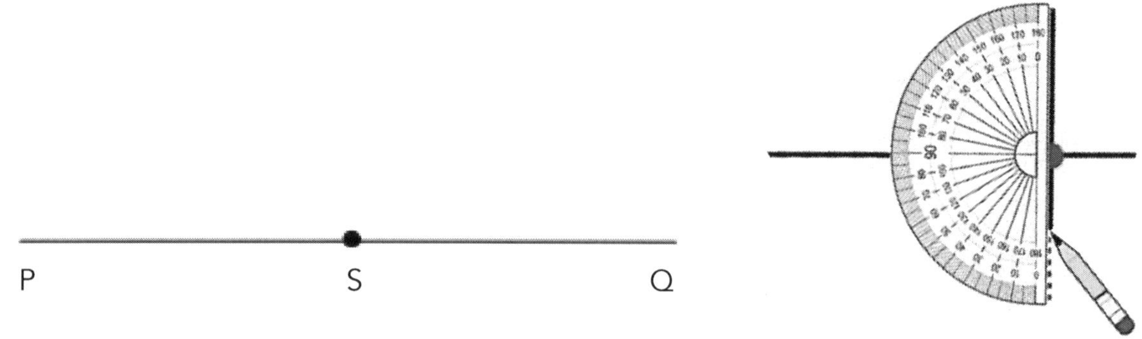

5. Here is another method to draw as many **parallel** lines as you need by using TWO set squares, OR a ruler and a set square. One of them should be pressed down, so it does not move. You slide the other and keep drawing lines.

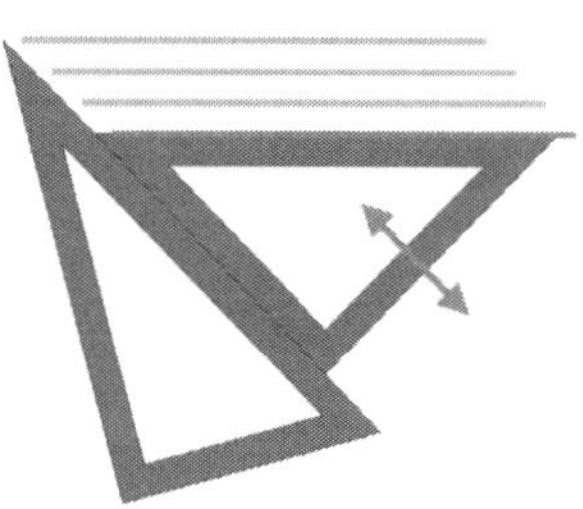

Try to keep the distances between the lines the same, just like the lines on the lined paper you have in your notebook.

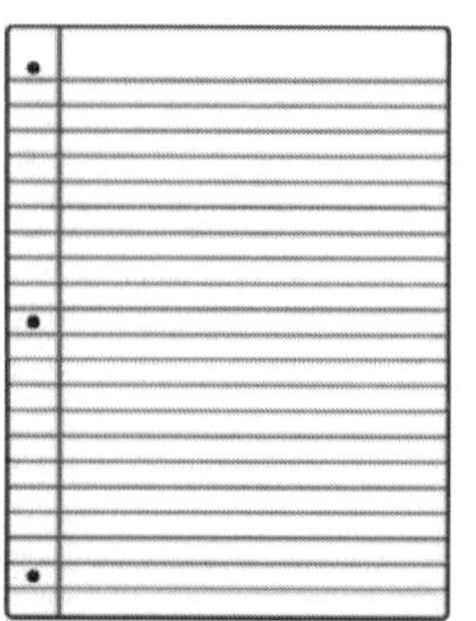

Drawing parallel and perpendicular lines

6. Draw a line **parallel** to line *m* that passes through point A.
   Draw ALSO a line **perpendicular** to line *m* that passes through point A.

   You may use any method you want, but be accurate.

A

m

7. Draw two lines that are perpendicular to line $\overline{XY}$, call them *Line4* and *Line5*. One must pass through point X, and the other through point Y.

   Use a protractor and follow the method that you see in the picture.

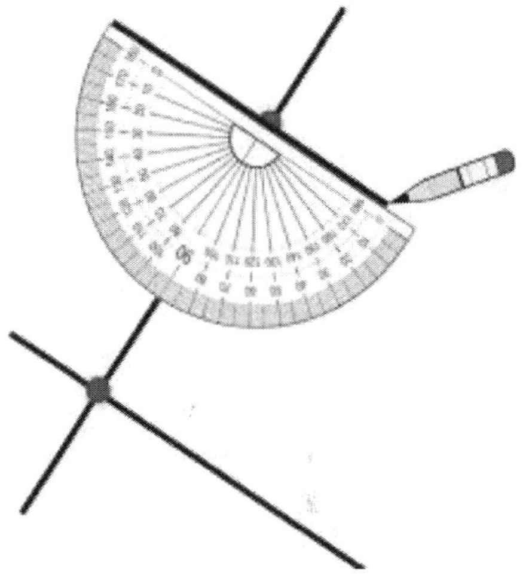

X
Y

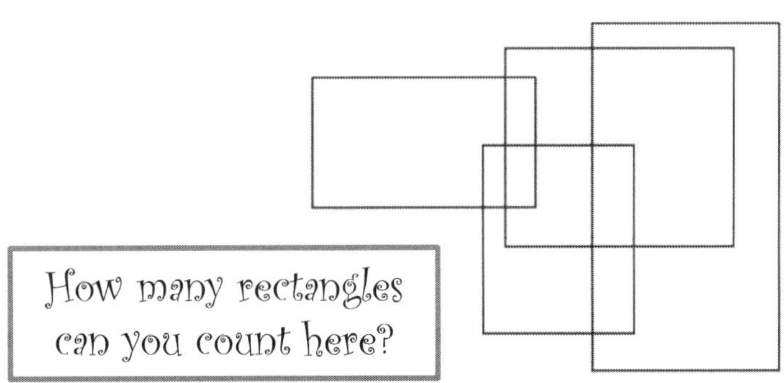
How many rectangles
can you count here?

8. State all pairs of **parallel** lines, and all pairs of perpendicular lines that you can find in this picture.

   Use proper notation in answering!

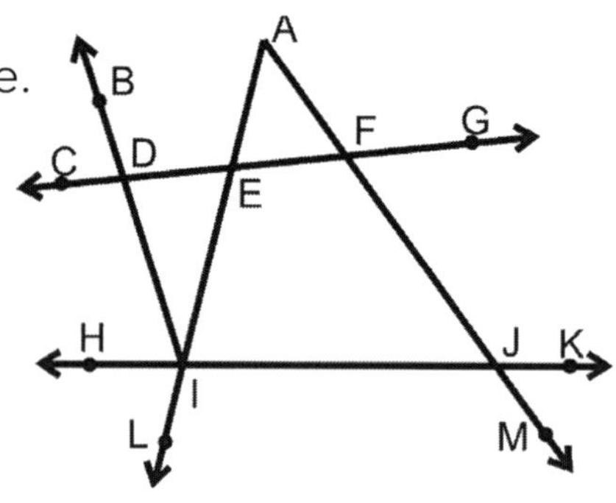

9. Below is a map of downtown Calgary. List 3 pairs of parallel roads and 3 pairs of perpendicular roads. Use proper notation!

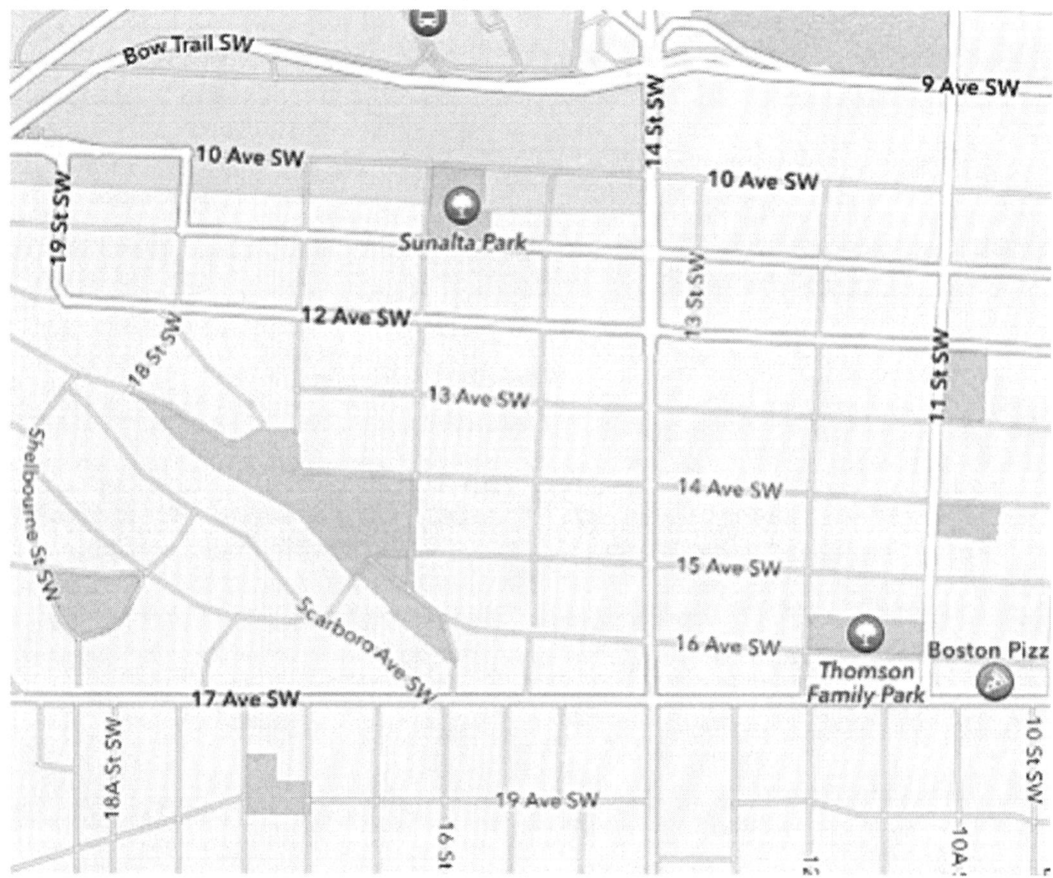

Example: 14Ave. || 15Ave.

10. Draw a **PERFECT square** with a side length of 5cm. Be sure to use a **sharpened pencil**, a ruler, and a set square or a protractor. Make sure the sides are EXACTLY 5cm and that each of the 4 angles is EXACTLY 90^0.

Take your time; this is harder than it sounds.

11. Draw a **PERFECT rectangle** that is 8cm by 3cm. Be sure to use a **sharpened pencil**, a ruler, and a set square or a protractor. Make sure the sides are EXACTLY 8cm and 3cm, and that each of the 4 angles is EXACTLY 90^0.

Take your time here as well; this is harder than it sounds.

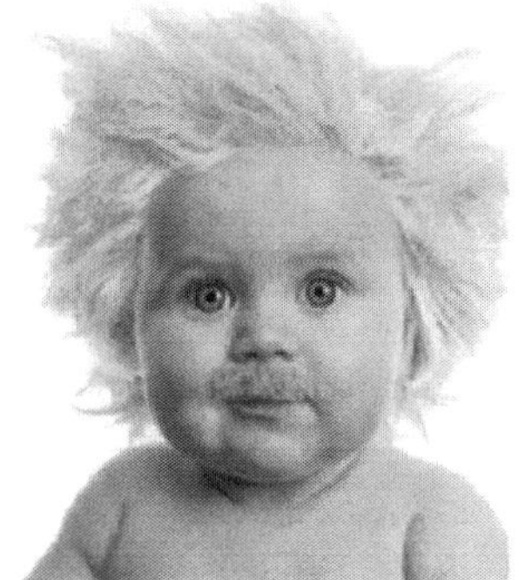

Renert's Bright Minds expresses its gratitude to Jack Hope, Barbara and Bob Reys for creating this wonderful resource and allowing our students to use it throughout the program.

A little mental math to keep us sharp

UNIT ONE REVIEW **(CLASS DISCUSSION)**

Mental Math Techniques
• **ADD FROM THE LEFT.** 245 + 138 = 300 + 70 + 13
• **SUBTRACT FROM THE LEFT.** 5.78 − 3.45
• **BREAK IT UP.** 140 + 285 = 140 + 200 + 80 + 5
• **BREAK UP AND BRIDGE.** 4.5 + 2.7 = 6.5 + 0.7
• **USE COMPATIBLES.** 3.85 + 1.99 = 3.84 + 2

Do the problems below in your head. Tell which techniques you find useful for each one.

1. 527 + 36
2. 2 − 1.95
3. 965 − 342
4. 1000 − 350
5. 145 + 38 + 56
6. 100 − 73
7. 0.15 + 0.65
8. 4.37 + 0.48 + 0.16
9. 457 + 298
10. 350 + 455

Talk about each problem below. What's an easy way to do it in your head? Tell how you would think it through.

1. 1000 − 475
2. 636 + 48
3. 465 + 236
4. 344 + 38 + 76
5. 4275 − 3160
6. 14.6 + 3.8 + 6.7
7. $4 − $2.27
8. 857 + 498
9. 1.55 + 3.45
10. 100 − 87

MENTAL MATH PROGRESS TEST

UNIT ONE
LESSONS 1–10

1. 150 + 172 = ______
2. 8.1 − 2.9 = ______
3. 375 + 226 = ______
4. 10 − 0.77 = ______
5. The difference in time from 9:15 A.M. to 12:30 P.M. = ______
6. 325 + 265 = ______
7. 74 − 35 = ______
8. 348 + 155 = ______
9. The difference in time from 8:00 A.M. to 11:45 A.M. = ______
10. 6.7 − 4.3 = ______
11. $10.00 − $4.69 = ______
12. 5 − 1.36 = ______
13. $20 − $15.50 = ______
14. 355 + 38 = ______
15. 476 − 125 = ______
16. 1000 − 829 = ______
17. $10 − $4.37 = ______
18. The difference in time from 11:15 A.M. to 7:30 P.M. = ______
19. 545 + 128 = ______
20. $0.65 + $0.25 = ______
21. 100 − 67 = ______
22. $20 − $1.78 = ______
23. 5.5 + 1.7 = ______
24. 23.7 + 5.5 = ______
25. 2.6 + 0.6 + 1.3 = ______
26. 500 − 275 = ______
27. 3 − 1.254 = ______
28. $1.45 + $0.25 + $1.30 + $1.15 = ______
29. 47 + 26 = ______
30. 1 − 0.67 = ______
31. 1000 − 455 = ______
32. The difference in time from 2:35 P.M. to 9:30 P.M. = ______
33. 9150 + 275 = ______
34. 800 − 445 = ______
35. 595 + 308 = ______
36. 9 + 16 + 25 + 18 = ______
37. 4.75 − 1.35 = ______
38. $100 − $75.88 = ______
39. 369 − 36 = ______
40. 75 + 27 = ______

Mental Math in Junior High

Jack A. Hope   Barbara J. Reys   Robert E. Reys

DATA ANALYSIS

1. Benito wrote down the number of grade 11 and 12 students at West Island College that play basketball, badminton, tennis and hockey. Study the results, and answer the questions.

		Indoor Sports		Outdoor Sports	
		Basketball	Badminton	Tennis	Hockey
Grade 11	Boys	12	18	22	17
	Girls	15	20	8	11
Grade 12	Boys	23	25	7	10
	Girls	11	21	16	20

A. How many students chose hockey? __________

B. How many grade 11 girls chose indoor sports? __________

C. How many boys chose indoor sports ? __________

D. How many grade 12 students chose indoor sports? __________

E. How many boys chose tennis? __________

F. How many students participate in these 4 sports? __________

2. 115 students are enrolled in 3 sports, as in the table below.
Fill in the missing information.

	Soccer	Volleyball	Basketball	TOTAL
Girls		17		55
Boys	24			
TOTAL	39	44		**115**

3. Evita has 50 students in her class. She recorded what each of them got on the most recent English and Math tests, and summarized the results in the table below:

Mark	21-30	31-40	41-50	51-60	61-70	71-80	81-90	91-100
English	3	4	10	12	10	6	3	2
Math	1	2	8	14	20	3	2	0

A. How many students got less than 41 in English or Math? ___________

B. How many got more than 60 in English? ___________

C. How many got 70 or less in Math? ___________

D. How many got between 51 and 70 in English or Math? ___________

E. Do you think these exams were hard? Why? ___________________________

____

4. Rudolph asked his 30 classmates how many brothers and sisters they each have. He kept track of the results. Help him draw a Bar Graph based on the data he collected:

0	1	2	1	0	0	1	2	1	1
2	0	0	1	1	2	3	4	1	1
2	1	2	0	0	3	2	1	5	1

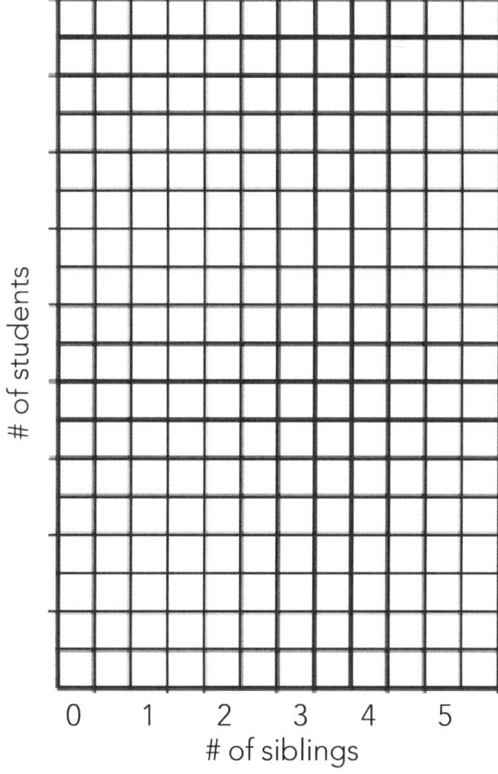

5. The pictogram shows the number of suitcases sold by the AMA store during 1991-1996. The information for 1995 is missing.

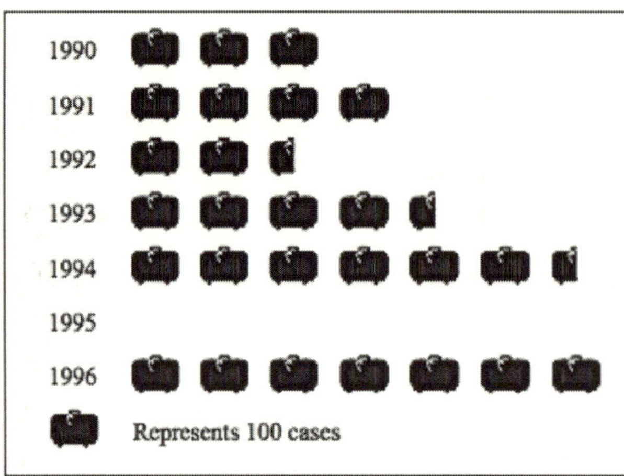

A. How many suitcases were sold in 1994? ___________

B. What was the the total number of suitcases sold during 1990-1992? _________

C. In what year were sales the greatest? ____________

D. If 1,700 suitcases were sold in 1994-1996, complete the pictogram for 1995.

6. In the chart below are the number of boys and girls in the three grade 2 classes at Renert School. Fill in the missing information.

	Boys	Girls	**Total**
Mrs. R	8	7	
Ms. Amy		11	
Mr. Sam	9		
Total	23		**51**

BRAINTEASER: You get out of jail. Your car does not move, so you push it until you stop at a hotel. You walk in, and realize that you are bankrupt.. Where are you?

Hint: This one is SO hard that we put a big hint on p.2

7. Heinrich conducted a survey among 40 senior high girls, collecting data on their shoe sizes. Here are the results:

10	7	7	10	11	9	8	7	8	9
7	9	11	11	8	8	9	7	10	10
11	8	9	7	10	11	11	11	11	7
7	7	8	7	8	9	10	10	9	8

Complete the Bar Graph to represent the data collected by Heinrich. Indicate clearly what each bar stands for.

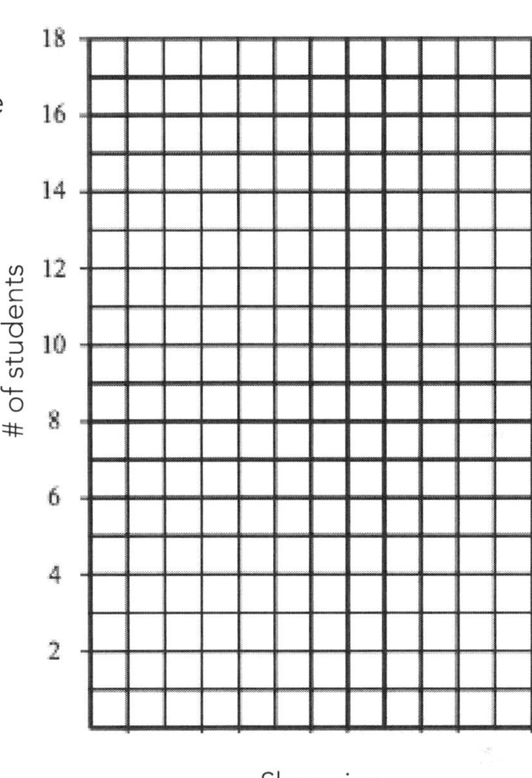

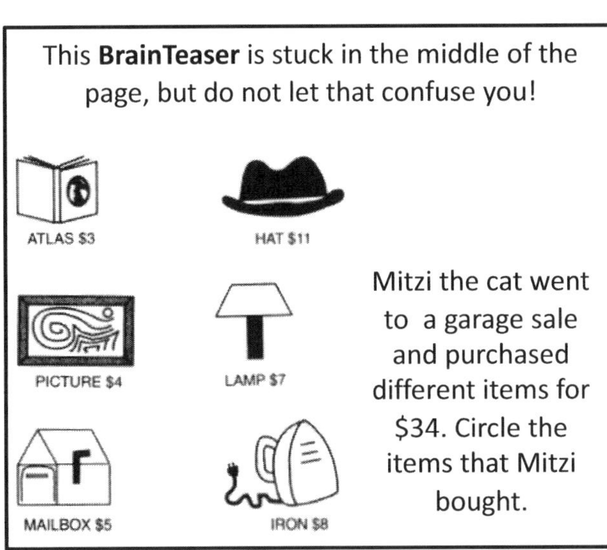

This **BrainTeaser** is stuck in the middle of the page, but do not let that confuse you!
ATLAS $3
HAT $11
PICTURE $4
LAMP $7
MAILBOX $5
IRON $8
Mitzi the cat went to a garage sale and purchased different items for $34. Circle the items that Mitzi bought.

8. The Bar Chart below shows the shoe sizes of all grade 11 boys at Rundolph College. How many boys are there in grade 11 at the college

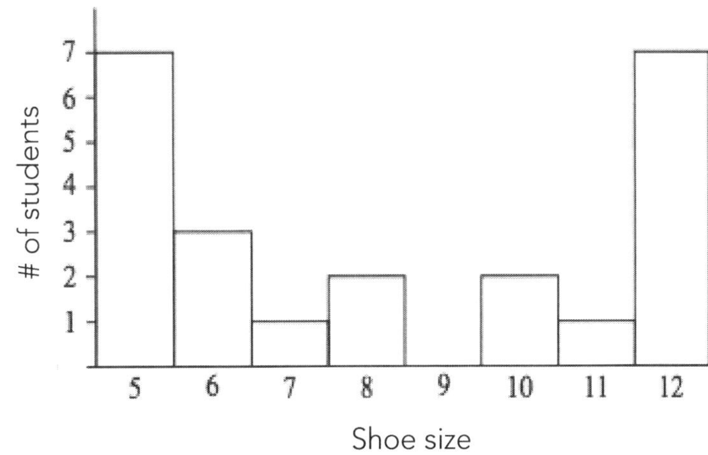

9. Neomi asked 30 of her classmates what their favorite colour was: white, blue, red or green. She wrote their answers in her little notebook→

w	w	r	w	g
r	w	r	b	r
r	r	w	r	r
b	w	r	r	w
w	g	r	w	r
g	w	w	b	r

Key:

w white
b blue
r red
g green

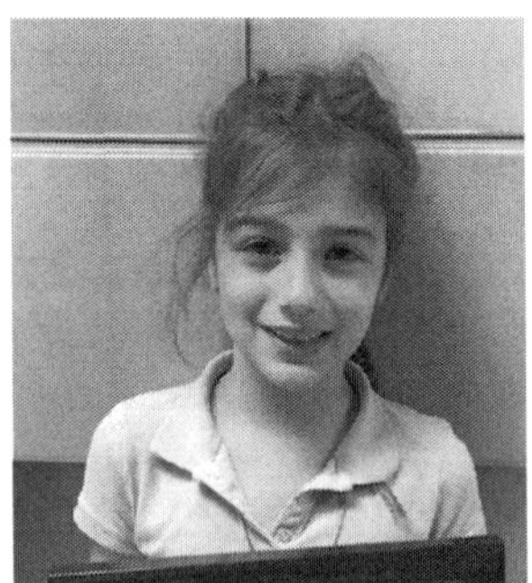

	Tally marks	How many?
White		
Blue		
Red		
Green		

Help Neomi complete her chart and to keep track of how many times each colour was chosen.

Start by using tally marks.

Complete the Bar Graph to represent the data collected by Neomi.

Indicate clearly what each bar stands for.

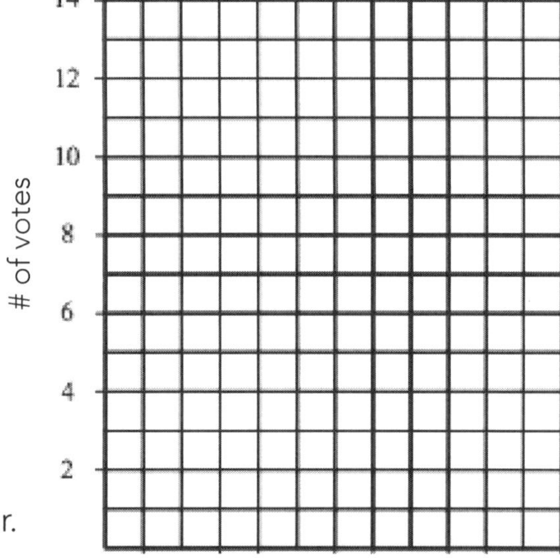

Colour

10. The Calgary Police recorded the number of accidents on Deerfoot Trail during winter *before* and *after* installing cameras for ticketing drivers who are speeding. The results are in the table below:

Type of accident	Before cameras	After cameras
Minor	185	144
Serious	94	81
Very serious	18	13

A. What was the total number of accidents **before** the cameras were installed?

B. What was the the total number of accidents **after** the cameras were installed?

C. Did the total number of accidents drop? If so, by how many accidents?

D. How many Minor accidents were there in total?

E. How many Very Serious accidents were there in total?

F. What was the total number of accidents during the entire winter?

Johnny's mother had four children.

The first was April, the second was May,

and the third was June.

What was the name of her fourth child?

11. Taliah conducted a survey at her school, asking students in grades 3-7 about their favorite sport. Students who participated chose their one favorite sport from among hockey, soccer, tennis and swimming.

Taliah recorded the results of the survey in a table:

	Hockey	Soccer	Tennis	Swimming	TOTAL
Grade 3	6	18	5	14	
Grade 4	5	16	8	14	
Grade 5	8	15	11	10	
Grade 6	11	12	4	19	
Grade 7	7	10	3	9	
TOTAL					

A. Complete the table by calculating the SUMS of the rows and the columns.

B. What information does the sum of each row give you?

C. What information does the sum of each column give you?

D. What was the most popular sport?

E. What is the least popular sport?

F. In which grade did Taliah have the biggest participation?

G. How many students participated in the survey altogether?

H. What is your favorite sport?

I. What are the 3 largest PARTICIPATION sports in Canada (in order)?

12. Hedwig conducted a survey at Hogwarts. He asked each students what grade they got in the **Magic** course and what grade they got in the **Care of Magical Creatures** course.

He recorded the results in a table:

	Care of Magical Creatures						TOTAL
Magic		**A**	**B**	**C**	**D**	**F**	
	A	5	7		3	1	
	B	4	6	8			
	C		10	5			
	D			4	2	1	
	F		3		2	1	
TOTAL							

A. Complete the table by calculating the SUMS of the rows and the columns.

B. What information does the sum of each row give you?

C. What information does the sum of each column give you?

D. How many students got AT LEAST one "A"?

E. How many students participated in the survey?

F. How many students need to repeat AT LEAST one course? [You need to repeat a course if your grade was a "D" or "F"].

G. How many students need to repeat BOTH courses?

H. What would be your top 3 course choices at Hogwarts?

13. The grade 3s went on a field trip to British Columbia. Below is the map of distances

	Banff	Calgary	Columbia Icefield	Edmonton	Field, B.C.	Jasper	Lake Louise	Radium Hot Springs	Golden	Revelstoke
Calgary	128									
Columbia Icefield	188	316								
Edmonton	423	295	461							
Field, B.C.	85	213	157	508						
Jasper	291	419	100	361	260					
Lake Louise	58	186	130	481	27	233				
Radium Hot Springs	132	260	261	555	157	361	130			
Golden	134	262	207	557	49	307	76	105		
Revelstoke	282	410	355	705	197	455	224	253	148	
Vancouver	856	984	928	1279	771	798	794	818	713	565

Distances shown are in Kilometres.

A. They first went from Calgary to Banff. What distance did they travel?

____

B. They passed Banff at 11:00 and continued to Lake Louise. If the bus traveled at 90km per hour, at what time ROUGHLY did they get to Lake Louise?

____

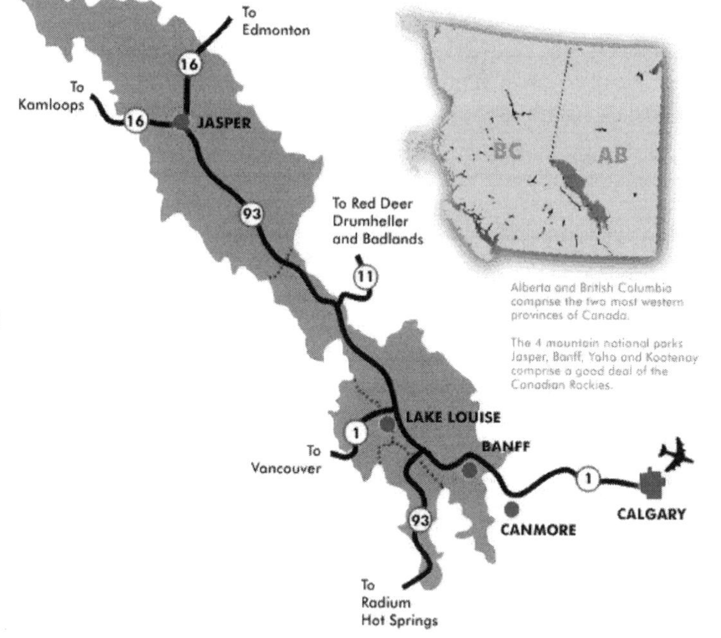

C. From Lake Louise the bus continued to Jasper, where they stayed for the night. If the bus uses 1 litre of gas for every 5km traveled, how many litres of gasoline were used on the way from Calgary to Jasper? ____________________

D. A litre of gasoline costs $1.15. What was the cost of the gas used on the drive from Jasper to Vancouver? ________________________

14. The table below gives the distances (in Kms), by air travel, between major cities in Finland. The national airline, Finnair, has flights connecting all these cities.

	Kc	R	O	T	V	Ku	J
Helsinki (H)	1050	1200	900	300	700	600	650
Joensuu (J)	750	850	600	900	700	200	
Kuopio (Ku)	600	700	500	700	600		
Vaasa (V)	600	750	550	500			
Turku (T)	1200	1300	1050				
Oulu (O)	200	300					
Rovaniemi (R)	150						
Kemi (Kc)							

A. Which town is closest to Helsinki? ____________________

B. Which town is farthest from Oulu? ____________________

C. If you fly from Oulu to Helsinki, through Rovaniemi and Kemi, how much MORE do you travel than if you were to fly directly from Oulu to Helsinki? ________________________

B. What distance was travelled by a plane that flew this journey:

Helsinki →Oulu →Kemi →Helsinki →Rovaniemi →Kuopio →Helsinki

KILLER Brainteaser

IF .. THEN .. ????
Monday = 617
Tuesday = 729
Wednesday = 9312
Thursday = 8412
Friday = 6511
Saturday = 8614
Sunday = ????

Quick review of angles

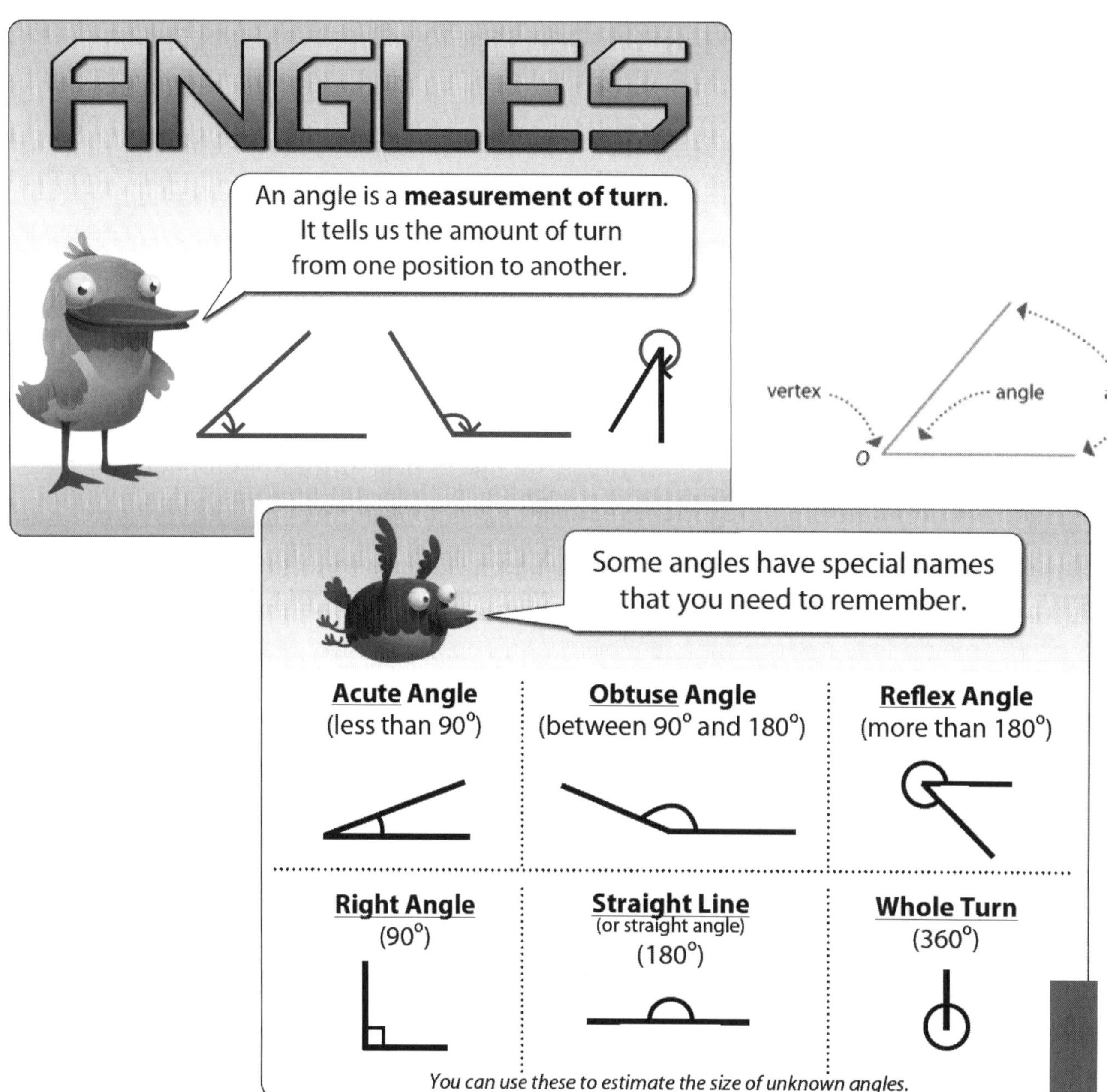

We use a **PROTRACTOR** to measure angles, and we measure them in *degrees*.

The symbol for degrees is a little circle °.

- There are 360° in the circular angle.
- A half circle or a straight angle is 180°.
- A quarter circle or a right angle is 90°

Classify each angle as Acute, Right, Obtuse, Straight or Reflex

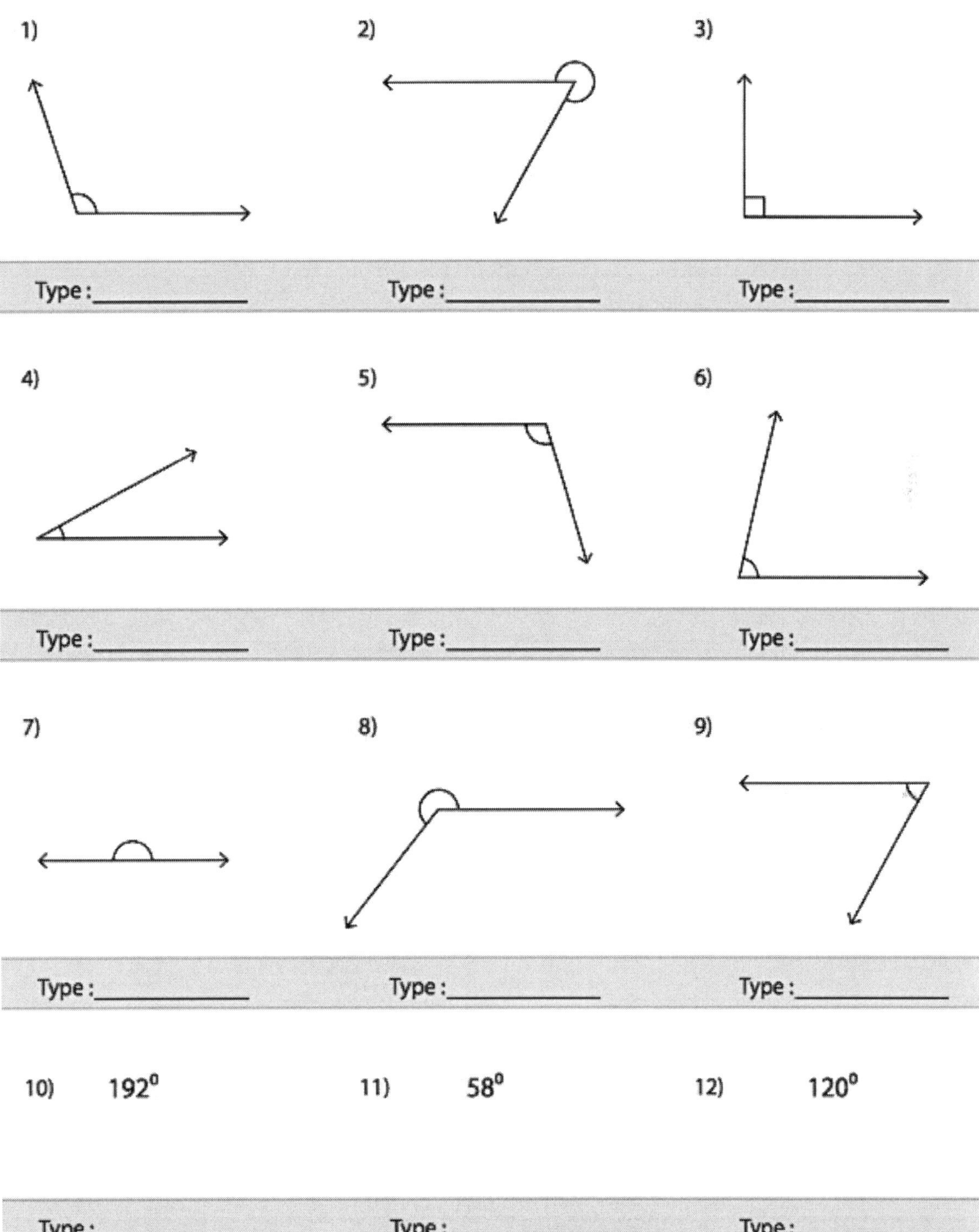

Count the number of interior angles of each type

1)

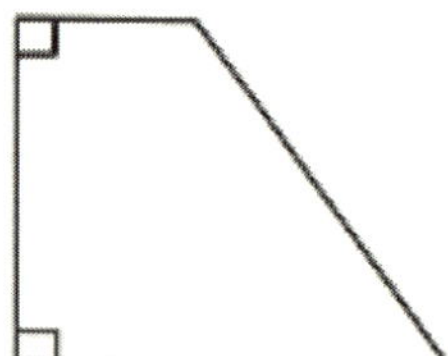

Number of acute angles: ________

Number of obtuse angles: ________

Number of right angles: ________

2)

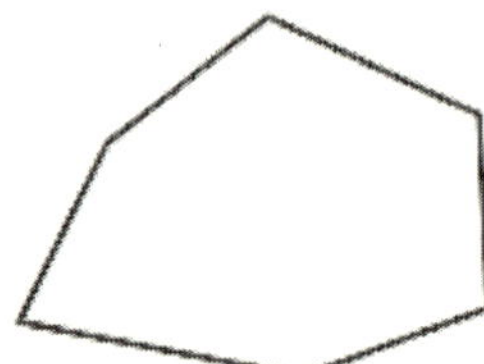

Number of acute angles: ________

Number of obtuse angles: ________

Number of right angles: ________

3)

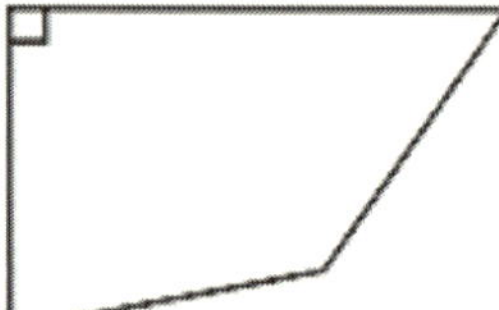

Number of acute angles: ________

Number of obtuse angles: ________

Number of right angles: ________

4)

Number of acute angles: ________

Number of obtuse angles: ________

Number of right angles: ________

5)

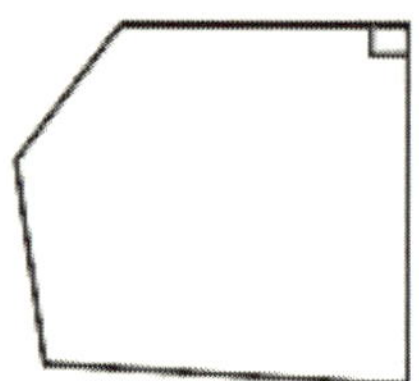

Number of acute angles: ________

Number of obtuse angles: ________

Number of right angles: ________

6)

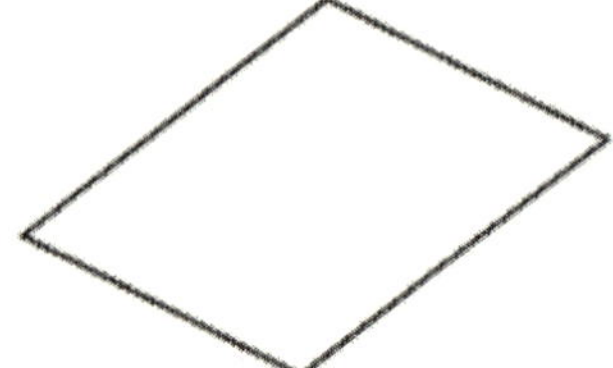

Number of acute angles: ________

Number of obtuse angles: ________

Number of right angles: ________

A break from angles: The ice cream BRAINTEASER

I bought a 5-scopp ice cream cone.
The flavours are Blueberry, Strawberry, Chocolate, Bubble Gum, and Vanilla

- The bottom flavour has 10 letters.
- The vanilla scoop touches both chocolate and the blueberry.
- Vanilla is below Chocolate but above bubble gum.

Can you figure out which is which?

Draw the following angles, and MEASURE them all accurately.

A. Draw 2 Acute angles.

B. Draw a Right angle. Make sure it is exactly 90^0.

C. Draw a Straight (180^0) angle.

D. Draw 2 Obtuse angles.

E. Draw 2 Reflex angles and mark them clearly.

Describing and measuring angles

A. Measure each of the 6 angles
Note: ∠ABC is the angle that you get when you go from A to B to C in this order (the vertex of the angle will always be at the middle letter (B in this case).

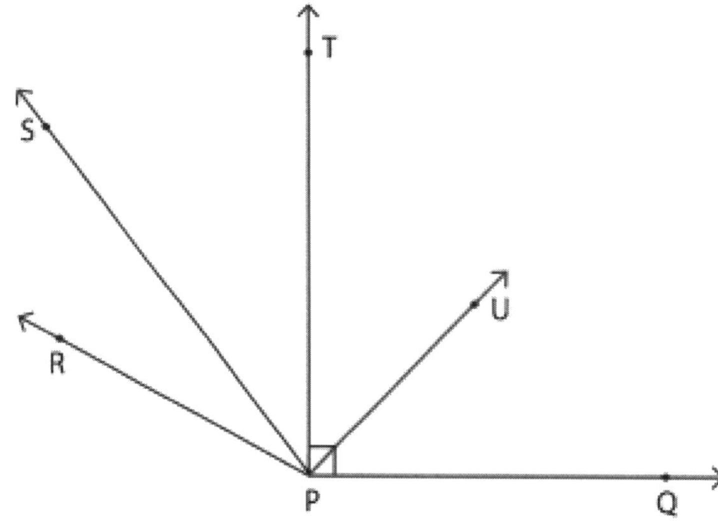

a) ∠QPT = ______________

d) ∠TPS = ______________

b) ∠UPQ = ______________

e) ∠QPR = ______________

c) ∠QPS = ______________

f) ∠RPT = ______________

B. Measure each of the 3 angles of ΔABC

∠ABC = __________

∠ACB = __________

∠BAC = __________

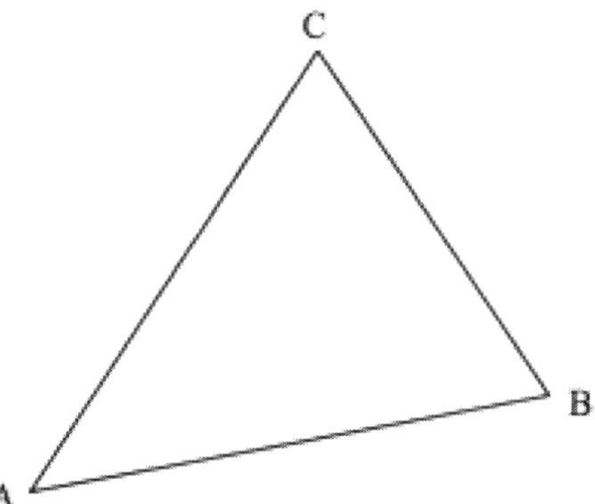

What do you get when you add the three angles up __________?

C. For each triangle measure the three angles and write them down.
For each triangle add up the three angles.
What do you observe?

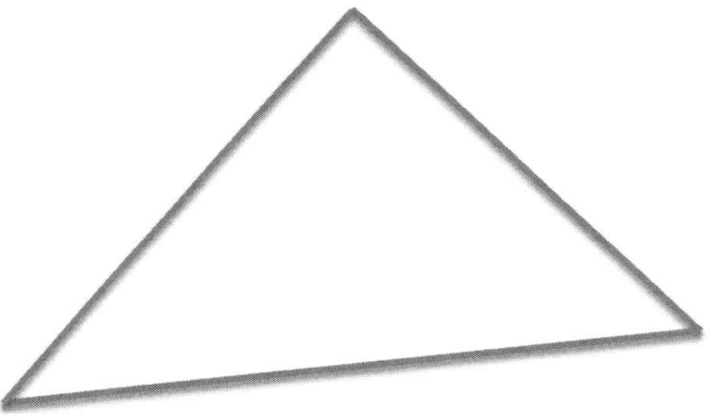

Sum of angles = ___________

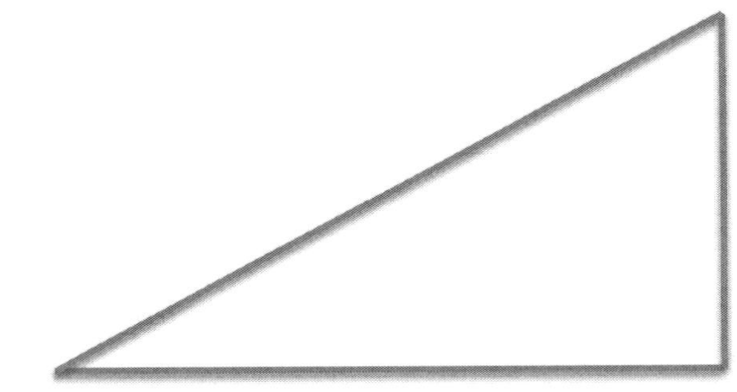

Sum of angles = ___________

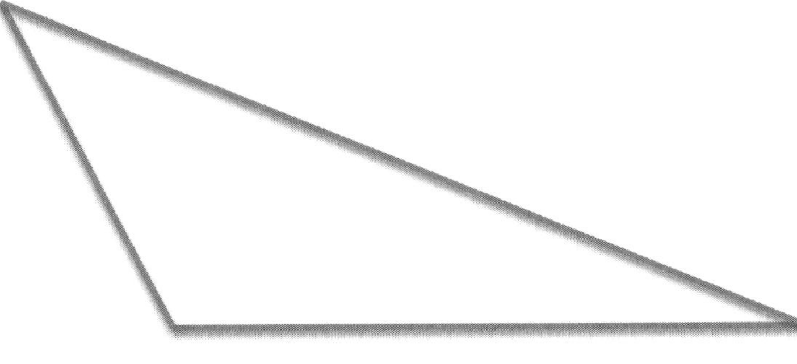

Sum of angles = ___________

Observation I made: ____

D. What do you think you will get if you measure angles *a* and *b* and add them up? Why? Try it!

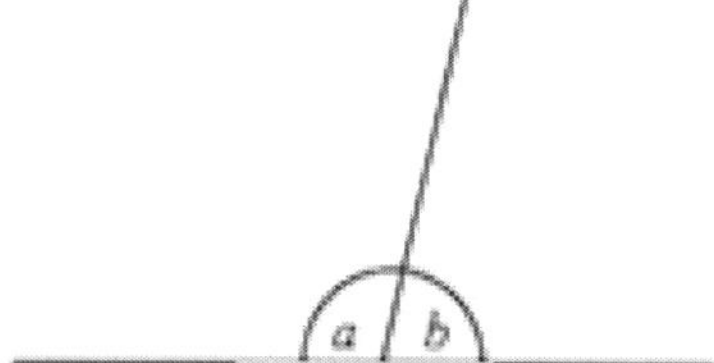

E. What do you think you will get if you measure angles *a*, *b* and *c* and add them up? Why? Try it!

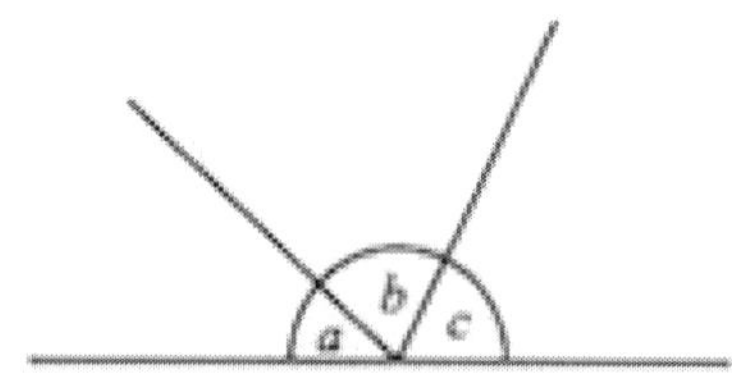

F. What do you think you will get if you measure angles *a*, *b* and *c* and add them up? Why? Try it!

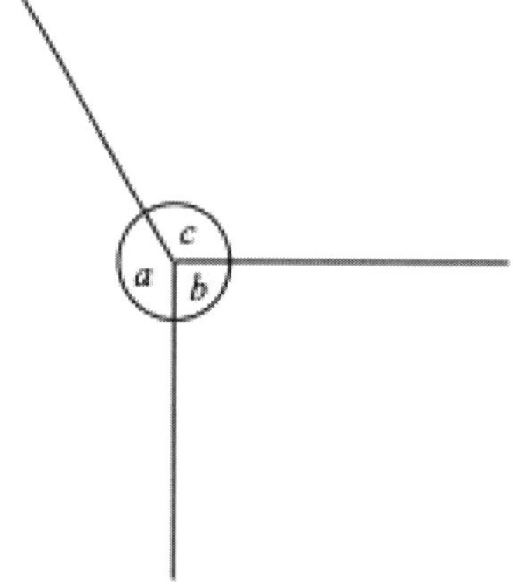

Hint: In answering the above questions, remember that:

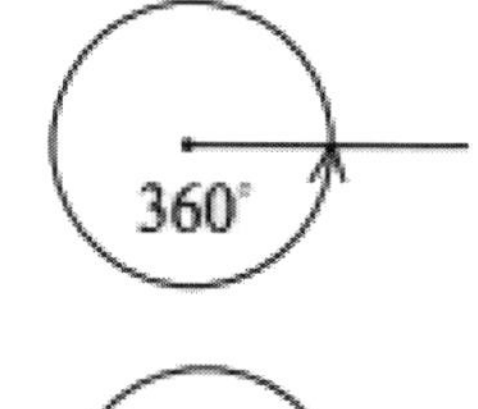

G. Find the missing angle in each.

(a)

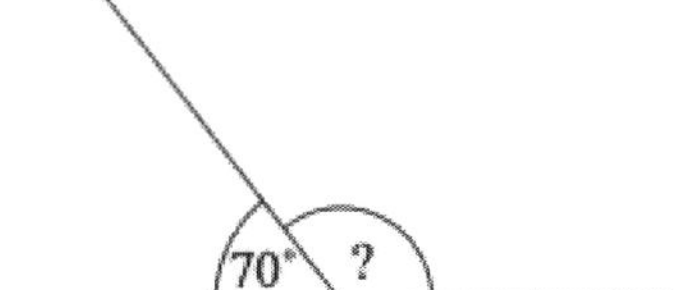

(b)

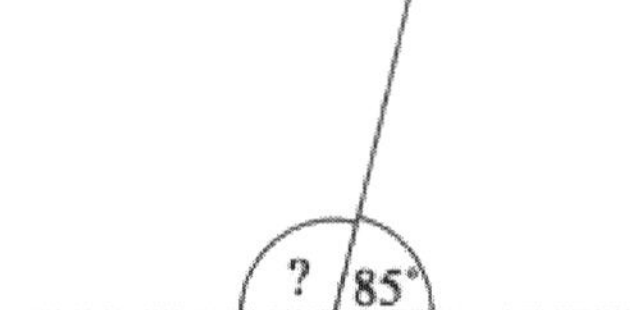

(c)

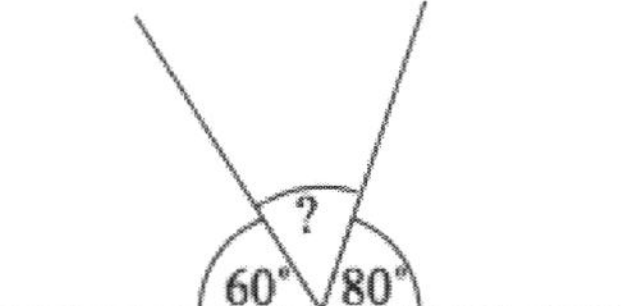

(d)

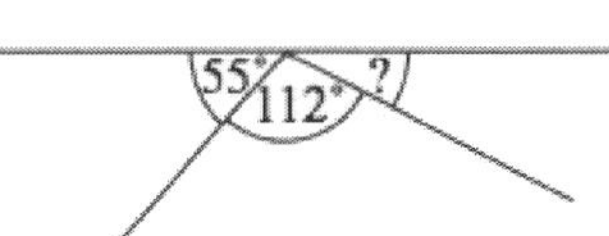

(e)

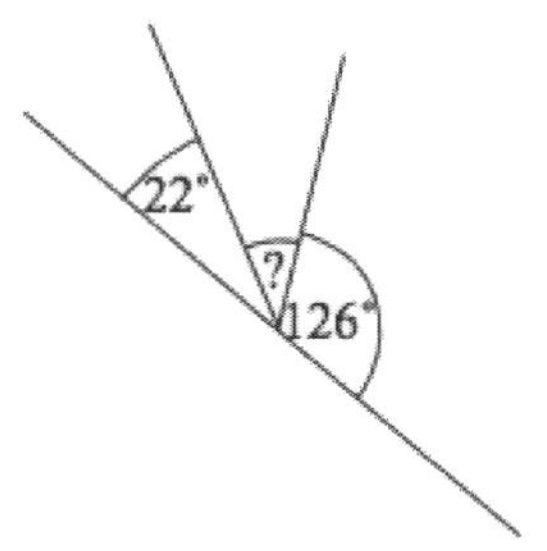

(f)

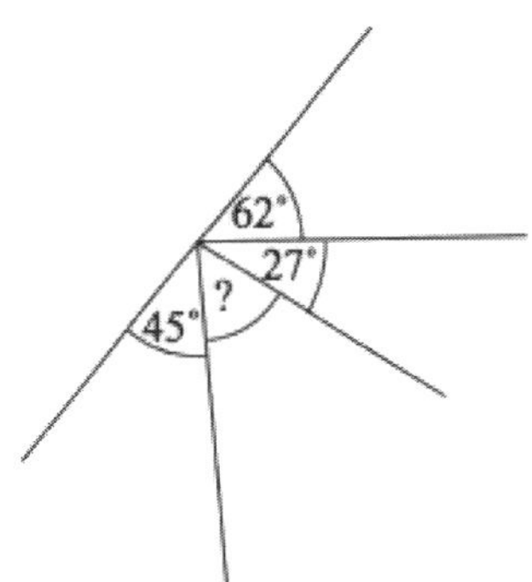

H. Find the missing angle in each.

(a)

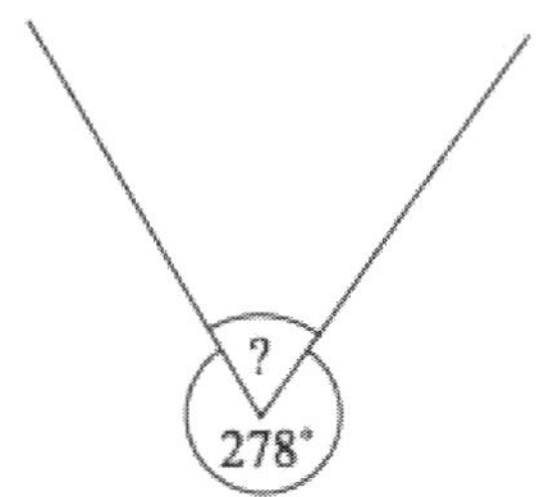

(b)

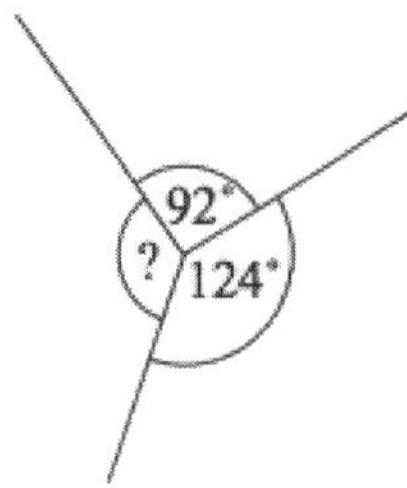

(c)

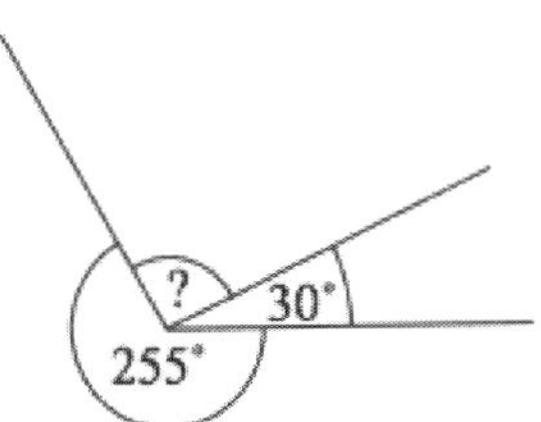

(d)

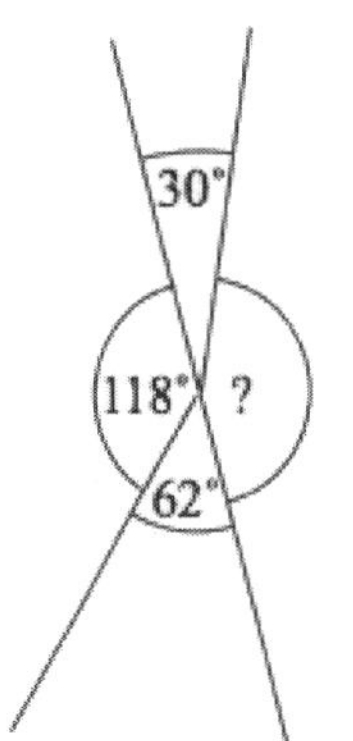

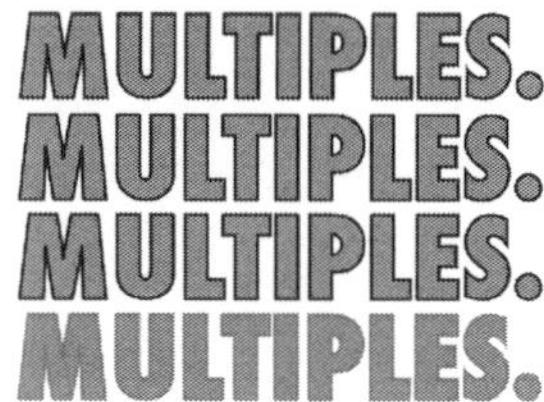

The number A is a *multiple* of the number B if B is a factor of A.
For example, 20 is a multiple of 4 because 4 is a factor of 20.

The number 20 is also a multiple of 2, 5 and 10 because they all divide 20.
The multiples of any number are the ones that are on the "count by" list of that number:

Examples:

- The multiples of 3 are 3, 6, 9, 12, ...
- The multiples of 20 are 20, 40, 60, 80, ...
- 35 is a multiple of 5, because 5 is a factor of 35
- 10 is not a multiple of 80, but 80 is a multiple of 10
- 17 is not a multiple of 4 because it is not on the "count by 4" list

1	2	3	4	5	6	7	8	9	10
11	12	13	14	15	16	17	18	19	20
21	22	23	24	25	26	27	28	29	30
31	32	33	34	35	36	37	38	39	40
41	42	43	44	45	46	47	48	49	50

Cross out all the multiples of 2

1	2	3	4	5	6	7	8	9	10
11	12	13	14	15	16	17	18	19	20
21	22	23	24	25	26	27	28	29	30
31	32	33	34	35	36	37	38	39	40
41	42	43	44	45	46	47	48	49	50

Cross out all the multiples of 3

1	2	3	4	5	6	7	8	9	10
11	12	13	14	15	16	17	18	19	20
21	22	23	24	25	26	27	28	29	30
31	32	33	34	35	36	37	38	39	40
41	42	43	44	45	46	47	48	49	50

Cross out all the multiples of 4

1	2	3	4	5	6	7	8	9	10
11	12	13	14	15	16	17	18	19	20
21	22	23	24	25	26	27	28	29	30
31	32	33	34	35	36	37	38	39	40
41	42	43	44	45	46	47	48	49	50

Cross out all the multiples of 5

TRUE OR FALSE?

- 12 is factor of 3 ____________________
- 3 is a factor of 30 ____________________
- 70 is a multiple of 15 ____________________
- 6 is a divisor of 3 ____________________
- 70 is divisible by 7 ____________________
- The numbers 1, 2, 3, 4... are all multiples of 1 ____________________
- Every whole number has infinitely many multiples ____________________
- The smallest multiple of a number is itself ____________________
- 44 is a multiple of 11 ____________________
- The multiples of 6 are all even ____________________

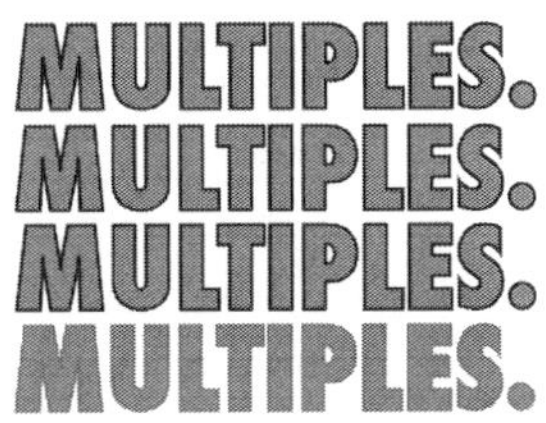

Here are the multiples of 7 all marked for you as an example. Now you do the ones below.
Use colours to make them look pretty.
Pay attention to the patterns!

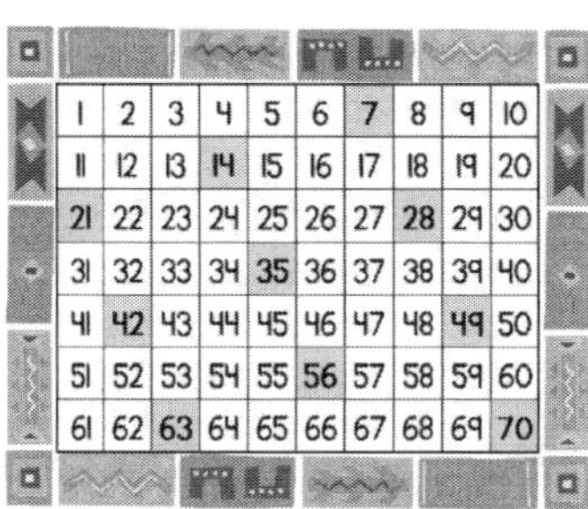

1	2	3	4	5	6	7	8	9	10
11	12	13	14	15	16	17	18	19	20
21	22	23	24	25	26	27	28	29	30
31	32	33	34	35	36	37	38	39	40
41	42	43	44	45	46	47	48	49	50
51	52	53	54	55	56	57	58	59	60
61	62	63	64	65	66	67	68	69	70

1	2	3	4	5	6	7	8	9	10
11	12	13	14	15	16	17	18	19	20
21	22	23	24	25	26	27	28	29	30
31	32	33	34	35	36	37	38	39	40
41	42	43	44	45	46	47	48	49	50
51	52	53	54	55	56	57	58	59	60
61	62	63	64	65	66	67	68	69	70
71	72	73	74	75	76	77	78	79	80
81	82	83	84	85	86	87	88	89	90
91	92	93	94	95	96	97	98	99	100

Cross out all the multiples of 6

1	2	3	4	5	6	7	8	9	10
11	12	13	14	15	16	17	18	19	20
21	22	23	24	25	26	27	28	29	30
31	32	33	34	35	36	37	38	39	40
41	42	43	44	45	46	47	48	49	50
51	52	53	54	55	56	57	58	59	60
61	62	63	64	65	66	67	68	69	70
71	72	73	74	75	76	77	78	79	80
81	82	83	84	85	86	87	88	89	90
91	92	93	94	95	96	97	98	99	100

Cross out all the multiples of 8

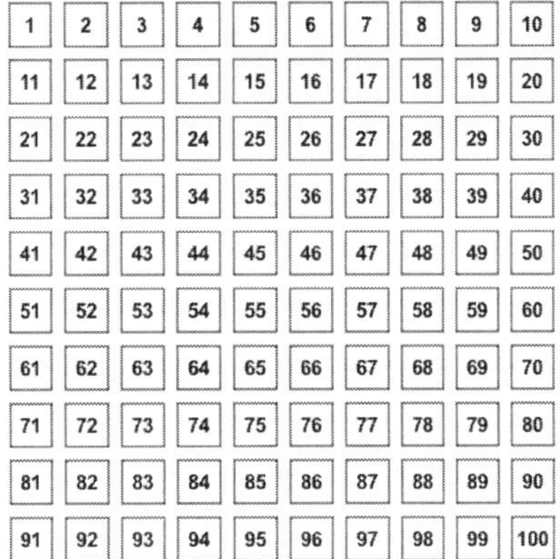

1	2	3	4	5	6	7	8	9	10
11	12	13	14	15	16	17	18	19	20
21	22	23	24	25	26	27	28	29	30
31	32	33	34	35	36	37	38	39	40
41	42	43	44	45	46	47	48	49	50
51	52	53	54	55	56	57	58	59	60
61	62	63	64	65	66	67	68	69	70
71	72	73	74	75	76	77	78	79	80
81	82	83	84	85	86	87	88	89	90
91	92	93	94	95	96	97	98	99	100

Cross out all the multiples of 9

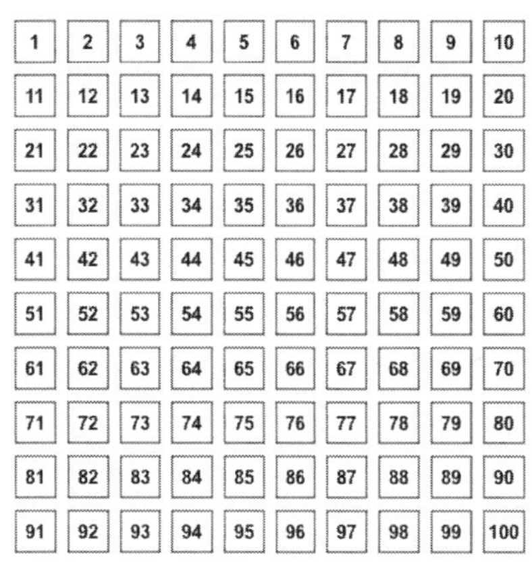

1	2	3	4	5	6	7	8	9	10
11	12	13	14	15	16	17	18	19	20
21	22	23	24	25	26	27	28	29	30
31	32	33	34	35	36	37	38	39	40
41	42	43	44	45	46	47	48	49	50
51	52	53	54	55	56	57	58	59	60
61	62	63	64	65	66	67	68	69	70
71	72	73	74	75	76	77	78	79	80
81	82	83	84	85	86	87	88	89	90
91	92	93	94	95	96	97	98	99	100

Cross out all the multiples of 10

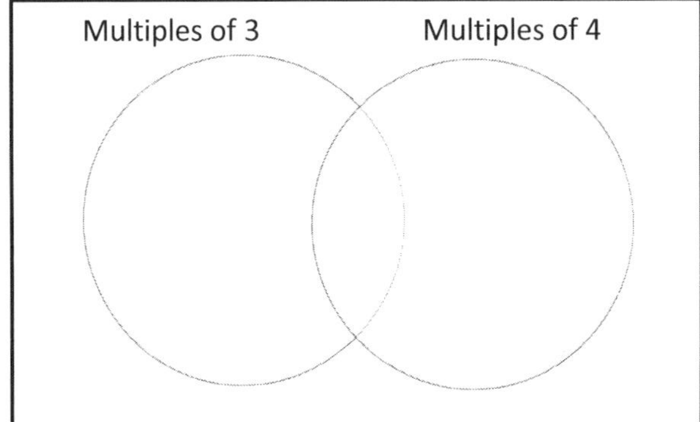

Place these numbers correctly in the diagram:
8 2 6 12 9 16 30 7 15 36 20 34 17 42

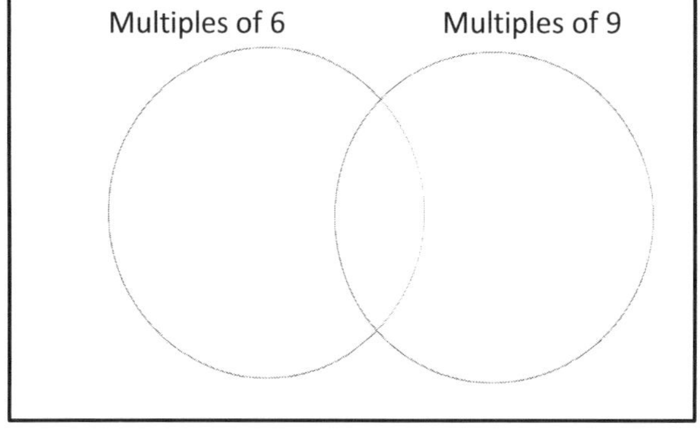

Place these numbers correctly in the diagram:
24 10 6 18 39 90 30 63 25 60 45 36 17

For the ones below put a 
if the answer is YES, and an ✗
if the answer is NO.
▼

1) Is 90 a multiple of 6?

2) Is 90 a multiple of 5?

3) Is 32 a multiple of 4?

4) Is 48 a multiple of 8?

5) Is 21 a multiple of 3?

6) Is 24 a multiple of 6?

7) Is 28 a multiple of 7?

8) Is 12 a multiple of 5?

9) Is 88 a multiple of 4?

10) Is 35 a multiple of 7?

11) Is 86 a multiple of 7?

12) Is 28 a multiple of 4?

13) Is 72 a multiple of 4?

14) Is 60 a multiple of 3?

15) Is 60 a multiple of 9?

16) Is 23 a multiple of 6?

17) Is 76 a multiple of 2?

18) Is 64 a multiple of 3?

19) Is 60 a multiple of 4?

20) Is 63 a multiple of 9?

For each number below decide if it is a multiple of 2, 3, 5, 6, 9 and 10, and place ✗ in the appropriate places, just like in the example.
▼

	2	3	5	6	9	10
Ex) 24	X	X		X		
1) 88						
2) 53						
3) 21						
4) 56						
5) 28						
6) 35						
7) 90						
8) 58						
9) 31						
10) 49						
11) 13						
12) 74						
13) 93						
14) 14						
15) 16						
16) 17						
17) 19						
18) 63						
19) 83						
20) 15						

Least Common Multiple

The **Least Common Multiple (LCM)** of two numbers is the **smallest** number that is a multiple of both.

Example: In order to find the LCM of 10 and 12, we could list the multiples of both, and then look for the **smallest** multiple that is on both lists:

- Multiples of 10: 10, 20, 30, 40, 50, **60**, 70, ...
- Multiples of 12: 12, 24, 36, 48, **60**, 72, ...

The smallest number that is common to both is 60, so LCM (10,12)=60

A. Find the following:

1. LCM (5, 7) = ________
2. LCM (4, 8) = ________
3. LCM (12, 18) = ________
4. LCM (50, 20) = ________
5. LCM (13, 5) = ________
6. LCM (10, 4) = ________
7. LCM (8, 12) = ________
8. LCM (6, 21) = ________
9. LCM (3, 5) = ________
10. LCM (4, 11) = ________
11. LCM (15, 25) = ________
12. LCM (4, 6) = ________
13. LCM (40, 60) = ________
14. LCM (8, 20) = ________
15. LCM (5, 30) = ________
16. LCM (6, 24) = ________

The **Least Common Multiple (LCM)** of three numbers (or more) is the **smallest** number that is a multiple of all of them.

Example: In order to find LCM (2, 3, 5) you could list the multiples of 5 one after the other, until you get to the first one that is also divisible by 2 and by 3:

Multiples of 5: 5, 10, 15, 20, 25, **30**, 35.....
The smallest multiple of 5 that is also divisible by 2 and 3 is 30, so LCM (2, 3, 5)=30

B. Find the following:

1. LCM (2, 3, 4) = ________
2. LCM (3, 4, 5) = ________
3. LCM (3, 6, 8) = ________
4. LCM (2, 4, 7) = ________
5. LCM (2, 3, 12) = ________
6. LCM (10, 15, 25) = ________

1. Write the numbers **1-40** in the Venn Diagram below. Make sure you place each number in its right place: common multiples should be placed in the middle, where the two circles intersect.

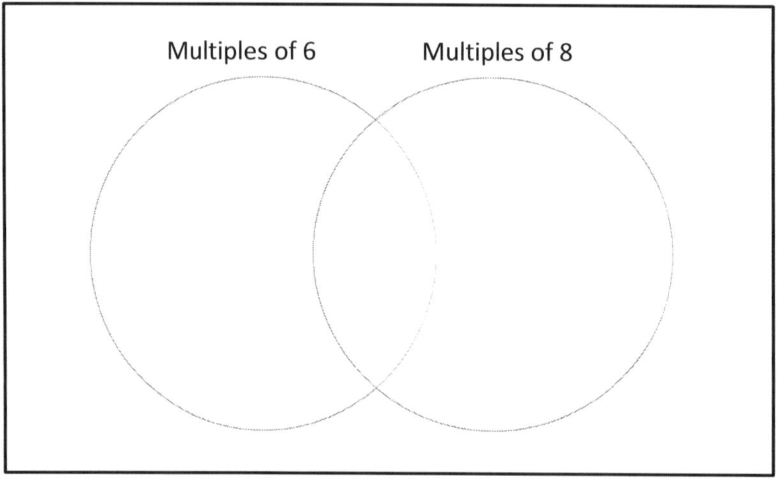

The common multiples of 6 and 8 (less than 60) are: ________________

The least common multiple (LCM) of 6 and 8 is: ______________

2. Write the numbers **1-30** in the Venn Diagram. Make sure you place each number in its right place: common multiples should be placed in the middle, where the two circles intersect.

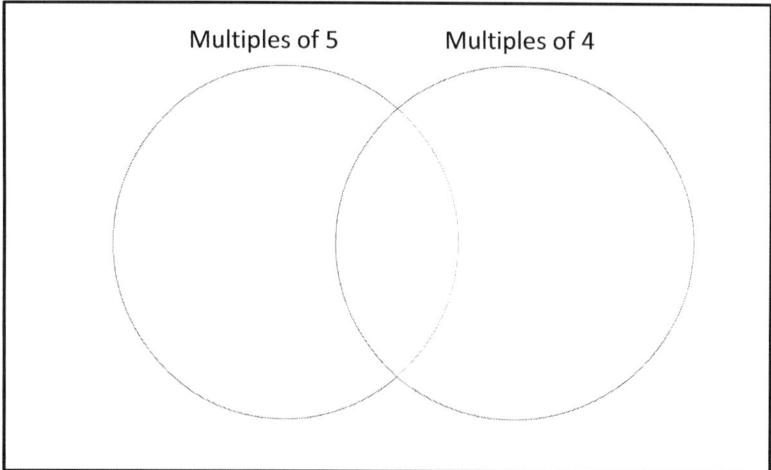

The common multiples of 4 and 5 (less than 30) are: ________________

The least common multiple (LCM) of 4 and 5 is: ______________

A. Find the following *without getting confused between LCM and GCD!*

GREATEST COMMON FACTOR

LEAST COMMON MULTIPLE

1. LCM (1, 8) = ________
2. GCD (1, 8) = ________
3. LCM (16, 24) = ________
4. GCD (16, 24) = ________
5. LCM (8, 15) = ________
6. GCD (8, 15) = ________
7. GCD (15, 45) = ________
8. LCM (15, 45) = ________

B. True or False? If you think it is false, give an example to prove it!

1. If a number is a multiple of 10, it must be a multiple of 5. ____________________
2. If a number is divisible by 5, it must be a multiple of 10. ____________________
3. If a number is divisible by 5 and 2, it must be a multiple of 10. ____________________
4. If a number is a multiple of 9, it must be a multiple of 3. ____________________
5. If a number is a multiple of 3, it must be a multiple of 9. ____________________
6. If a number is a multiple of 4 and 6, it must be a multiple of 24. ____________________

C. Below each number write the remainder when it is divided by 6.

24	25	26	27	28	29	30
☐	☐	☐	☐	☐	☐	☐

Select from these 2-digit numbers:

a) **two** numbers so that their sum is divisible by 6 ☐, ☐
b) **two** numbers so that their difference is divisible by 6 ☐, ☐
c) **two** numbers so that their product is divisible by 6 ☐, ☐
d) **three** numbers so that their sum is divisible by 6 ☐, ☐, ☐
e) **three** numbers so that their sum is **not** divisible by 6 ☐, ☐, ☐
f) **three** numbers so that their product is divisible by 6 ☐, ☐, ☐
g) **three** numbers so that their product is **not** divisible by 6. ☐, ☐, ☐

LEAST COMMON DENOMINATOR

1. List the first 10 multiples of the following numbers:

(a) 6: ____________________

(b) 4: ____________________

(c) 7: ____________________

2. What is the **Least Common Multiple (LCM)** of

(a) 4 and 6: ____________________

(b) 4 and 7: ____________________

(c) 6 and 7: ____________________

(d) 4, 6 and 7: ____________________

3. Find the **Least Common Denominator** for the following:

(a) $\frac{2}{3}$ and $\frac{1}{6}$: ____________________

(b) $\frac{5}{6}$ and $\frac{1}{10}$: ____________________

(c) $\frac{1}{2}$ and $\frac{5}{9}$: ____________________

(d) $\frac{3}{8}$ and $\frac{1}{6}$: ____________________

4. Convert the following to equivalent fractions that have the same denominator. Always try to work with the **Least Common Denominator**

(a) $\frac{1}{4}$ and $\frac{1}{6}$: ______________________________

(b) $\frac{3}{4}$ and $\frac{1}{7}$: ______________________________

(c) $\frac{1}{4}$ and $\frac{5}{6}$: ______________________________

(d) $\frac{1}{4}$, $\frac{1}{6}$ and $\frac{3}{7}$ ______________________________

5. For each pair of fractions write the Least Common Denominator (LCD) in the box.

a) $\frac{3}{7}$ $\frac{7}{4}$ LCD = ☐

b) $\frac{1}{9}$ $\frac{6}{7}$ LCD = ☐

c) $\frac{2}{9}$ $\frac{3}{8}$ LCD = ☐

d) $\frac{4}{10}$ $\frac{4}{9}$ LCD = ☐

e) $\frac{4}{5}$ $\frac{3}{4}$ LCD = ☐

6. For each pair of fractions write the Least Common Denominator (LCD) in the box.

a) $\frac{8}{3}$ $\frac{1}{2}$ LCD = ☐

b) $\frac{5}{3}$ $\frac{4}{10}$ LCD = ☐

c) $\frac{6}{8}$ $\frac{3}{6}$ LCD = ☐

d) $\frac{8}{7}$ $\frac{5}{8}$ LCD = ☐

e) $\frac{7}{28}$ $\frac{11}{8}$ LCD = ☐

This page was way too easy, so here is something extra…
Write the whole numbers from 10 to 30 correctly in each of the two Venn Diagrams.

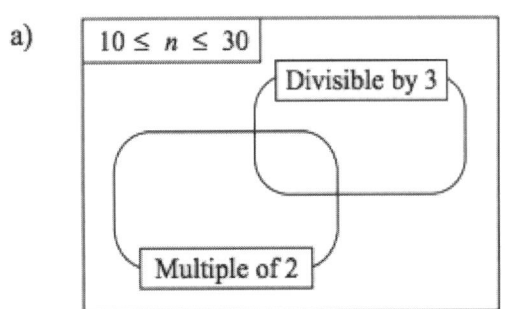

a) $10 \le n \le 30$

Divisible by 3

Multiple of 2

b)

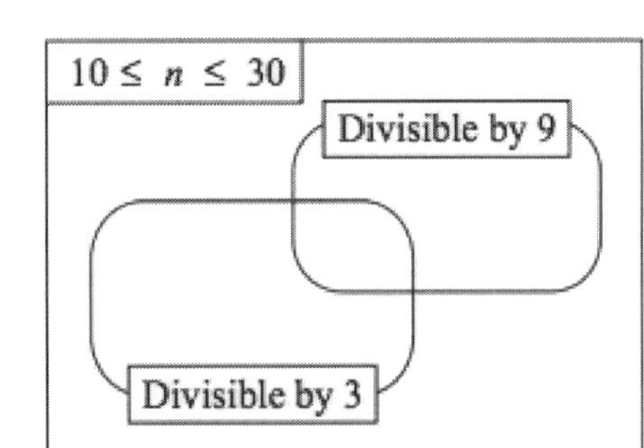

7. Convert to equivalent fractions with equal denominators, then circle the BIGGER fraction.

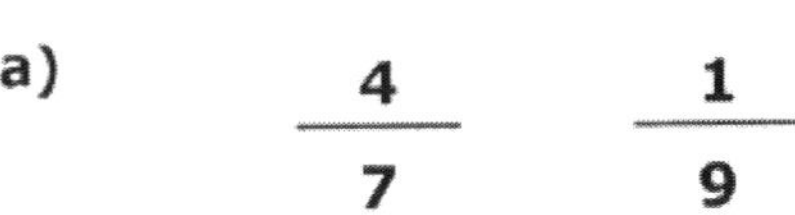

a) $\frac{4}{7}$ $\frac{1}{9}$

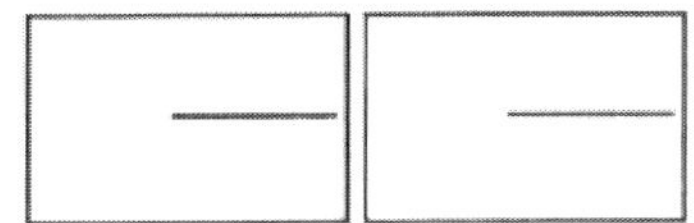

b) $\frac{2}{3}$ $\frac{7}{8}$

c) $\frac{6}{9}$ $\frac{6}{8}$

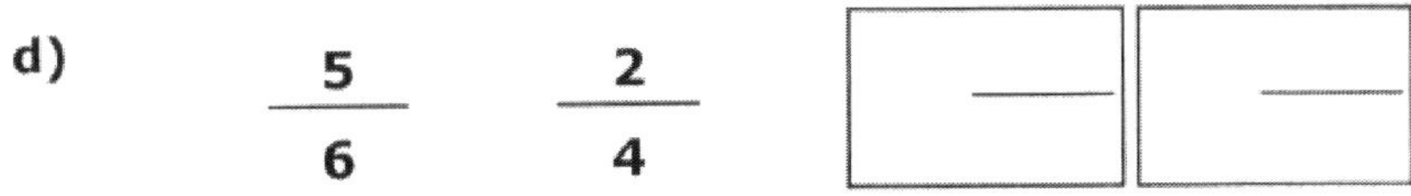

d) $\frac{5}{6}$ $\frac{2}{4}$

e) $\frac{2}{10}$ $\frac{3}{7}$

8. Convert to equivalent fractions with equal denominators, then circle the SMALLER fraction

a) $\frac{5}{9}$ $\frac{1}{2}$

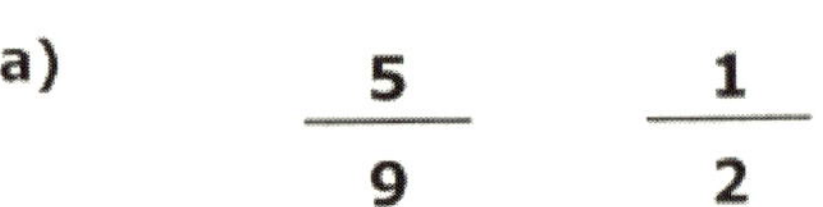

b) $\frac{4}{5}$ $\frac{4}{7}$

c) $\frac{4}{7}$ $\frac{2}{8}$

d) $\frac{1}{4}$ $\frac{5}{9}$

e) $\frac{3}{6}$ $\frac{1}{9}$

BrainTeaser: Look at the original shape, as well as the 9 shapes on the right side. Some of the 9 shapes can be obtained by **rotating** (turning) the original shape, without flipping it. <u>Circle them.</u>

Others can be obtained by **reflecting** ("flipping" it to its backside), and then rotating it. <u>Put a box around them.</u>

<u>Cross out</u> all shapes that you cannot get to from the original shape, no matter what you do.

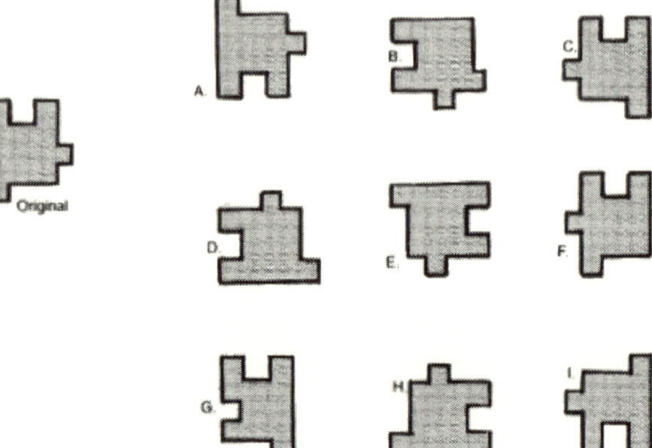

9. Convert to equivalent fractions with equal denominators, and calculate the DIFFERENCE between each two.

a) 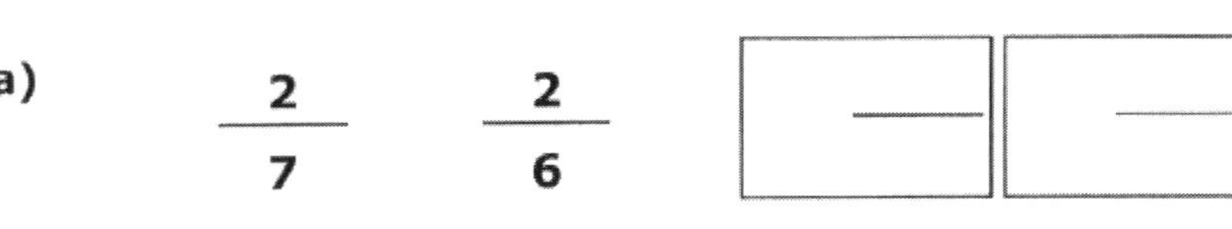

b) $\frac{5}{6}$ $\frac{3}{10}$

c) $\frac{7}{10}$ $\frac{2}{3}$

d) $\frac{4}{8}$ $\frac{7}{10}$

e) $\frac{4}{9}$ $\frac{1}{6}$

10. ORDER from small to big. Use common denominators if needed.

a) $\frac{3}{5}$ $\frac{1}{9}$ $\frac{2}{3}$ $\frac{2}{5}$ $\frac{1}{10}$

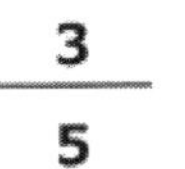

$\frac{1}{2} + \frac{3}{4}$ LEAST COMMON DENOMINATOR

b) $\frac{2}{3}$ $\frac{1}{4}$ $\frac{8}{9}$ $\frac{1}{2}$ $\frac{1}{3}$

c) $\frac{3}{4}$ $\frac{2}{3}$ $\frac{4}{7}$ $\frac{6}{7}$ $\frac{1}{7}$

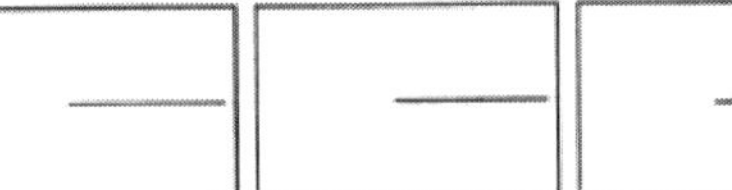

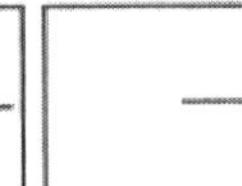

d) $\frac{1}{5}$ $\frac{4}{7}$ $\frac{4}{5}$ $\frac{1}{2}$ $\frac{3}{5}$

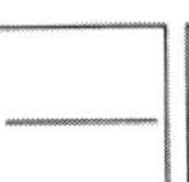

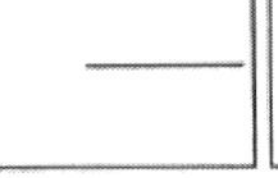

11. ORDER from big to small. Use common denominators if needed.

½ + ¾
LEAST COMMON DENOMINATOR

a) $\frac{2}{5}$ $\frac{8}{3}$ $\frac{7}{9}$ $\frac{8}{10}$ $\frac{7}{6}$

b) $\frac{3}{4}$ $\frac{17}{6}$ $\frac{1}{6}$ $\frac{5}{9}$ $\frac{8}{9}$

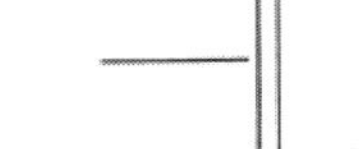

c) $\frac{5}{10}$ $\frac{5}{8}$ $\frac{11}{5}$ $\frac{2}{8}$ $\frac{4}{10}$

d) $\frac{1}{5}$ $\frac{3}{4}$ $\frac{8}{3}$ $\frac{2}{6}$ $\frac{8}{10}$

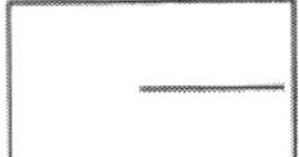

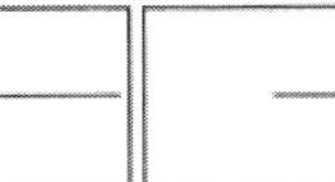

BrainTeaser: Flotsim and Pookim

Each of these is a Flots:  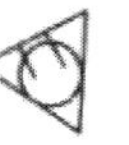  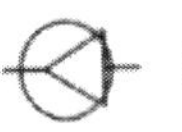 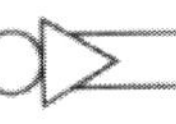

And each of these is Pook:    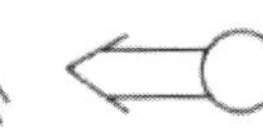 

Which of the following is a Flots, and which is a Pook?

A.  B.  C.  D.  E.

12. Write each group in ascending order.

½ + ¾

LEAST COMMON DENOMINATOR

a) $\frac{4}{10}$ $\frac{7}{9}$ $2\frac{1}{5}$ $1\frac{1}{3}$ $\frac{19}{9}$

b) $\frac{7}{8}$ $1\frac{1}{5}$ $\frac{4}{5}$ $\frac{3}{10}$ $2\frac{1}{2}$

c) $\frac{5}{10}$ $\frac{8}{9}$ $2\frac{2}{3}$ $\frac{1}{6}$ $\frac{5}{2}$

d) $\frac{8}{10}$ $\frac{1}{4}$ $\frac{18}{8}$ $\frac{1}{2}$ $\frac{3}{10}$

BrainTeaser

Claire is boarding a flight from Manila to return home to Calgary. It in Thursday, and Claire's flight leaves at 4:05PM Manila time. Calgary clock is 14 hours behind Manila's. The total flying time is 15 hours and 35 minutes, and she will also has a 4 hours stopover in Hawaii. It will take Claire about half an hour after the plane lands in Calgary to pick up the luggage and clear customs. **When should Mary be at the Calgary airport to pick up her sister?**

13. Write each group is descending order.

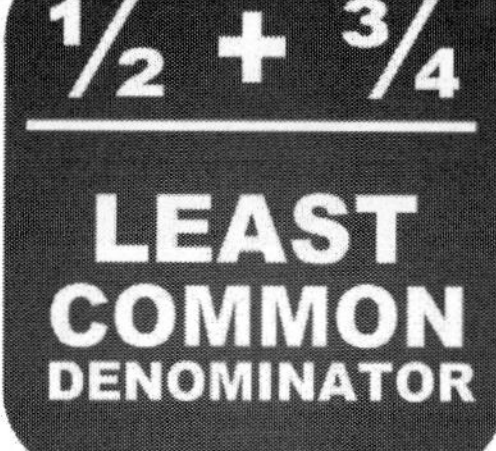

a) $\frac{2}{7}$ $\frac{1}{4}$ $\frac{4}{3}$ $\frac{5}{7}$ $\frac{2}{6}$

b) $\frac{1}{4}$ $\frac{7}{8}$ $\frac{11}{6}$ $\frac{1}{2}$ $\frac{7}{3}$

c) $\frac{5}{7}$ $\frac{1}{2}$ $1\frac{2}{3}$ $3\frac{1}{2}$ $\frac{3}{2}$

d) $\frac{2}{7}$ $1\frac{1}{3}$ $\frac{1}{7}$ $3\frac{1}{2}$ $1\frac{5}{7}$

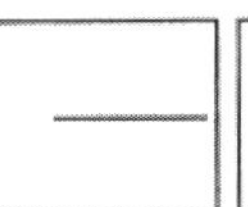
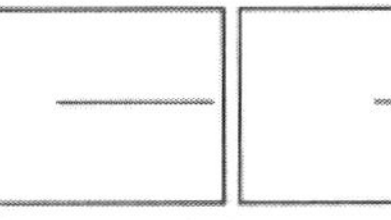

Adding fractions with different denominators

Give your final answer in simplest form

Example: $\frac{1}{2}+\frac{2}{3}=\frac{3}{6}+\frac{4}{6}=\frac{7}{6}=1\frac{1}{6}$

1. $\frac{1}{2}+\frac{5}{6}=$ ______________________

2. $\frac{3}{5}+\frac{3}{4}=$ ______________________

3. $\frac{3}{11}+\frac{2}{3}=$ ______________________

4. $\frac{2}{3}+\frac{7}{9}=$ ______________________

5. $\frac{3}{4}+\frac{4}{3}=$ ______________________

6. $\frac{1}{3}+\frac{3}{10}=$ ______________________

7. $\frac{4}{5}+\frac{3}{2}=$ ______________________

8. $\frac{5}{3}+\frac{1}{2}=$ ______________________

9. $\frac{2}{21}+\frac{3}{7}=$ ______________________

10. $\frac{7}{12}+\frac{1}{8}=$ ______________________

11. $\frac{1}{10}+\frac{1}{15}=$ ______________________

12. $\frac{3}{5}+\frac{2}{7}=$ ______________________

Where can you find rivers with no water, cities with no buildings and forests with no trees?

Hint: Look at p.96

Adding mixed numbers with different denominators

Give your final answer in simplest form

Example: $7\frac{1}{2} + 9\frac{2}{3} = 7\frac{3}{6} + 9\frac{4}{6} = 16\frac{7}{6} = 16 + 1\frac{1}{6} = 17\frac{1}{6}$

1. $5\frac{1}{2} + 8\frac{1}{6} =$ ______________________________

2. $10\frac{3}{5} + 6\frac{1}{4} =$ ______________________________

3. $7\frac{3}{8} + 6\frac{2}{3} =$ ______________________________

4. $12\frac{2}{3} + 1\frac{7}{9} =$ ______________________________

5. $1\frac{3}{4} + 2\frac{5}{6} =$ ______________________________

6. $8\frac{11}{12} + \frac{3}{8} =$ ______________________________

7. $3\frac{4}{5} + 11\frac{1}{2} =$ ______________________________

8. $4\frac{4}{6} + \frac{7}{9} =$ ______________________________

9. $5\frac{7}{11} + \frac{5}{6} =$ ______________________________

10. $8\frac{7}{12} + 9\frac{5}{8} =$ ______________________________

11. $20\frac{7}{10} + 3\frac{4}{15} =$ ______________________________

12. $9\frac{3}{5} + 22\frac{6}{7} =$ ______________________________

Subtracting fractions with different denominators

Find a common denominator. Give your final answer in simplest form

Example: $\frac{4}{3}-\frac{1}{2}=\frac{8}{6}-\frac{3}{6}=\frac{5}{6}$

1. $\frac{5}{6}-\frac{1}{2}=$ ____________________

2. $\frac{3}{4}-\frac{2}{5}=$ ____________________

3. $\frac{2}{3}-\frac{4}{11}=$ ____________________

4. $\frac{8}{9}-\frac{2}{3}=$ ____________________

5. $\frac{5}{3}-\frac{1}{2}=$ ____________________

6. $\frac{9}{10}-\frac{3}{4}=$ ____________________

7. $\frac{14}{5}-\frac{3}{2}=$ ____________________

8. $\frac{5}{3}-\frac{3}{4}=$ ____________________

9. $\frac{17}{21}-\frac{3}{7}=$ ____________________

10. $\frac{7}{12}-\frac{1}{8}=$ ____________________

11. $\frac{7}{10}-\frac{4}{15}=$ ____________________

12. $\frac{4}{5}-\frac{2}{7}=$ ____________________

We can use **NEGATIVE NUMBERS** to subtract mixed numbers with different denominators. We first convert to a common denominator and then subtract as we did before, working with negative numbers (if needed). Study the examples carefully.

Examples:

a. $3\frac{7}{11} - 1\frac{1}{2} = 3\frac{14}{22} - 1\frac{11}{22} = 2 + \left(\frac{14}{22} - \frac{11}{22}\right) = 2\frac{3}{22}$

b. $5\frac{1}{4} - 1\frac{2}{3} = 5\frac{3}{12} - 1\frac{8}{12} = 4 + \left(\frac{3}{12} - \frac{8}{12}\right) = 4 - \frac{5}{12} = 3\frac{7}{12}$

c. $13\frac{2}{5} - 4\frac{6}{7} = 13\frac{14}{35} - 4\frac{30}{35} = 9 + \left(\frac{14}{35} - \frac{30}{35}\right) = 9 - \frac{16}{35} = 8\frac{19}{35}$

Try these on your own following the above examples:

d. $12\frac{2}{3} - 10\frac{5}{7} =$ ______________________________

e. $7\frac{1}{5} - 1\frac{3}{4} =$ ______________________________

f. $12\frac{1}{2} - 10\frac{2}{3} =$ ______________________________

g. $10\frac{6}{7} - 1\frac{3}{4} =$ ______________________________

h. $5\frac{2}{5} - 1\frac{7}{8} =$ ______________________________

i. $2\frac{1}{2} - \frac{7}{10} =$ ______________________________

j. $4\frac{3}{4} - 1\frac{11}{12} =$ ______________________________

k. $5\frac{2}{6} - 4\frac{5}{8} =$ ______________________________

***MENTAL MATH**: Add or subtract in your head
[Watch out! These ones really require you to concentrate]

Examples: $\frac{7}{11} - \frac{1}{2} = \frac{14}{22} - \frac{11}{22} = \frac{3}{22}$ $\frac{8}{15} + \frac{1}{20} = \frac{32}{60} + \frac{3}{60} = \frac{35}{60} = \frac{7}{12}$

$\frac{8}{15} + \frac{11}{30} = \square$ $\frac{19}{16} - \frac{25}{24} = \square$ $\frac{7}{18} + \frac{2}{27} = \square$

$\frac{19}{14} - \frac{6}{21} = \square$ $\frac{9}{8} + \frac{1}{12} = \square$ $\frac{7}{10} - \frac{8}{25} = \square$

$\frac{5}{12} + \frac{7}{18} = \square$ $\frac{13}{35} - \frac{5}{21} = \square$ $\frac{9}{5} + \frac{16}{15} = \square$

$\frac{14}{9} - \frac{7}{6} = \square$ $\frac{6}{11} + \frac{1}{22} = \square$ $\frac{14}{15} - \frac{13}{20} = \square$

$\frac{3}{28} + \frac{1}{21} = \square$ $\frac{13}{8} - \frac{7}{12} = \square$ $\frac{9}{14} + \frac{8}{12} = \square$

Fraction of a Set: for each picture write down the fraction of the set that is shaded.

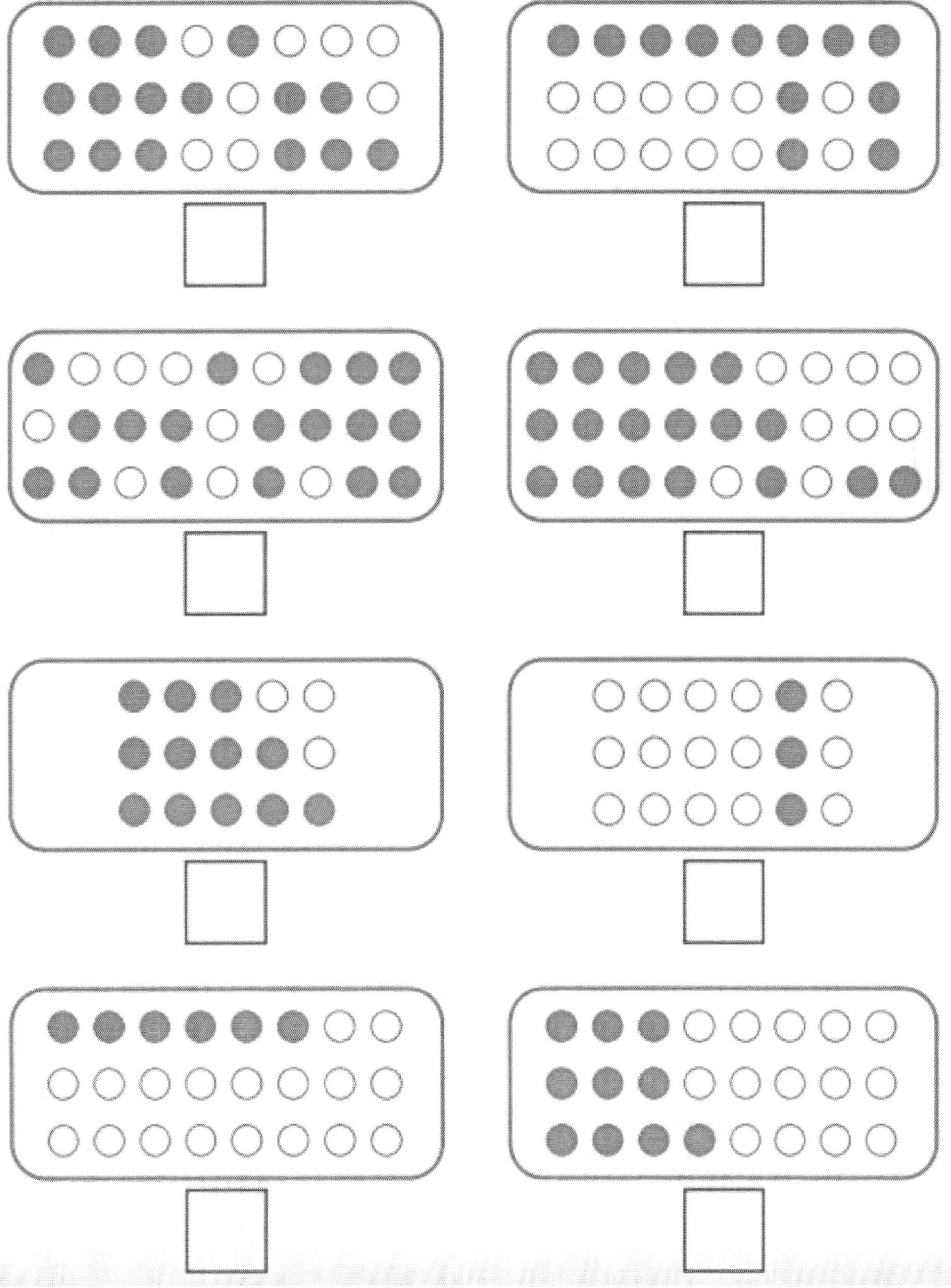

Fraction of a Set: for each picture write down the fraction of the set that is NOT shaded.

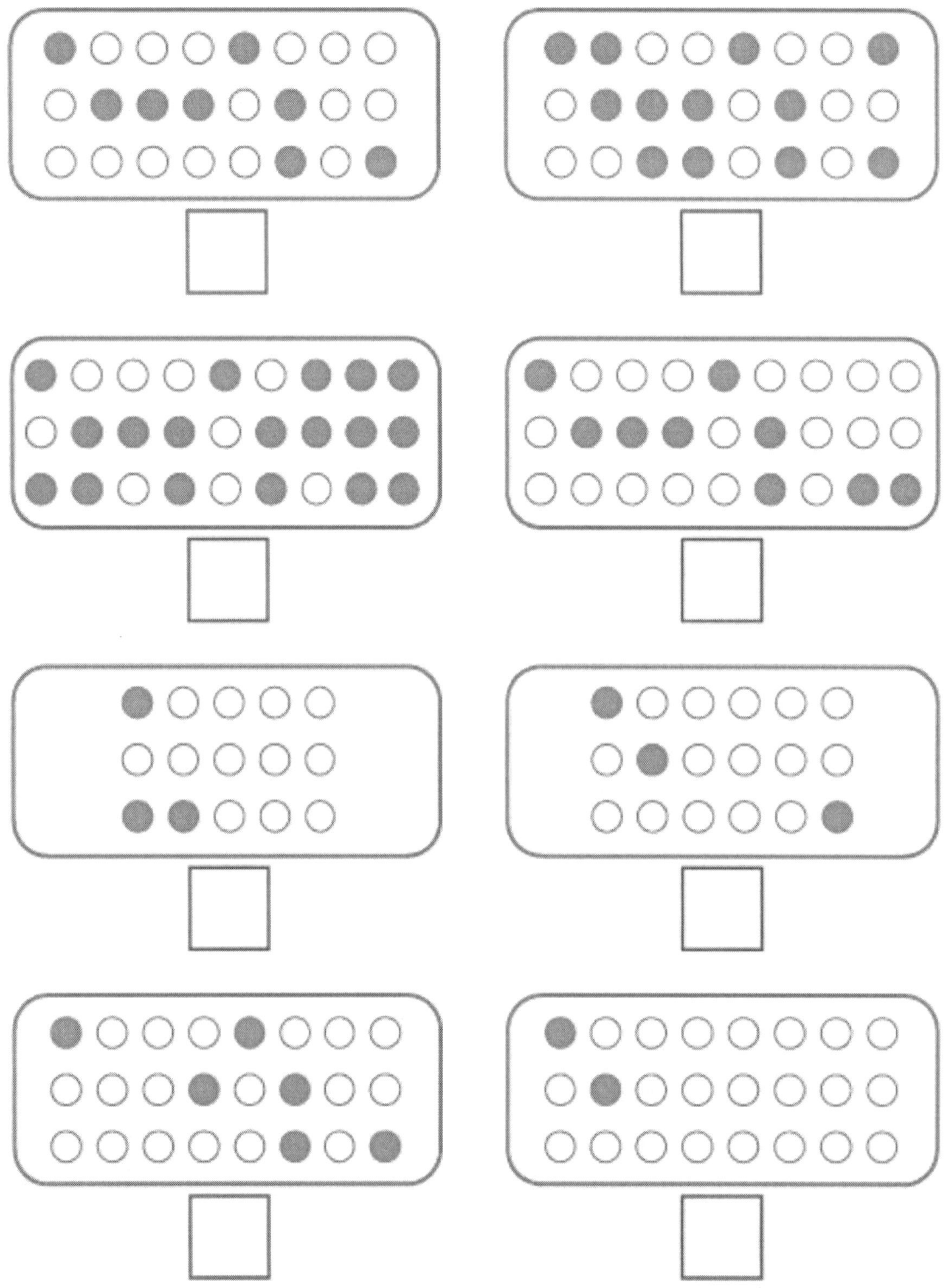

Multiplying a whole number by a fraction

Examples: $\frac{1}{3}\times 6 = \frac{1}{3}$ of $6 = 6\div 3=2$ $30\times\frac{1}{5} = \frac{1}{5}\times 30 = \frac{1}{5}$ of $30 = 30\div 5=6$

The word "of" in mathematics always means multiplication.

For example, $\frac{1}{4}\times 32$ is the same as $\frac{1}{4}$ of 32, which is the same as $32\div$ 4, which is 8.

1. $\frac{1}{3}$ of $12 = 12\div 3=$ _____
2. $\frac{1}{5}$ of $40 = 40 \div$ _____ $=$ _____
3. $\frac{1}{4}$ of $44 = 44 \div$ _____ $=$ _____
4. $\frac{1}{10}$ of $70 = 70 \div$ _____ $=$ _____
5. $\frac{1}{7}$ of $35 = 35\div$ _____ $=$ _____
6. $\frac{1}{8}$ of $40 = 40 \div$ _____ $=$ _____
7. $\frac{1}{6}$ of $60 = 60 \div$ _____ $=$ _____
8. $\frac{1}{2}$ of $32 = 32\div$ _____ $=$ _____
9. $\frac{1}{5}$ of $75 = 75 \div$ _____ $=$ _____
10. $\frac{1}{7}$ of $63 = 63\div$ _____ $=$ _____

1. Kanika has 30 hockey sticks. She gives $\frac{1}{6}$ of them to Raunak, and gives $\frac{1}{10}$ of them to Lekha. How many hockey sticks does she have left?

2. Kanika has 40 hockey sticks. She gives $\frac{1}{5}$ of them to Raunak, and then gives $\frac{1}{2}$ of **the remainder** to Lekha. How many hockey sticks does she have left?

Fraction of a Set: a little harder

Examples: $\frac{1}{5}$ of $16 = 16 \div 5 = \frac{16}{5} = 3\frac{1}{5}$ $\frac{1}{7}$ of $40 = 40 \div 7 = \frac{40}{7} = 5\frac{5}{7}$

Remember that one answer to the question A÷B is the fraction $\frac{A}{B}$

$\frac{1}{2}$ of 100 =	$\frac{1}{2}$ of 120 =	$\frac{1}{2}$ of 125 =	$\frac{1}{3}$ of 50 =
$\frac{1}{3}$ of 150 =	$\frac{1}{2}$ of 140 =	$\frac{1}{3}$ of 70 =	$\frac{1}{4}$ of 60 =
$\frac{1}{2}$ of 180 =	$\frac{1}{2}$ of 160 =	$\frac{1}{2}$ of 165 =	$\frac{1}{3}$ of 180 =
$\frac{1}{5}$ of 150 =	$\frac{1}{4}$ of 160=	$\frac{1}{2}$ of 92 =	$\frac{1}{2}$ of 167 =
$\frac{1}{5}$ of 120 =	$\frac{1}{3}$ of 180 =	$\frac{1}{5}$ of 156 =	$\frac{1}{3}$ of 85 =
$\frac{1}{4}$ of 200 =	$\frac{1}{4}$ of 320 =	$\frac{1}{6}$ of 115 =	$\frac{1}{10}$ of 125 =
$\frac{1}{2}$ of 110 =	$\frac{1}{3}$ of 210 =	$\frac{1}{4}$ of 235 =	$\frac{1}{8}$ of 150 =
$\frac{1}{5}$ of 220 =	$\frac{1}{6}$ of 120 =	$\frac{1}{4}$ of 124 =	$\frac{1}{9}$ of 60 =
$\frac{1}{7}$ of 140 =	$\frac{1}{8}$ of 160 =	$\frac{1}{6}$ of 80 =	$\frac{1}{8}$ of 190 =
$\frac{1}{9}$ of 270 =	$\frac{1}{5}$ of 250 =	$\frac{1}{7}$ of 140 =	$\frac{1}{4}$ of 224 =
$\frac{1}{2}$ of 130 =	$\frac{1}{7}$ of 280 =	$\frac{1}{9}$ of 80 =	$\frac{1}{6}$ of 100 =
$\frac{1}{9}$ of 180 =	$\frac{1}{6}$ of 240 =	$\frac{1}{8}$ of 200 =	$\frac{1}{6}$ of 200 =

Multiplying a whole number by a fraction

Examples: $\frac{1}{7}\times14=\frac{1}{7}$ of $14=14\div7=2$ → $\frac{4}{7}\times14=\frac{4}{7}$ of $14=4\times2=8$

$\frac{1}{4}\times20=\frac{1}{4}$ of $20=20\div4=5$ → $\frac{3}{4}\times20=\frac{3}{4}$ of $20=3\times5=15$

1. $\frac{1}{3}$ of $21=$ _____
2. $\frac{2}{3}\times21=$ _____
3. $\frac{1}{8}$ of $40=$ _____
4. $\frac{3}{8}$ of $40=$ _____
5. $\frac{5}{8}\times40=$ _____
6. $\frac{1}{5}\times35=$ _____
7. $\frac{4}{5}$ of $35=$ _____
8. $\frac{3}{5}$ of $35=$ _____
9. $\frac{1}{6}\times42=$ _____
10. $\frac{5}{6}$ of $42=$ _____
11. $\frac{3}{10}\times60=$ _____
12. $\frac{7}{10}\times60=$ _____
13. $\frac{4}{7}$ of $49=$ _____
14. $\frac{2}{7}\times49=$ _____
15. $\frac{2}{3}\times27=$ _____
16. $\frac{4}{5}$ of $45=$ _____
17. $\frac{5}{11}\times33=$ _____
18. $\frac{2}{5}$ of $60=$ _____

1. Lekha has 40 hockey pucks. She gives $\frac{2}{5}$ of them to Raunak, and gives $\frac{3}{8}$ of them to Kanika. How many pucks does she have left?

2. Lekha has 40 hockey pucks. She gives $\frac{2}{5}$ of them to Raunak, and gives $\frac{3}{8}$ **of the remaining ones** to Kanika. How many pucks does she have left?

Cross-number Puzzle

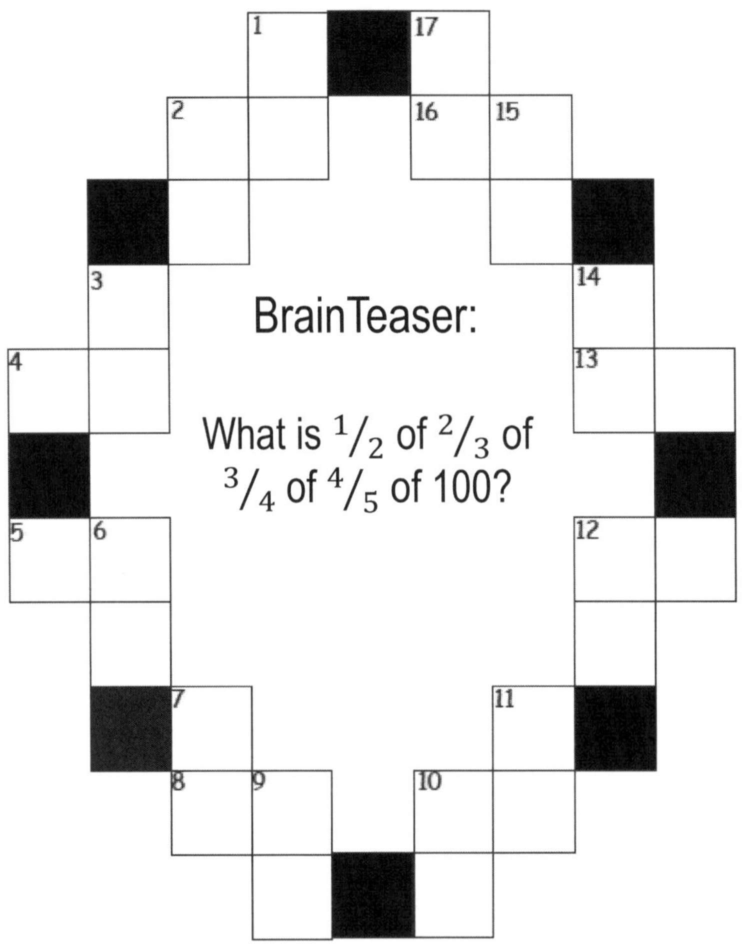

Across

2. half of 50
4. seven-tenths of 50
5. three-fourths of 28
8. two-fifths of 30
10. four-eights of 40
12. one-third of 96
13. one-fourth of 200
16. four-fifths of 30

Down

1. three-fourths of 20
2. three-eighths of 64
3. one-fifth of 125
6. one-sixth of 108
7. three-sevenths of 49
9. four-fifths of 25
10. three-ninths of 81
11. two-fifths of 25
12. six-twentieths of 100
14. one-third of 45
15. four-ninths of 90
17. three-fifths of 20

Fraction of a Set: Word Problems

1. Jeena has 60 My-Little-Pony toy horses. She keeps two thirds of them under her bed and another one fifth in a drawer. The rest of them are in her backpack. How many are there in her backpack?

2. Marlea also has 60 My-Little-Pony toy horses. She keeps two fifth of them under her bed and one third **of the remaining ones** in a drawer. She gave the rest of them to her sister Chelsea, but Chelsea lost half of the ones she got. How many toy horses does Chelsea have left?

3. Here is a very **beautiful, ancient, tricky**, and **well-known** riddle:

An old Arab Sheikh in the Arabian desert passed away and gave his herd of camels to his 3 sons. To the eldest son he left half the camels, to his middle son he left one third of the camels, and to the youngest one he left one ninth of the camels. The only problem is that when he died, there were exactly 17 camels in the herd. The sons did not know what to do. Finally their uncle came, riding his own camel, and gave them an excellent advise on how to do it. ***What was the uncle's advice?***

Fraction of a Set: Word Problems

1. Mrs. Cumming had 1Kg of flour. She used ¾ of it to bake a cake, and 1/5 of what was left to bake a muffin for Emori. How much flour was left at the end? [HINT: 1Kg =1,000mg]

2. Mrs. R. had 1Kg of flour. She used ¼ of it to bake muffins, another 2/5 of it to bake cookies, and finally she used another 200g of the flour to bake a tart. How much flour was left at the end?

3. Mrs. Purdy had 2Kg of flour. She used ½ of it to bake a wedding cake for her wedding, and another ¼ of it to bake a loaf of bread for her husband Brad. She then used ¾ of the flour that was left to bake 5 scones for her daughter Isla. How much flour did she use for each scone?

4. Grandpa Moose gives his 4 grandchildren (Mandy, Sandy, Randy and Andy) a total of $120 for Hanukkah. He give Mandy ¼ of everything. He then gives Sandy 1/3 of what is left. He then gives Randy ¼ of what is left. He then gives Andy all the money that he has left. How much money did Andy get?

5. Mr. C. participated in the last Calgary Marathon (a 42km run). He ran the first half of the course at a pace of 5 minutes per km. He then slowed down and ran the next one third of the course at a pace of 5½ minutes per km. He completed the rest of it at a pace of 6½ minutes per km. How long did it take him to complete the entire race?

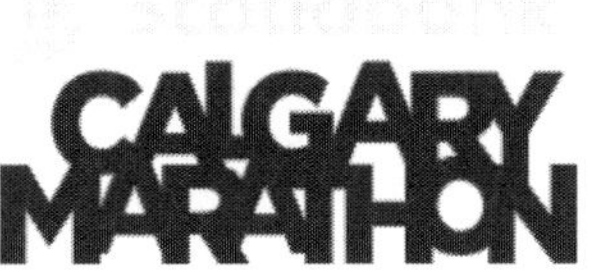

6. Ali is a short distance runner, and his favorite run is the 800m dash. In the most recent track and field meeting he completed the first 2/5 of the run in 20s and 3/4 of the remaining distance in another 45s. What distance did he still have to run in order to complete the race after the first 65 seconds?

7. A race track is 400m long. How many laps do you need to complete if you compete in any of the following distances?

a. 800m dash ____________

b. 1,000m dash ____________

c. 200m dash ____________

d. 100m dash ____________

e. 1,500m run ____________

f. 3,000m run ____________

g. 5km run ____________

h. 42km (Marathon) run ____________

Multiplying a whole number by a fraction: Revisit

Give your final answer in simplest form

Example: $6\times\frac{1}{3}=\frac{1}{3}+\frac{1}{3}+\frac{1}{3}+\frac{1}{3}+\frac{1}{3}+\frac{1}{3}=\frac{6}{3}=2$

But also $6\times\frac{1}{3}=\frac{1}{3}\times 6=\frac{1}{3}$ of $6=6\div 3=2$

It is important that you understand both ways of solving . **The word "of" in mathematics always translates into multiplication.** For example, $\frac{1}{4}\times 32$ means $\frac{1}{4}$ of 32, which is the same as $32\div 4$, which is 8.
A little harder is a question like $\frac{3}{4}\times 32$, which means $\frac{3}{4}$ of 32, but if we already know that one quarter of 32 is 8, then three quarters of 32 will be 3×8, which is 24.

1. $\frac{1}{3}$ of $12=12\div 3=$ _____ $\frac{2}{3}\times 12=$ ________

2. $\frac{1}{5}$ of $30=30\div$ _____ $=$ _____ $\frac{2}{5}\times 30=$ ________

3. $\frac{1}{7}\times 42=$ ________ $\frac{3}{7}$ of $42=$ ________ $\frac{6}{7}\times 42=$ ________

4. $\frac{3}{5}$ of $30=$ ________ $\frac{5}{3}\times 30=$ ________ $\frac{5}{6}$ of $30=$ ________

5. $\frac{3}{8}$ of $24=$ ________ $\frac{5}{8}\times 24=$ ________ $\frac{9}{8}$ of $24=$ ________

6. $\frac{4}{9}\times 36=$ ________ $\frac{2}{9}$ of $36=$ ________ $\frac{6}{9}\times 36=$ ________

FINALLY, what about something like $\mathbf{6\times\frac{4}{7}}$, which seems really difficult?

It is not really all that hard, because $6\times\frac{4}{7}=\frac{4}{7}+\frac{4}{7}+\frac{4}{7}+\frac{4}{7}+\frac{4}{7}+\frac{4}{7}=\frac{24}{7}=3\frac{3}{7}$

Try a few on your own:

$7\times\frac{4}{9}=$ ________ $6\times\frac{2}{5}=$ ________ $10\times\frac{5}{8}=$ ________

$\frac{6}{11}\times 9=$ ________ $4\times\frac{7}{8}=$ ________ $\frac{6}{7}\times 5=$ ________

$\frac{3}{4}\times 13=$ ________ $8\times\frac{3}{5}=$ ________ $\frac{9}{5}\times 4=$ ________

Final assessment – Level 4A

But first let's warm our brain up with a few easy Inkies™

Inky #1

7 +		1 -	1 -
	2 /		
12 ×		7 +	
	3 ×		

Inky #2

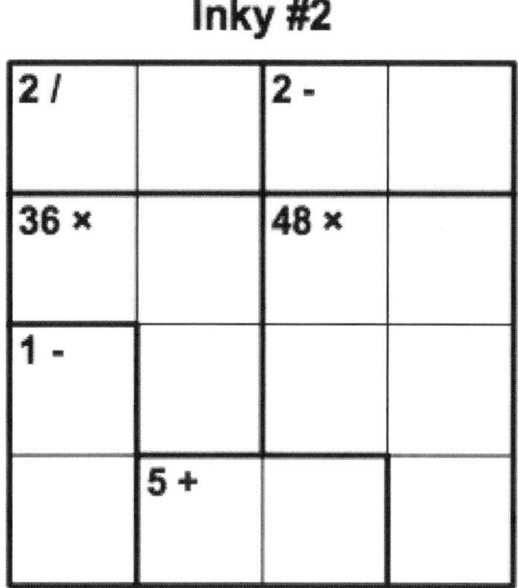

2 /		2 -	
36 ×		48 ×	
1 -			
	5 +		

Inky #3

2 ×		1 -	
1 -		7 +	
	1 -		
12 ×		2 /	

Inky #4

10 +			4 ×
	6 ×	2 -	
2 /			9 +

And also a few harder Inkies™

Inky #5

14 +		2 /		8 +
	8 +	30 ×	5 ×	
1 -				
			2 /	
1 -		60 ×		

Inky #6

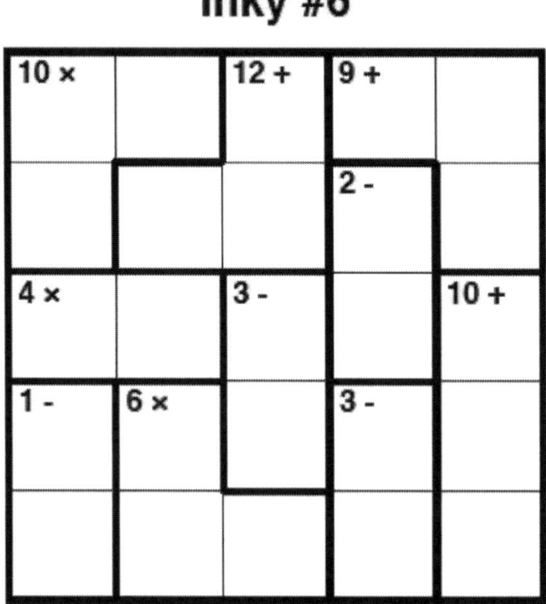

Inky #7

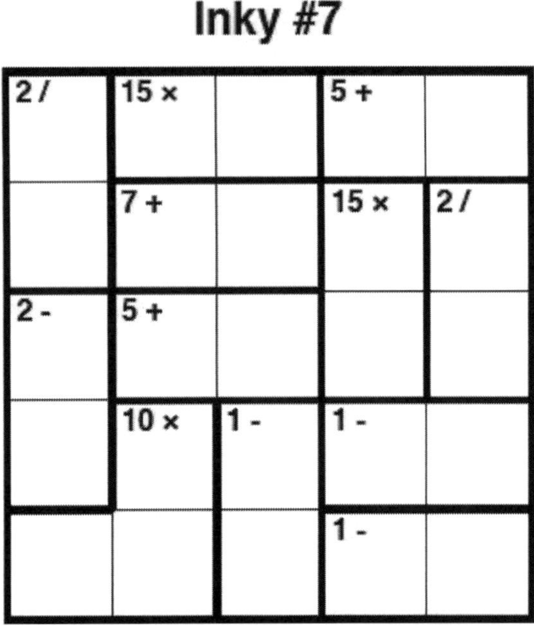

Inky #8

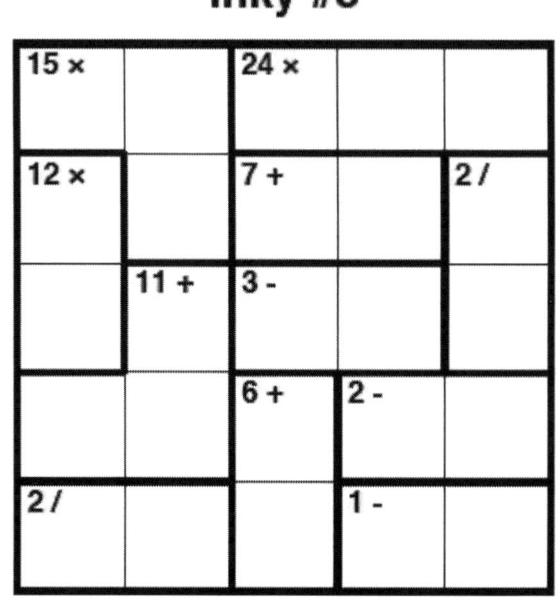

1. In 86,749, the digit _______ is in the hundreds place.

a) 6 b) 9 c) 7 d) 4

2. In 8,582 the digit 5 is in the __________ place.

a) ones b) tens c) hundreds d) thousands

3. In which of the following numbers does the digit 7 stand for 700.

a) 24,377 b) 937,427 c) 47,372 d) 74,732

4. 50 thousands and 3 tens is the same as ______________.

a) 5,030 b) 5,300 c) 50,030 d) 50,300

5. The value of 5 ten thousands, 9 thousands and 2 ones is ___________________.

6. Write 38,829 in words.

____

7. A grocer sold 807 mangoes on Monday and 658 mangoes on Tuesday. How many mangoes were sold on both days? **Round off your answer to the nearest ten.**

8. Round off 5495 to the nearest hundred.

a) 5,000 b) 5,400 c) 5,500 d) 6,000

9. The number of people who took part in a singing competition was 263 849. What is this number when rounded to the nearest hundred?

a) 263,000 b) 263,800 c) 264,000 d) 264,800

10. Round off the value of A to the nearest ten.

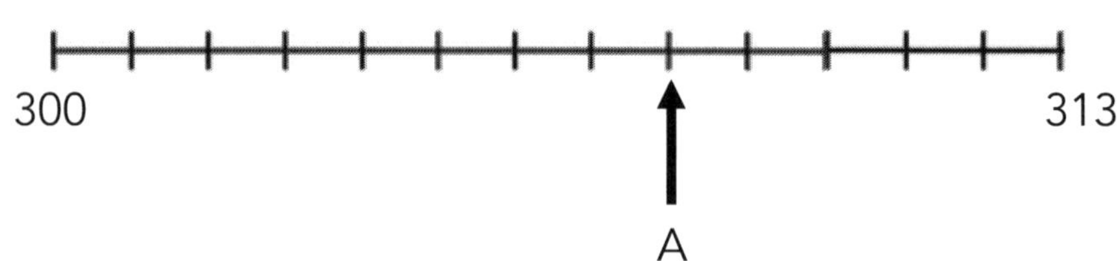

11. What is the largest number that when rounded to the nearest 100 is equal 6,000?

12. Study the pattern below and fill in the blank.

1, 2, 5, 10, ________, 26, 37, 50

13. Complete the following number pattern.

401, 408, 422, 443, ________, ________

14. What is the missing number in the pattern below?

32423, 32763, __________, 33443, 33783

15. What is the greatest four-digit odd number less than 5,000 that can be made with the digits 6, 4, 3, and 9?

16. Use all the digits 8, 0, 9 and 6 to form the smallest possible even number.

17. I am an even number. I am a multiple of 4 and a factor of 64.
I am smaller than 20 but bigger than 10.

What number am I? ______________________

18. Study the clues to find the following 5-digit number:

1. The digit 6 is in the thousands place.
2. The value of the digit 8 is 80.
3. The digit in the ones place is one quarter of the digit in the tens place.
4. The digit in the hundreds place is the only even prime.
5. The digit in the ten thousands place is equal to the sum of all other digits, divided by 6.

The number is ________________.

19. 20,000 + 1,000 + 40 + 3 = ______________

20. 23 thousands + 9 hundreds + 54 tens = ________________

a) 23,990 b) 23,954 c) 24,440 d) 32,540

21. Subtract 762 from 4,020 mentally.

22. For every 4 beads that Mena has, Venus has 7.
They have 88 beads altogether. How many beads does Venus have?

23. Heart-shaped and diamond-shaped beads were arranged in a long necklace in the pattern HHHDDHHHDD..... If 120 beads were used altogether. How many heart-shaped beads were used?

24*. Samit wants to give sweets to his friends.
If he gives each friend 3 sweets, he would have 2 sweets left over.
If he gives each friend 4 sweets, he would need another 3 sweets.
How many friends does Samit have?

25. Mrs. Birchall bought sweets to send to her Facebook friends on her birthday. She packed all the sweets into 193 packets and had 8 sweets left. If each packet contained 12 sweets, how many sweets did she buy?

26. Irmak had 2,504 pennies, and her mother gave her another 1,789. How many more pennies would she need in order to fill up her piggy bank if it can hold 10,000 pennies?

*27. Six students are standing in a circle in Phys-Ed, and each one is allowed to pass the ball to each other of the students only once. What is the maximum number of passes that can be made?

28. Find the value of 907 x 57 by using long multiplication.

29. Which one of the following is the best estimate for 609 × 29?

a) 600 x 20 b) 600 x 30 c) 610 x 20 d) 650 x 30

30. Li Ping had 4,420 red beads and 1,836 blue beads. She mixed them together and packed them equally into 8 boxes.

How many beads are there in each box?

a) 323 b) 657 c) 782 d) 6,256

31. What is the missing digit?

$$\begin{array}{r} 2\ 3\ \square\ 4 \\ \times \quad\quad 3 \\ \hline 7\ 1\ 8\ 2 \end{array}$$

a) 6 b) 7 c) 8 d) 9

32. Multiply 379 by 7 tens. The answer is ______________.

33. Ms. Doina makes 227 honey-layered cupcakes every day of the year. How many cupcakes does she make in a year? Use long multiplication.

Round your answer to the nearest 1,000.

34. Divide 5,649 by 7. Use short division.

35. Which of the following is divisible by 8?

a) 184 b) 246 c) 358 d) 404

36. What is the quotient when 7,645 is divided by 6?

a) 1,027 b) 1,074 c) 1,274 d) 1,277

37. The sum of all the factors of 9 is .

a) 16 b) 13 c) 12 d) 6

38. What is the common factor of 12 and 16?

a) 6 b)8 c) 3 d) 4

39. Which of the following is a common factor of 16 and 28?

a) 14 b) 8 c) 7 d) 4

40. Which of the following are common factors of 36 and 45?

a) 3 and 6 b) 3 and 9 c) 5 and 6 d) 6 and 9

41. Which one of the following statements is incorrect?

a) 4 is a common factor of 12 and 48
b) 2 is a common factor of 18 and 36
c) 3 is a common factor of 27 and 33
d) 6 is a common factor of 26 and 42

42. 42 children were divided into 7 equal groups. Each child got 12 stickers and each group received an extra 10 stickers. How many stickers did they receive altogether?

43. The first 2 common multiples of 3 and 4 are

a) 12 and 24 b) 10 and 18 c) 9 and 16 d) 6 and 8

44. Which of the following numbers is a multiple of 6?

a) 16 b) 26 c) 36 d) 46

45. What is the first common multiple of 6 and 8?

a) 12 b) 16 c) 24 d) 48

46. What are the next 3 multiples of 9?

99, _____, ______, _______

47. What is the sum of the 4th and 6th multiples of 8?

a) 24 b) 32 c) 48 d) 80

48. What fraction of the figure is shaded?

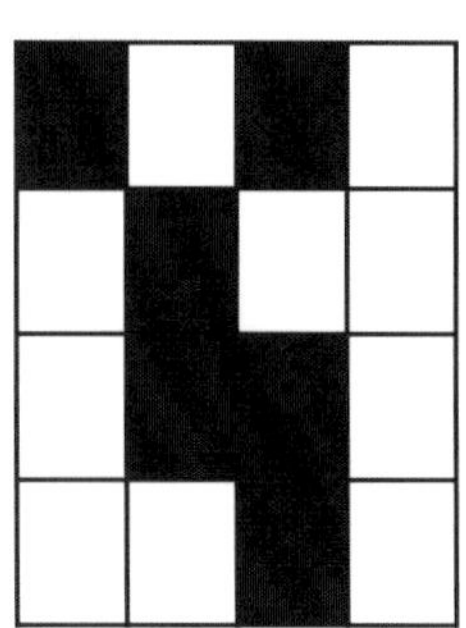

a) $\frac{1}{3}$ b) $\frac{1}{2}$ c) $\frac{3}{8}$ d) $\frac{5}{8}$

49. What fraction of each figure is shaded?

a) 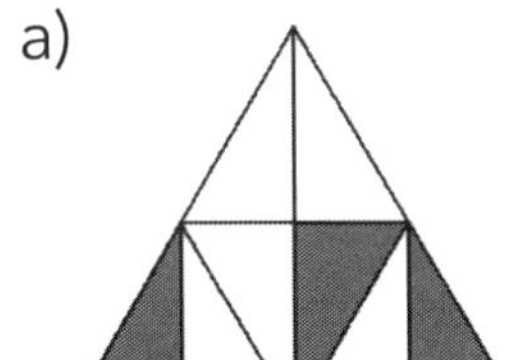 ______________

b) 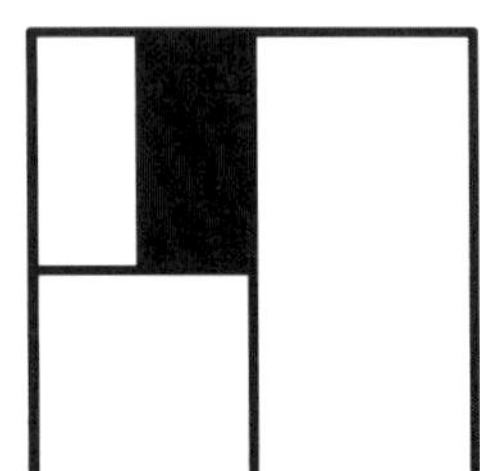 ______________

c) 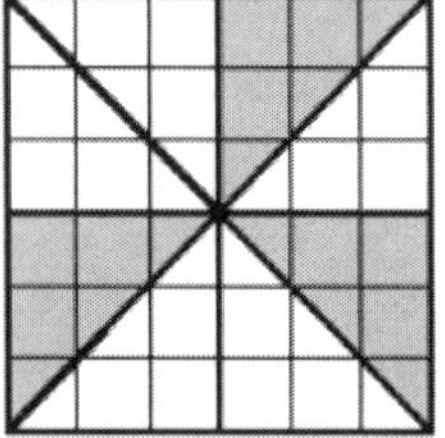 ______________

50. What fraction of each figure is shaded?

a) 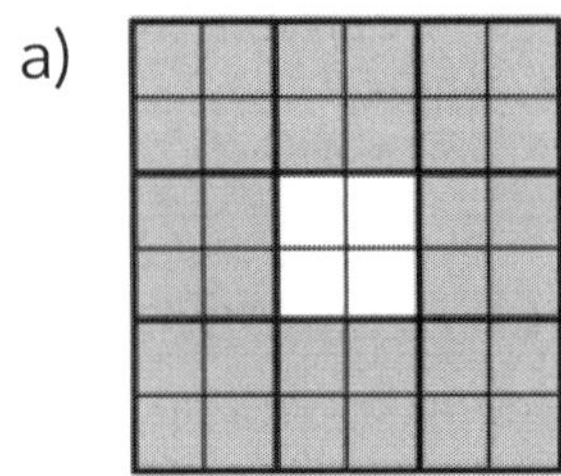 ______________

b) 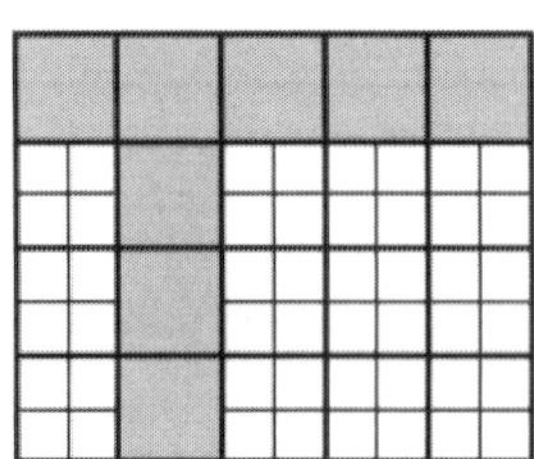 ______________

c*) 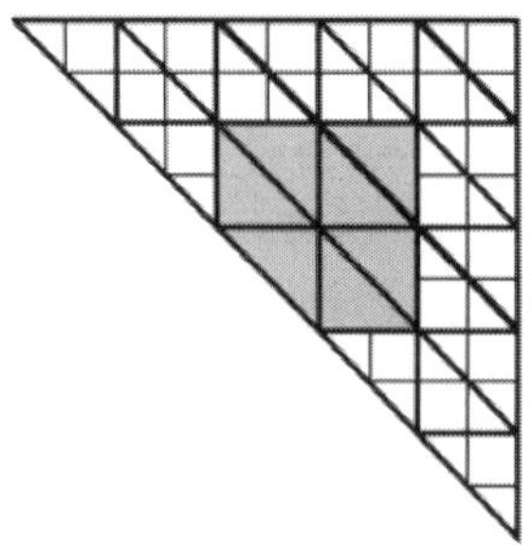 ______________

What lets you look through a wall? __________________

51. Arrange the following fractions in ascending order.

$\frac{7}{12}$, $\frac{3}{4}$, $\frac{1}{3}$, $\frac{1}{2}$

52. Arrange the following fractions from the greatest to the smallest.

$\frac{2}{17}$, $\frac{2}{3}$, $\frac{2}{9}$

53. $\frac{3}{5} + \frac{1}{10} =$

a) $\frac{2}{5}$ b) $\frac{4}{15}$ c) $\frac{7}{10}$ d) $\frac{4}{5}$

54. Calculate the sum of $4\frac{3}{5}$ and $1\frac{2}{10}$

a) $5\frac{4}{5}$ b) $5\frac{3}{10}$ c) $5\frac{5}{10}$ d) $5\frac{5}{15}$

55. The shaded area as an improper fraction is:

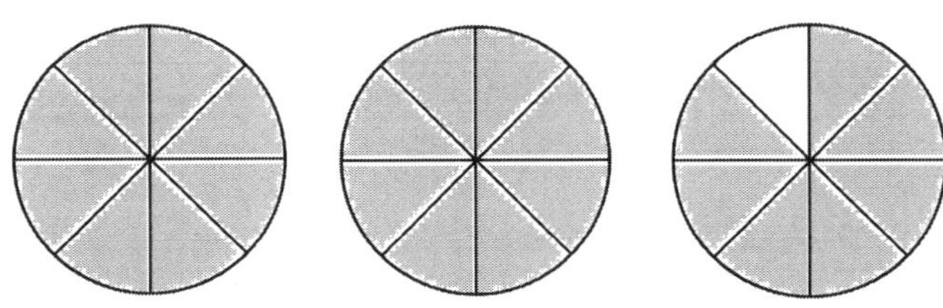

a) $2\frac{5}{8}$ b) $\frac{16}{8}$ c) $\frac{23}{8}$ d) $2\frac{7}{8}$

56. Which of the fractions below is the smallest?

a) $\frac{1}{2}$ b) $\frac{1}{3}$ c) $\frac{1}{4}$ d) $\frac{3}{8}$

57. What is the missing number?

$3\frac{3}{8} = \frac{}{24}$

58. What is the missing number?

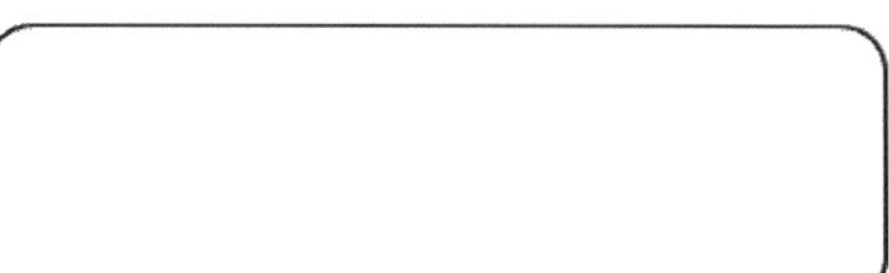

$\frac{11}{12} = \frac{1}{6} + \frac{}{6} + \frac{1}{12}$

59. Fill in the missing number.

$4 + 3\frac{1}{8} = \frac{}{8}$

60. Find the value of $4\frac{3}{10} - 1\frac{2}{5}$

a) $2\frac{1}{10}$ b) $2\frac{9}{10}$ c) $3\frac{1}{10}$ d) $3\frac{9}{10}$

True or false?

Every EVEN number from 4 and up can be written as the sum of 2 primes.

[Hint: This is Goldbach's Conjecture, and is one of the best known open questions in mathematics.]

61. Find the value of $2 - \frac{3}{4} - \frac{1}{6}$

a) $\frac{1}{12}$ b) $\frac{11}{12}$ c) $1\frac{1}{12}$ d) $1\frac{11}{12}$

62. What is the missing number?

$1 + \frac{3}{10} = 1\frac{3}{5} - \frac{\quad}{10}$

a) 5 b) 10 c) 3 d) 18

63. Express $\frac{28}{6}$ as a mixed number in the simplest form.

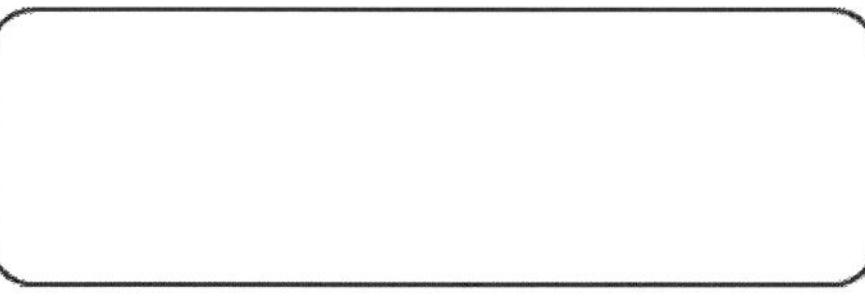

64. Find the value of $5 - \frac{5}{8} - 1 - \frac{1}{2}$.
Give your answer in the simplest form.

65. Express $2\frac{8}{24}$ in its simplest form.

66. Express $2\frac{5}{7}$ as an improper fraction.

67. Jenny had 4 red beads and 8 purple beads at first.
She bought another 4 red beads.
What fraction of her beads was red in the end?

a) $\frac{1}{2}$ b) $\frac{1}{3}$ c) $\frac{2}{3}$ d) $\frac{3}{4}$

68. Mrs. Lim baked some cookies and muffins. $\frac{3}{8}$ of her items were cookies.
She baked 115 muffins. How many cookies did she bake?

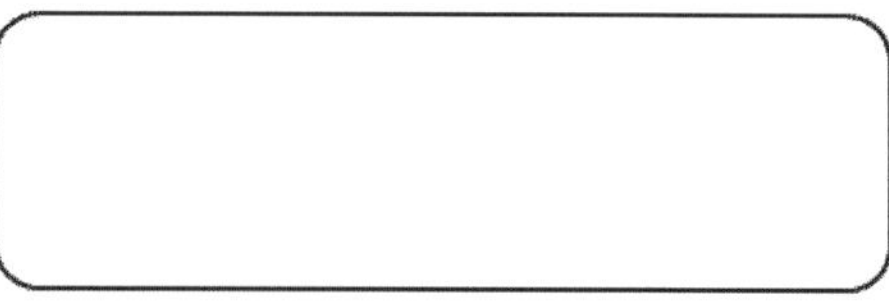

69. Ishan had 36 stickers. He gave $\frac{1}{3}$ of the stickers to his friends, and $\frac{1}{4}$ of the stickers he had left to his sister. How many stickers does he have at the end?

a) 12 b) 15 c) 18 d) 21

70. $5 \times \frac{3}{4} = \frac{1}{8} \times \square$ What number should go in the box?

71. Tom gave $\frac{1}{4}$ of his pizza to Alice and $\frac{5}{12}$ of it to Ms. Ruth.
What is fraction of the pizza was left for him to eat?

72. Two pizzas were cut into 12 pieces each and shared equally among 8 friends. What fraction of a pizza does each of the friends receive?

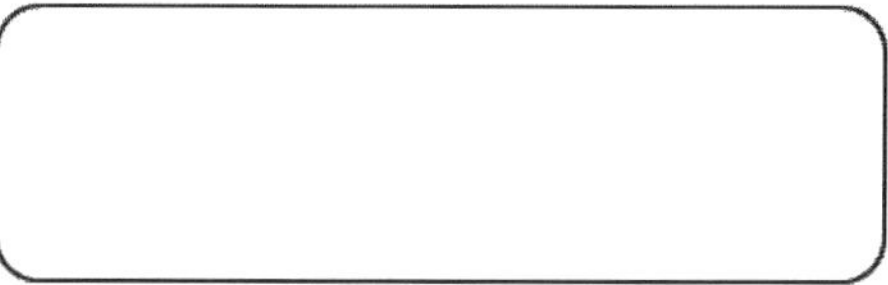

73*. Dave has $\frac{1}{2}$ as many stamps as Tom. After Tom gave 85 stamps to Dave, they had the same number of stamps. How many stamps do they have altogether?

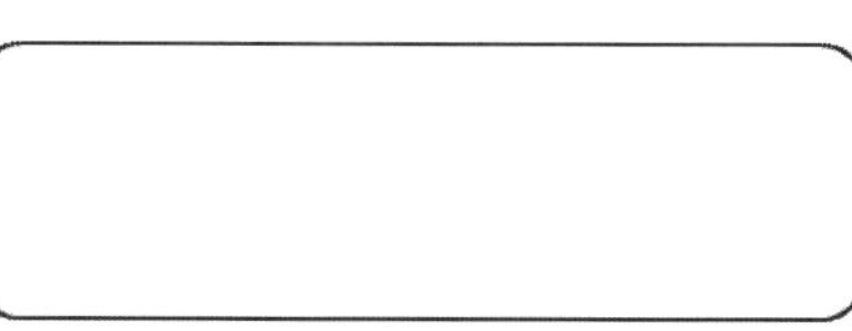

74. Joan bought 3 bags of candies. Each bag contained 20 candies. She gave 18 candies to May and 6 candies to June. What fraction of the candies did she have left?

a) $\frac{5}{6}$ b) $\frac{1}{3}$ c) $\frac{2}{5}$ d) $\frac{3}{5}$

75. What mixed number does the letter X represent on the line?

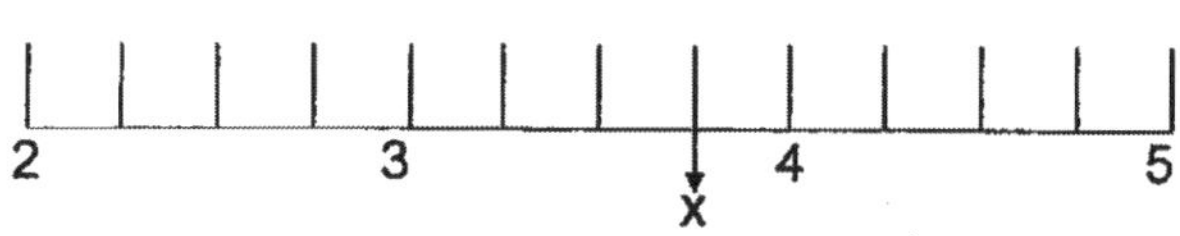

76. How many sixths are there in $1\frac{2}{3}$?

77. Which fractions below add up to 1 whole? Circle them.

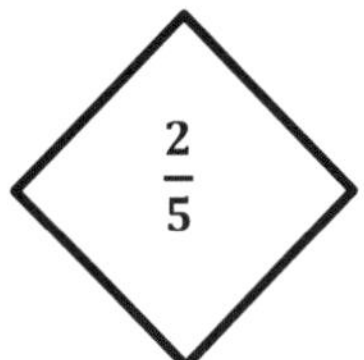

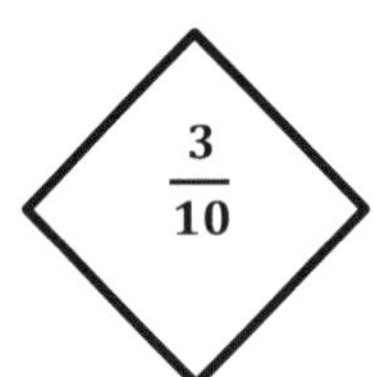

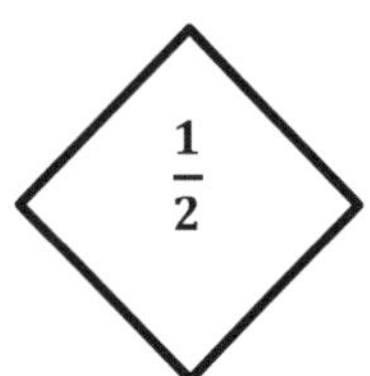

78. Shade the correct number of triangles such that $\frac{5}{8}$ of the figure is shaded.

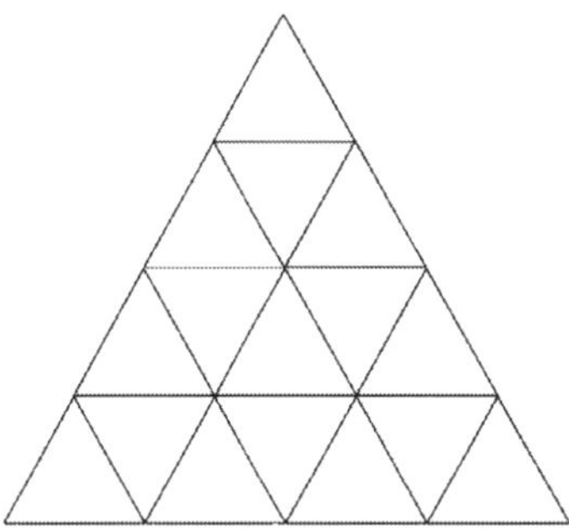

79. P and Q are two numbers on the number line below. Find P + Q. Give your answer in its simplest form.

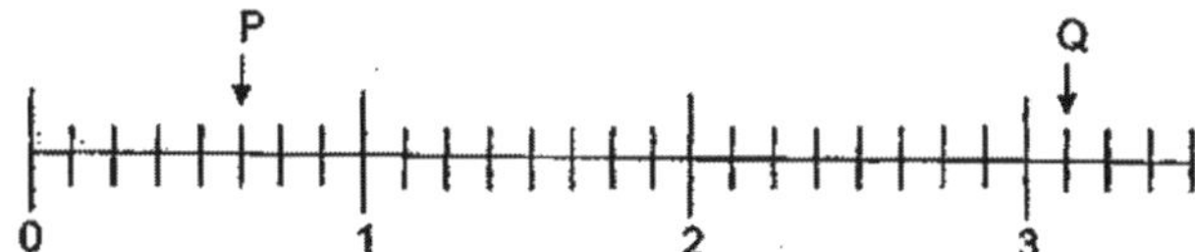

80. WXYZ is a square. Find the area of the shaded part.

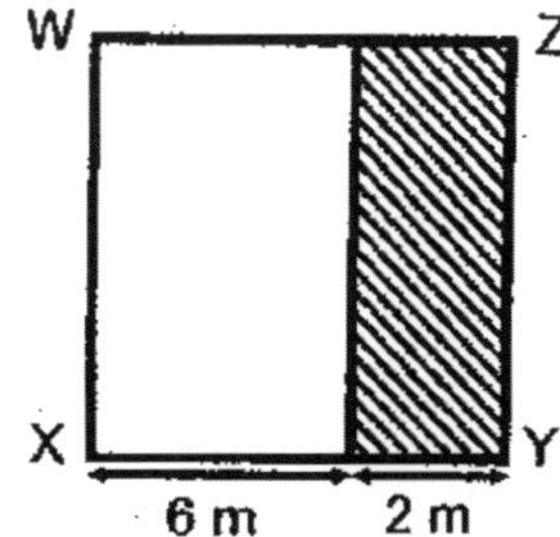

81. Find the area of the figure below. All lines meet at right angles. (The figure is not drawn to scale.)

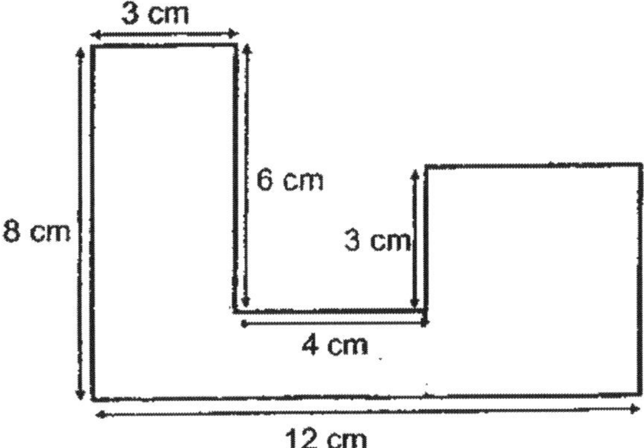

Answer _______________ cm^2

82. The figure below is made up of identical squares. What is the area of the figure?

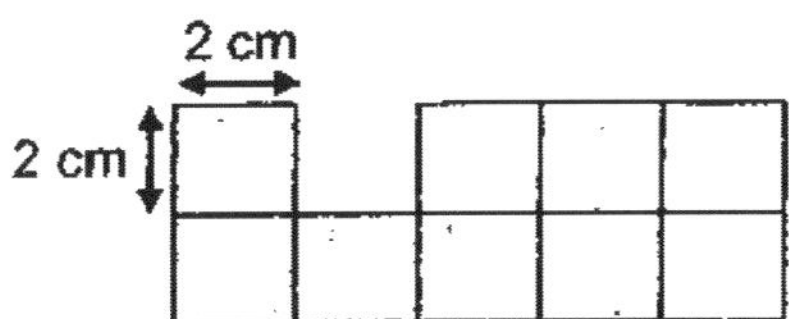

Answer _______________ cm^2

83. The length of rectangle ABCD is three and a half times as long as its width. What is the area of the triangle ABC if the width is 4cm?

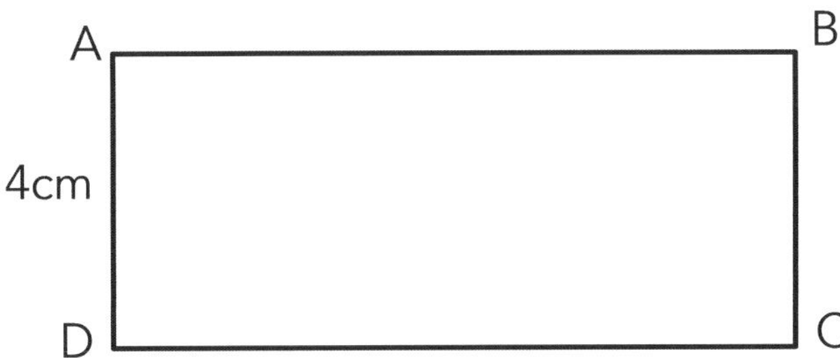

Answer _______________ cm^2

84. The figure of a cross is drawn on a square grid of size 6 cm. It is divided into equal parts as shown below. What is the area of the shaded part?

a) 6 cm² b) 18 cm² c) 30 cm² d) 45 cm²

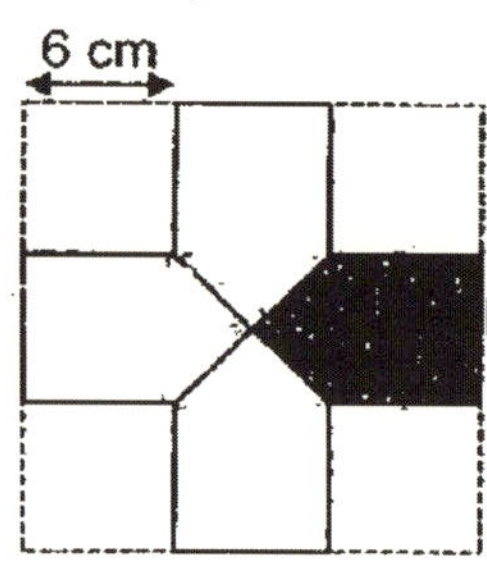

85. A rectangular field has a length of 10m and width of 8m. After a 2m pavement was built around the field, the area of the field became smaller. What is the area of the new, smaller field?

a) 16 m²
b) 24 m²
c) 64 m²
d) 80 m²

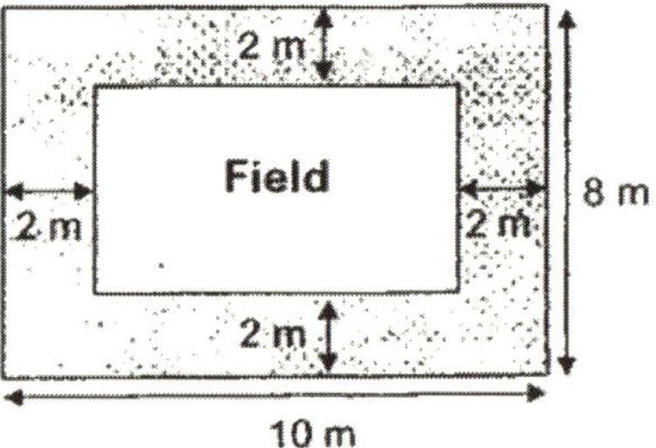

86. The diagram below shows a rectangle PRSU, which is made up of square PQTU and rectangle QRST. Figure D, E and F are squares and the area of square F is 1m² . The area of square D is equal to the shaded area in rectangle QRST and QA=AT.

(a) Find the area of square E.
(b) Find the total area of the unshaded parts in rectangular field PRSU.

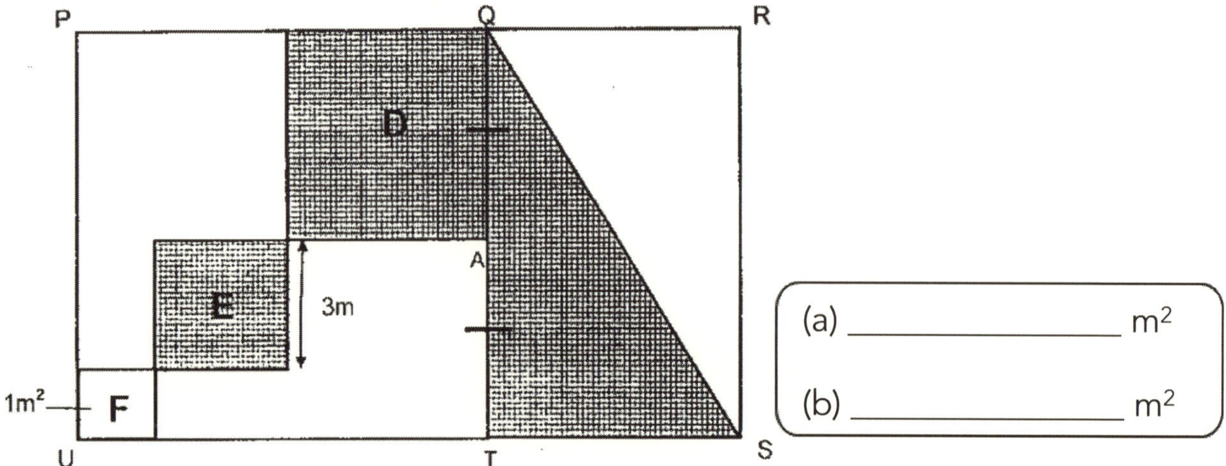

87. Find the perimeter of the figure below.

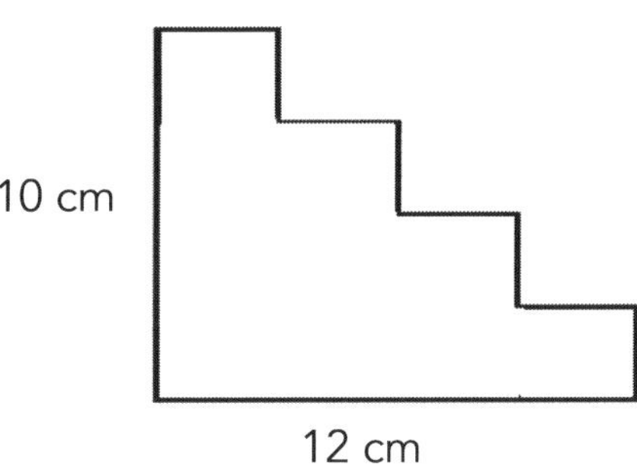

Answer _______________ cm

88. The perimeter of a rectangle is 7 times its width. If the perimeter is 35 cm, find its area.

Answer _______________ cm^2

89. The figure below is made up of a rectangle and 2 identical squares. What is the perimeter of the figure ?

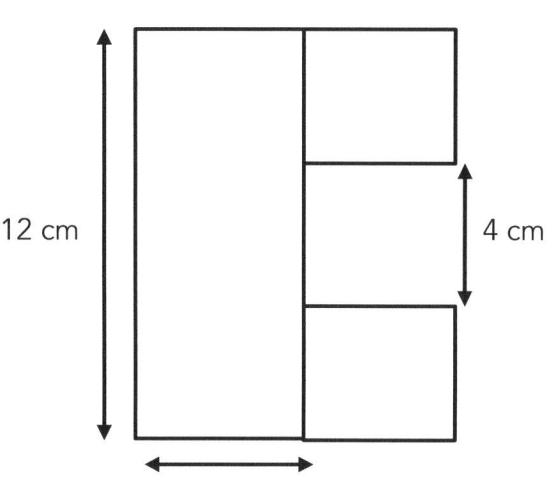

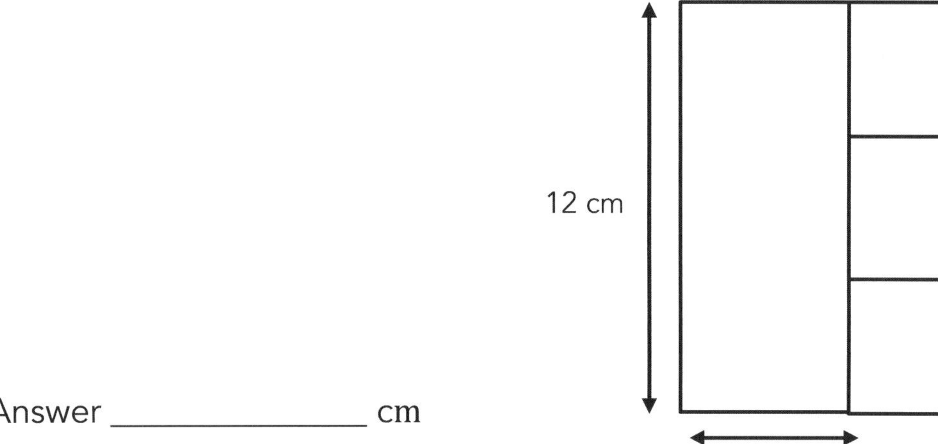

Answer _______________ cm

90. The figure below is made up of a square and 3 identical rectangles.

(a) Find the perimeter of the figure.
(b) Find the area of the shaded rectangle.

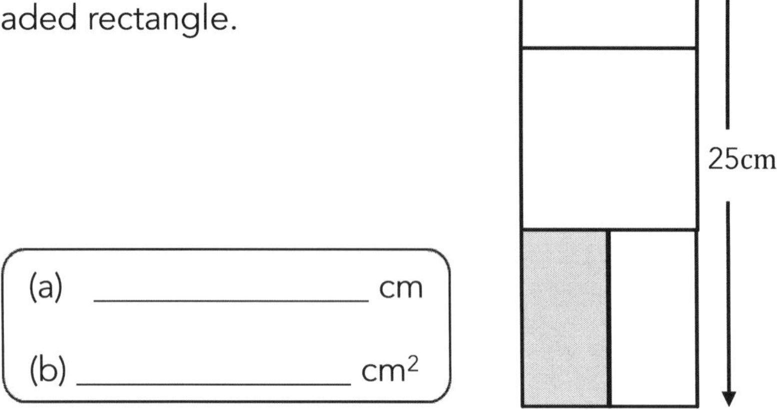

91. The figure shown is made up of three rectangles. The figure is not drawn to scale.
(a) Find the perimeter of the figure.
(b) Find the area of the figure.

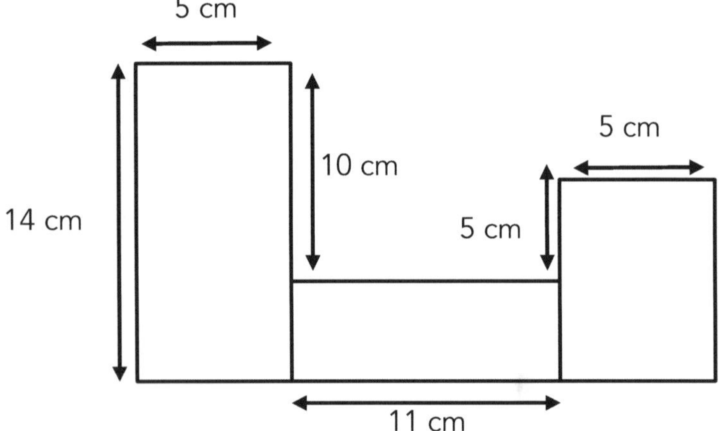

(a) ______ m

(b) ______ m^2

92. Two books cost as much as 3 magazines. Ms. Lora paid $36 for 6 books. How much must she pay if she wants to buy 15 magazines?

Answer ______

93. The figure below is made up of a square and a rectangle. Find the length of AF.

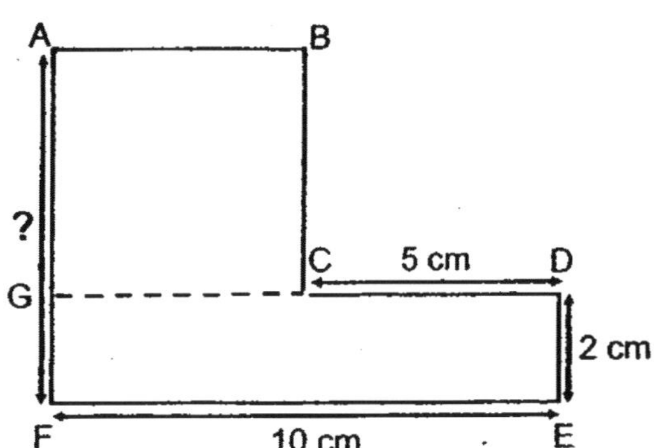

a) 5 cm b) 7 cm c) 8 cm d) 10 cm

94. The figure in the picture is made up of 4 identical rectangles. Find the length of AB.

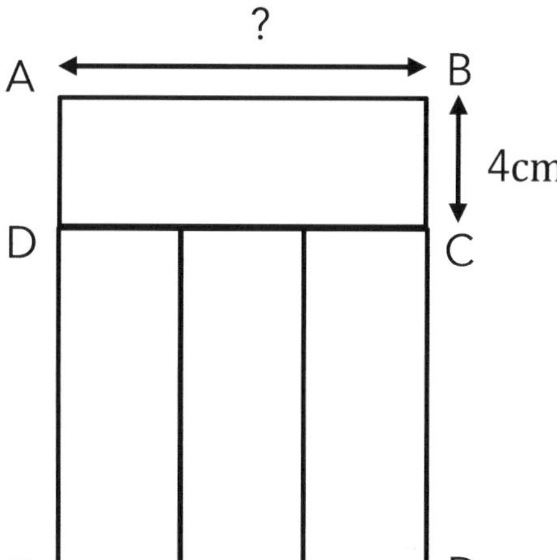

Answer ______________ cm

95. The diagram below is made up of three squares A, B and C. The area of square B is four times the area of square A. Find the side length of square C.

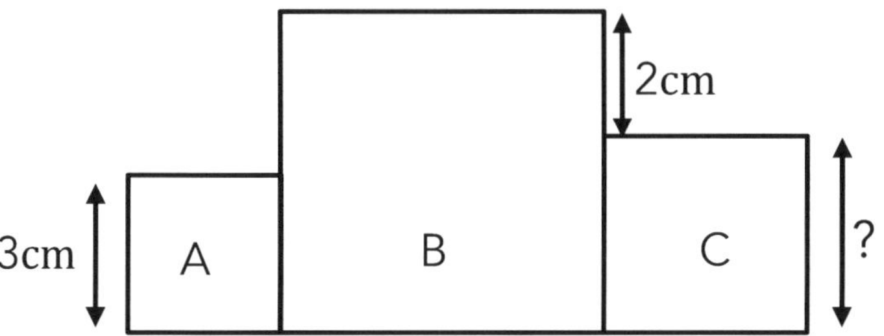

Answer __________ cm

96. Square P and Rectangle Q have the same perimeter.
What is the length of Rectangle Q ?

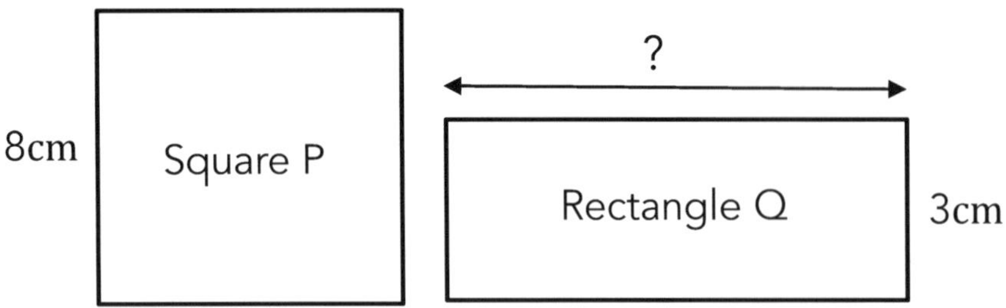

Answer _______________ cm

97. Area of square X is the same as the area of rectangle Y.
Find the difference between their perimeters.

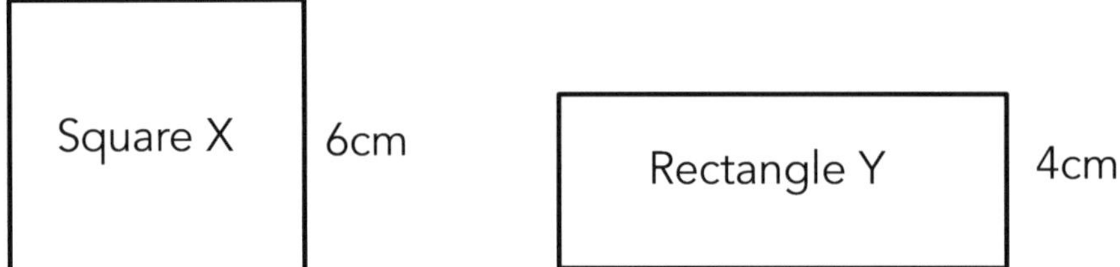

Answer _______________ cm

98. An empty basket weighs 400g. When it is filled with 23 apples of the same size, the weight of the basket and apples is 5kg. What is the weight of an apple?

a) $\frac{2}{5}$ kg b) $\frac{3}{5}$ kg c) $\frac{1}{5}$ kg d) $\frac{4}{5}$ kg

99. Study the pattern below. Matchsticks are used to form each pattern.

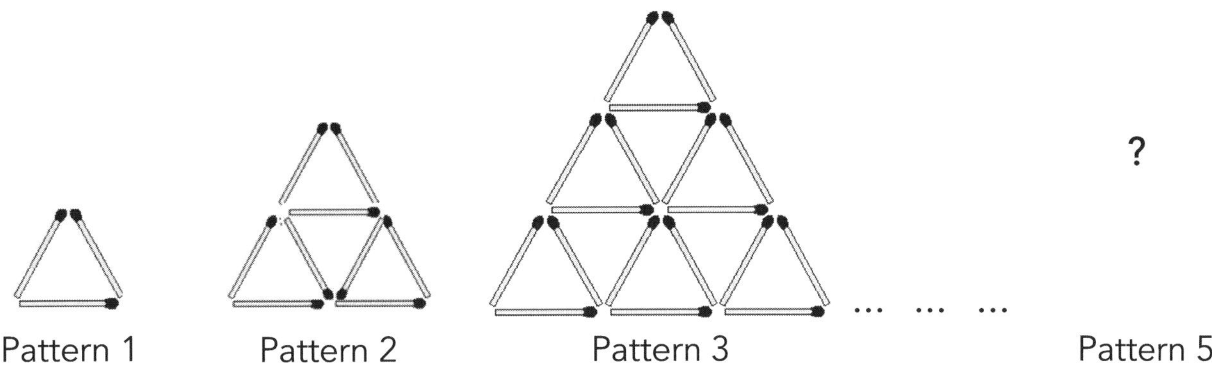

Find out the number of matchsticks needed to form pattern 5.

Pattern	1	2	3	4	5
Number of matches	3	9	18		?

Answer _______________

100*. Mr. Erikson paid $120 for 3 identical shirts and a pair of pants. The pants cost twice as much as each shirt. How much did Mr. Erikson pay for each shirt?

Answer _______________

101. The price of a glue stick is $3. When you buy 3 glue sticks, you get one more at half price. What is the greatest number of glue sticks you can buy with $51?

Answer _______________

102. Ali, Ben and Yonatan have $620 altogether. Ali has $90, and Ben has $42 more than Yonatan. How much money does Ben have?

Answer ________________

103. Kanika and Lekha each save an equal sum of money each day.
Kanika can save $25 in 4 days. Lekha can save $48 in 6 days.
How many days will it take Lekha to save $100 more than Kanika?

Answer ________________

104. Arjun has a pet store. He sells clownfish for $2 each and koi for $16 each.
He has 280 fish of both types, and $\frac{2}{7}$ of them are koi.
How much money will Arjun collect if he sells all his fish?

Answer ________________

105*. Marina and Emori had $60. After giving Emori $8, Marina had half as much as Emori. Who had more money at first and by how much?

Answer ________________

106. Johan spent \$33 on a shirt, a belt and a tie. The shirt cost \$5 more than the tie, and the belt cost \$8 more than the shirt. Find the cost of 6 ties.

Answer ______________

107. Jacintha spent $\frac{5}{9}$ of her money on a skirt. The price of the skirt was \$35. How much money did she have at first?

Answer ______________

108. Measure the size of ∠ x.

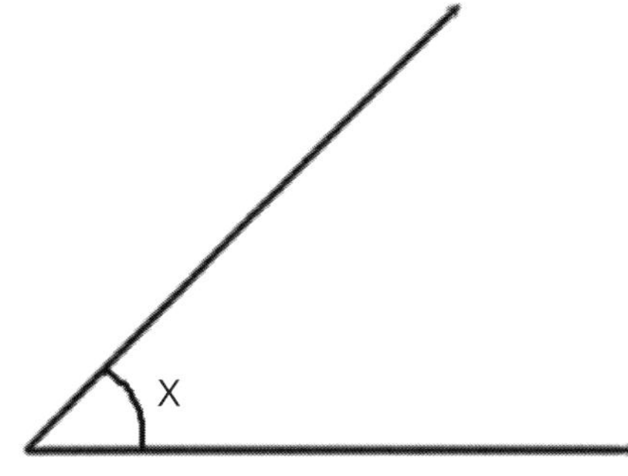

Answer ______________

109. Measure ∠ ABC.

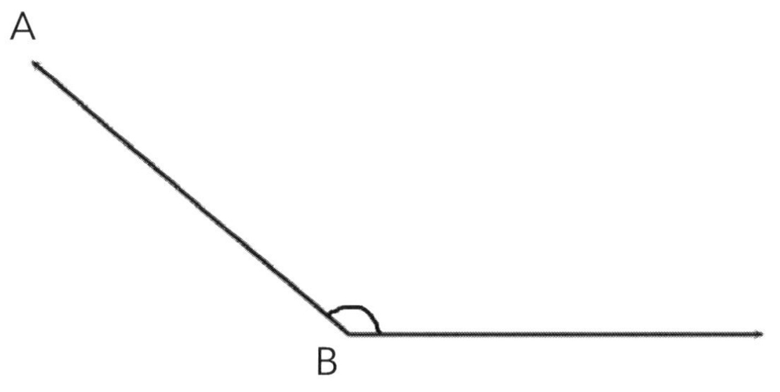

Answer ______________

110. Use a protractor to measure the obtuse angle in the figure below.

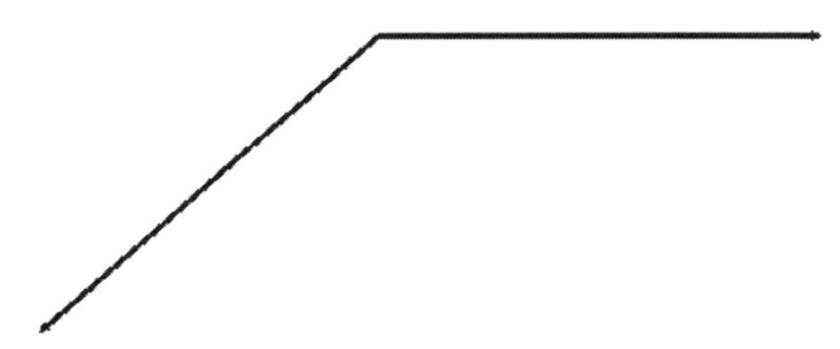

Answer ________________

111. Find ∠ a.

a) 42°
b) 90°
c) 138°
d) 180°

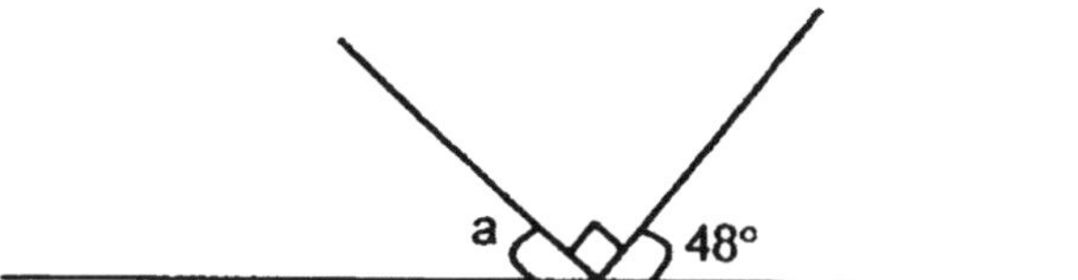

Answer ________________

112. A rectangular piece of paper is folded at two of its corners as shown:

How many right angles can are there ?

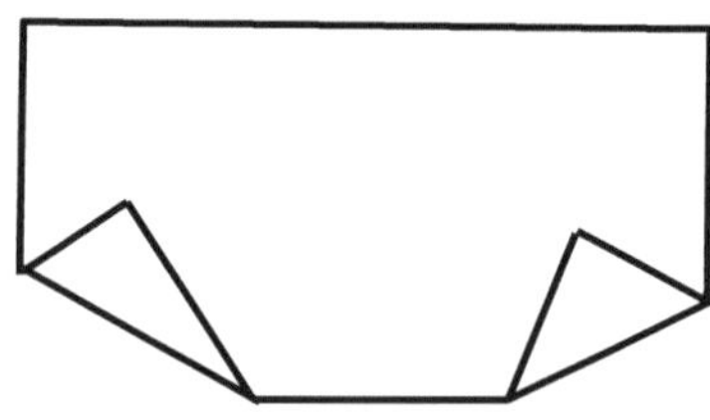

Answer ________________

113. How many angles inside the figure shown below are greater than a right angle?

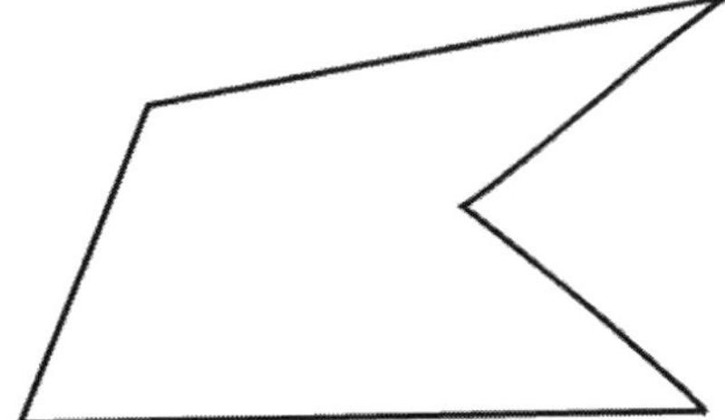

Answer ________________

114. Which of the angles is greater than a right angle?

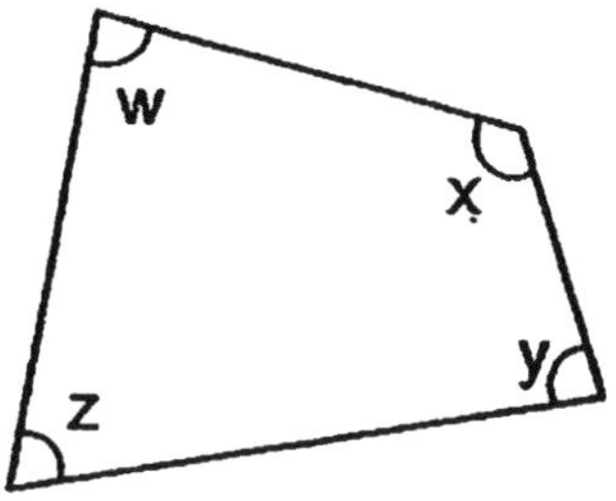

1) w
2) x
3) y
4) z

115. The rectangle below is not drawn to scale. What is ∠ x?

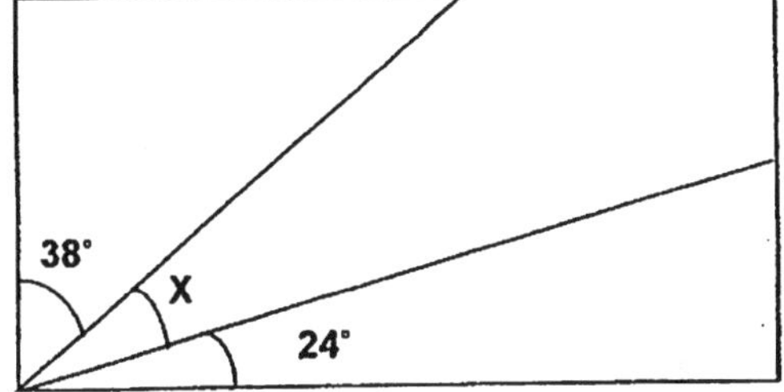

a) 24°
b) 28°
c) 38°
d) 62°

116. Figure CDEF is a square. What is ∠ y?

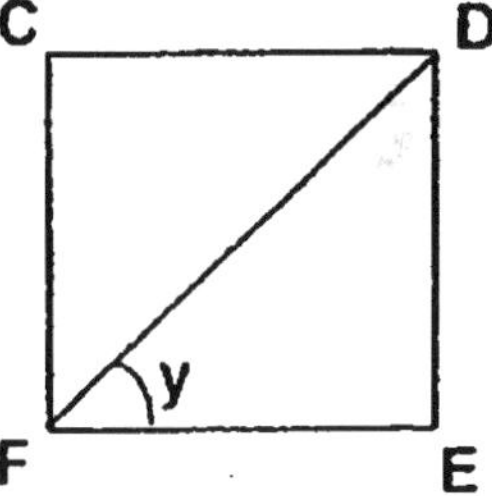

a) 30°
b) 45°
c) 60°
d) 90°

117. ABCD is a square. What is ∠ x + ∠ y?

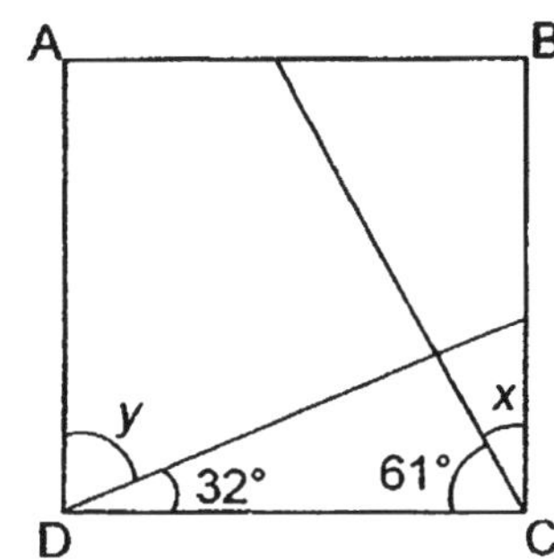

Answer ______________

118. How many of the marked angles inside the figure are less than a right angle?

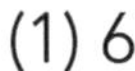

(1) 6
(2) 8
(3) 10
(4) 4

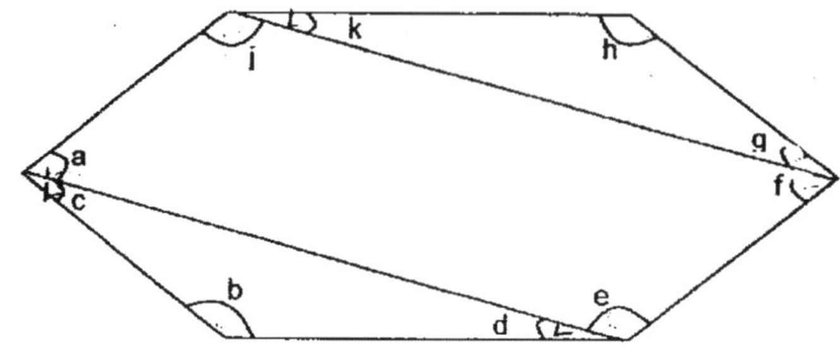

119. The figure is made up of 2 squares. What is the value of ∠AEC?

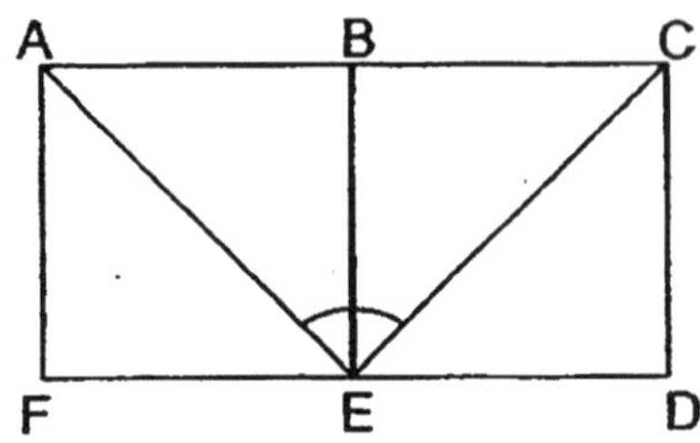

Answer ________________

120. The picture below shows a game board. Which object lies southeast of the letter F.

(1) 

(2) 

(3) 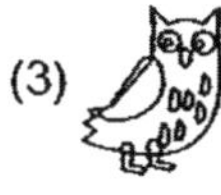

(4) 

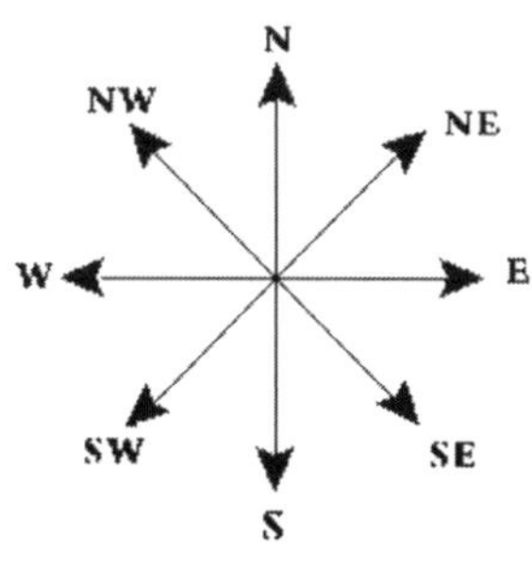

121. How many right angles are there inside the figure below?

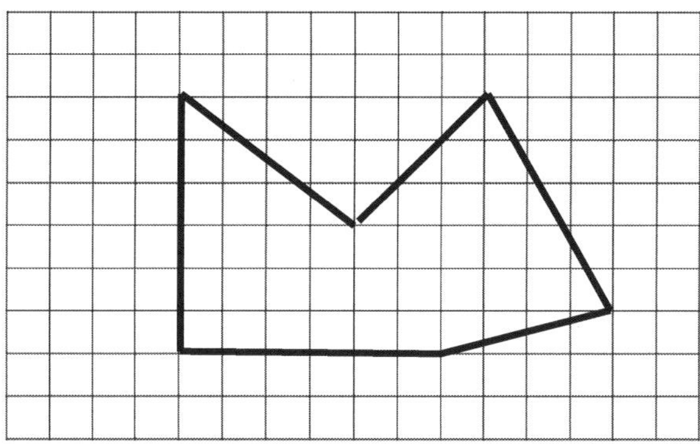

Answer __________

122*. What is the area of the figure in question 121?

Answer _______ units^2

123. Janice is facing south-west, if she makes a 270° clockwise turn, where will she be facing?

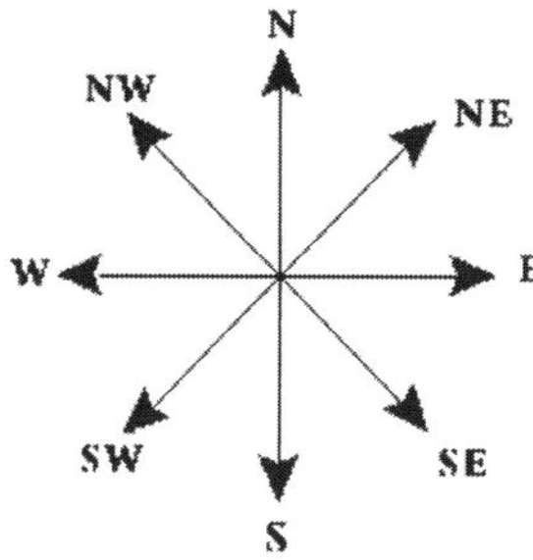

a) North
b) East
c) South-East
d) North-East

124. Kelly bought 28m of cloth. She used a $\frac{1}{4}$ of it to sew a dress.
Then she used another 3m of cloth to sew a scarf.
How many meters of cloth were left?

Answer __________

125. Sammy is standing at point X and is facing the library. He turns 225° in a clockwise direction. Where will he be facing?

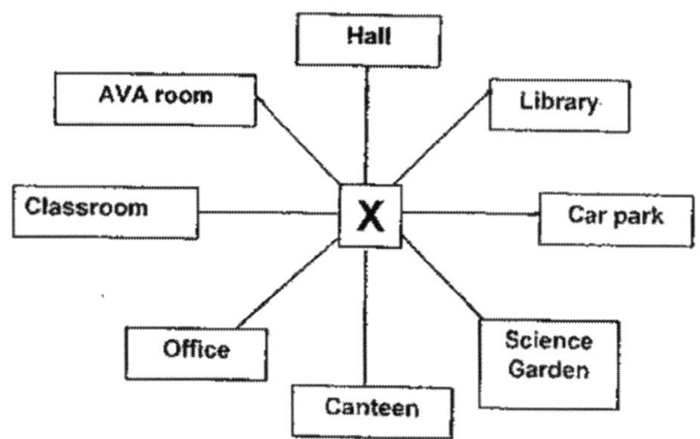

Answer ____________

126. Madam Kinley is standing at the point marked X in the figure below. She is facing Tekka Mall. What will she face when she turns 135° counter-clockwise?

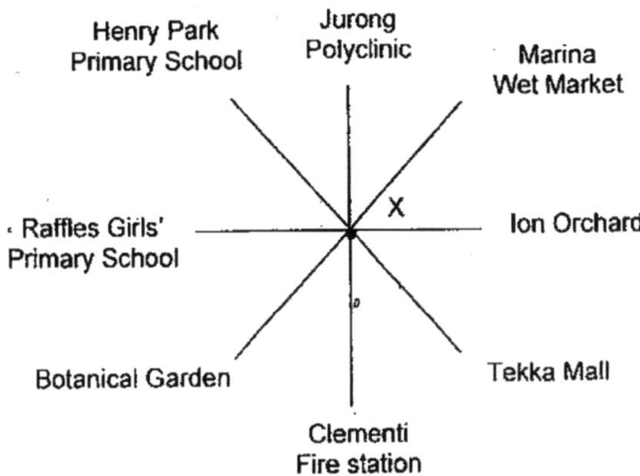

Answer ____________

127. A $\frac{3}{4}$ turn is equal to __________ degrees.

128. Study the diagram below and answer the questions.

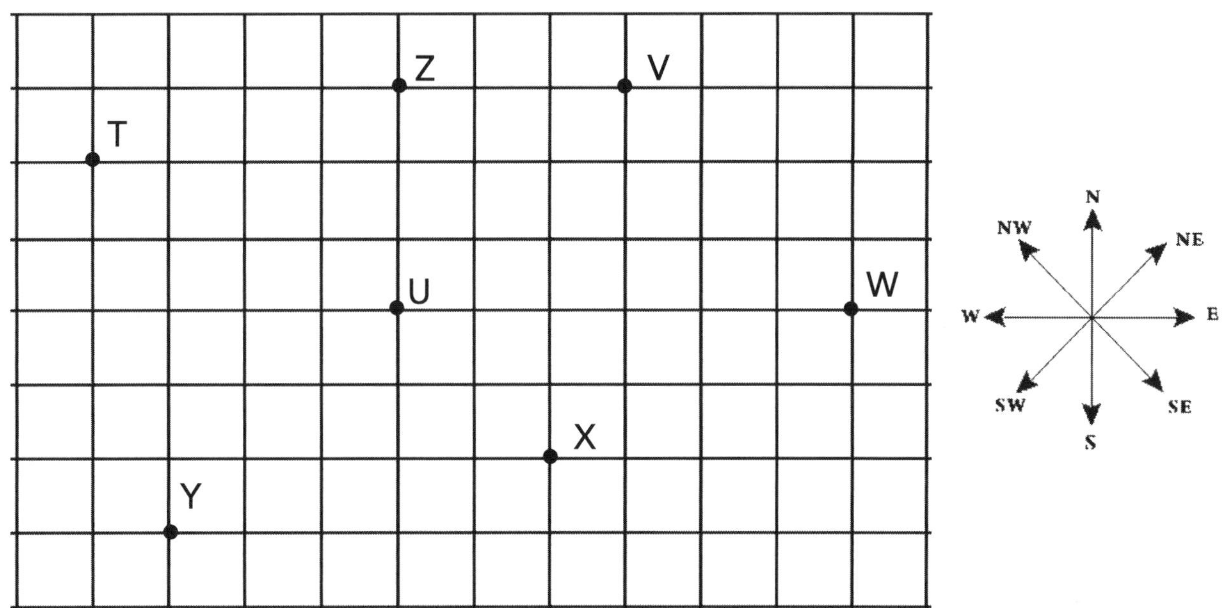

a) Point **U** is North-West of point _______

b) Andrew started at point T, and took 3 steps South. Next he took 4 steps East followed by 2 steps South. Finally he moved 3 steps West. At which point would he be at the end of his journey? ________

c) Sarina started at point Z, and took 5 steps South-West. Next she took 3 steps East followed by 5 steps North-East. Finally she moved 3 steps South-East. Which points did she visit along her journey? ____________

129. Nolan bought 2kg 50g of meat. Avery bought 30g of meat less than Nolan, and Moses bought 550g of meat more than Avery. How much meat did the 3 of them buy altogether?

Answer ____________

130. I have exactly one pair of parallel lines. Which is my shape?

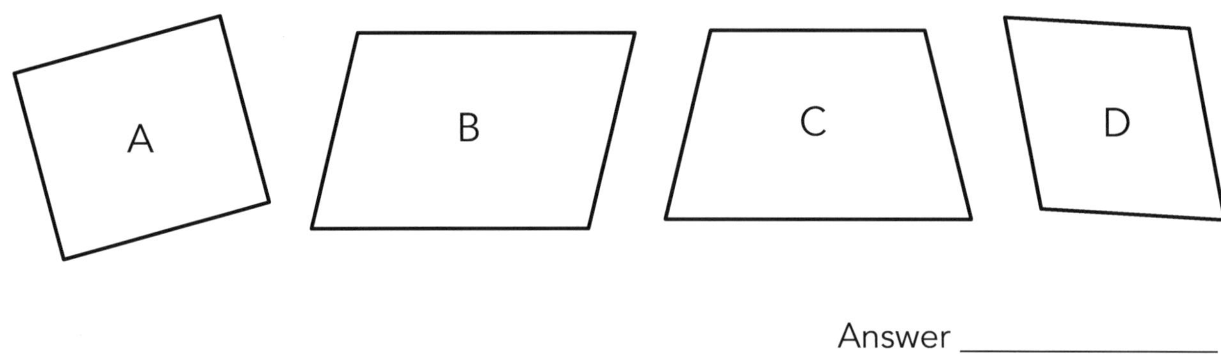

Answer _______________

131. Which of the following figures have more than 1 pair of parallel lines?

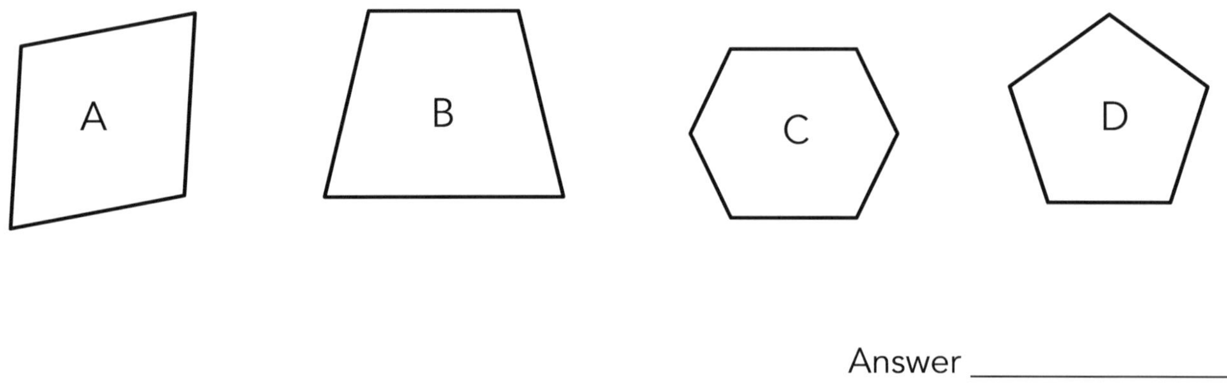

Answer _______________

132. In the, figure below, how many line(s) are parallel to AB? **Look carefully!**

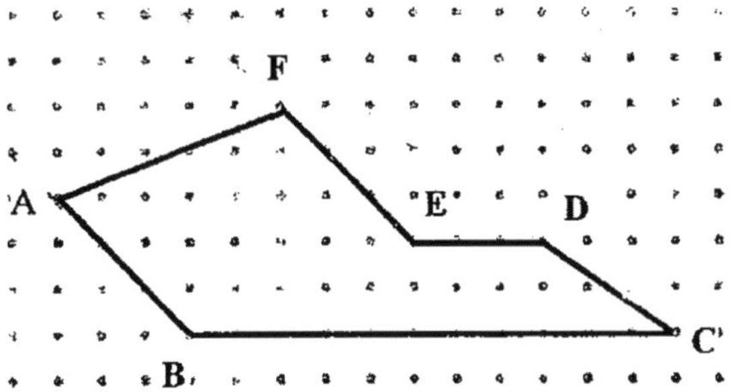

Answer _______________

133. Draw a line parallel to line AB through the point X.

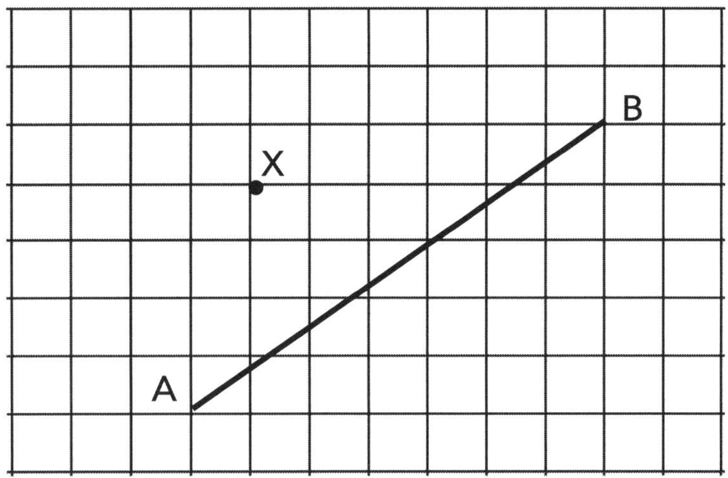

134. Draw a line perpendicular to XY through point Z.

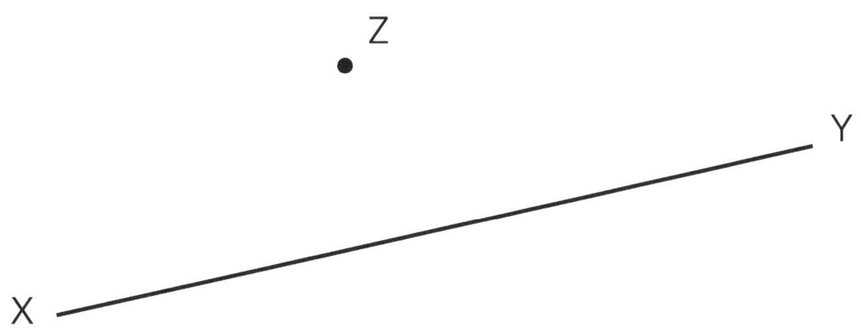

135. Which line is perpendicular to AB?

a) AD
b) AE
c) BC
d) ED

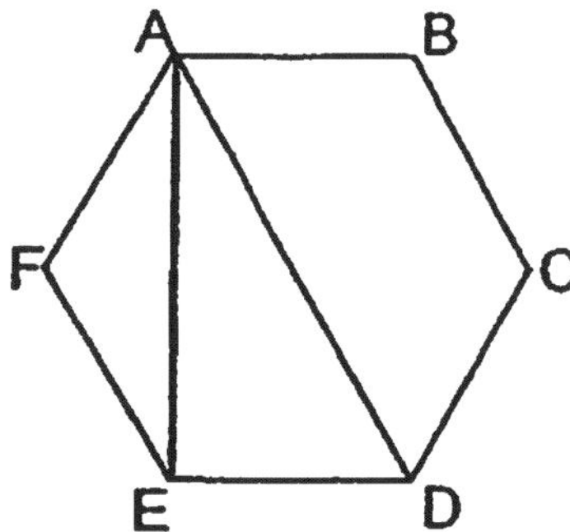

136. Study the figure below.

How many pairs of perpendicular lines are there? Use a protractor!

a) 1
b) 2
c) 3
d) 4

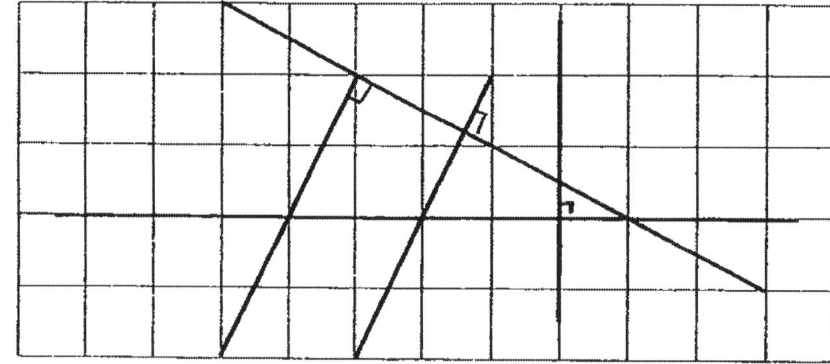

137. A shopkeeper has four 50Kg bags of rice. He packed all the rice into smaller packets weighing 5Kg and 2Kg.

He wants to have the same number of 5Kg packets and 2Kg packets.

(a) How many packets of rice can he pack altogether? ________________

(b) How much rice is left over? ____________________

138. John is 15 years old this year. Two years ago, he was $\frac{1}{3}$ of his father's age. How old is his father now?

Answer ______________

There are 22 blue and 35 black socks in a drawer. How many socks do you need to take out of the drawer to find a matching pair?

____

139. In the figure below, draw a line perpendicular to BC, and mark it L_1.

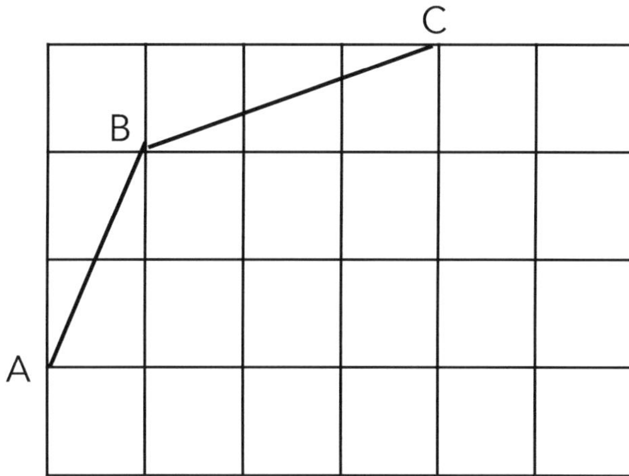

140. In the figure above, draw a line parallel to AB, and mark it L_2.

141. Which dot A, B or C, when joined to point G, could form a line perpendicular to line XY?

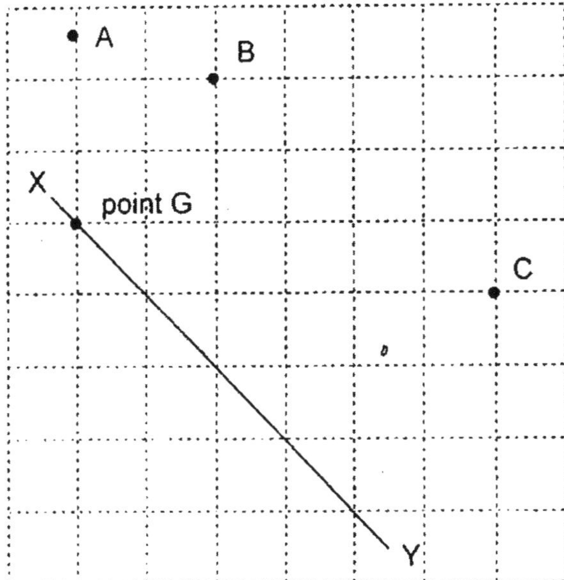

Answer: ______________

142. Place the right number in the box.

500 x 24 = 1,600 + ☐

143. Beyonce used all the 4 digits below to form two different 2-digit numbers that have the **largest** possible difference. What is this largest difference?

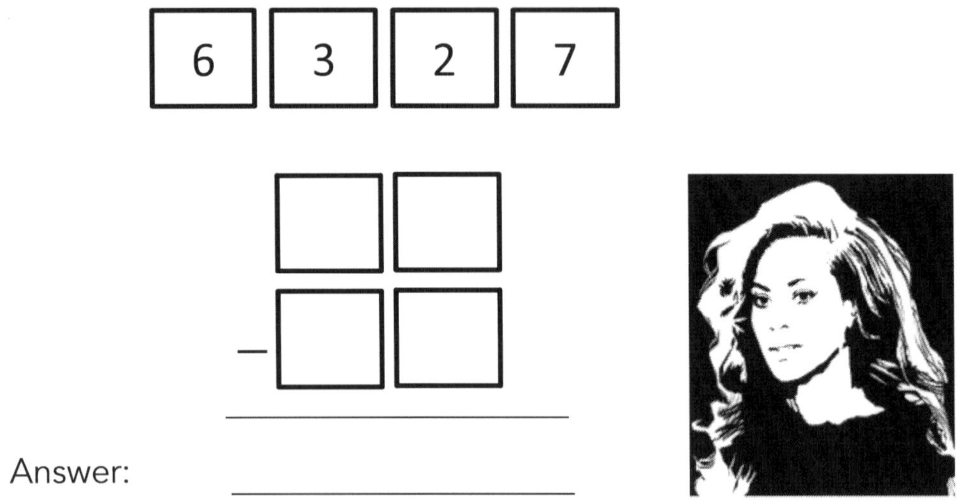

Answer: ______________

144. How many sixths of a pizza are there in two and a half pizzas?

Answer: __________

145. Jay-Z used all the 4 numbers below to form two different 2-digits numbers that have the **smallest** possible difference.
What is this smallest positive difference?

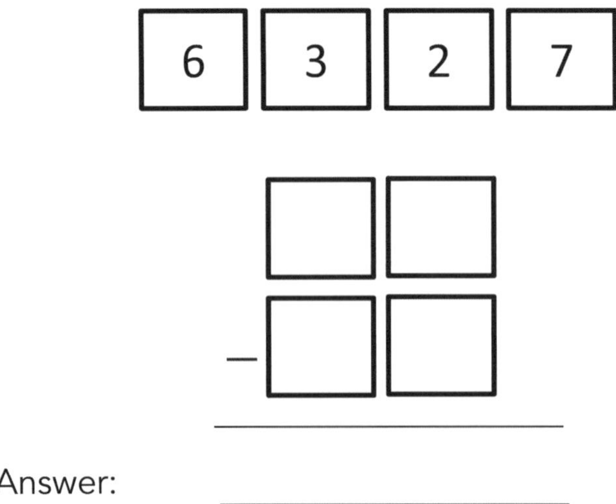

Answer: ______________

146. ♡ + ☆ + ☆ = 150

♡ × ♡ = 36

☆ ÷ ♡ = ?

Answer: __________

147*. Stevie Wonder has two photo albums. There are 18 photos on each page. His first album is full, and has 1,044 photos. His second album has 20 pages more than the first one, but is only two thirds full.

How many photos does Stevie have in his second album?

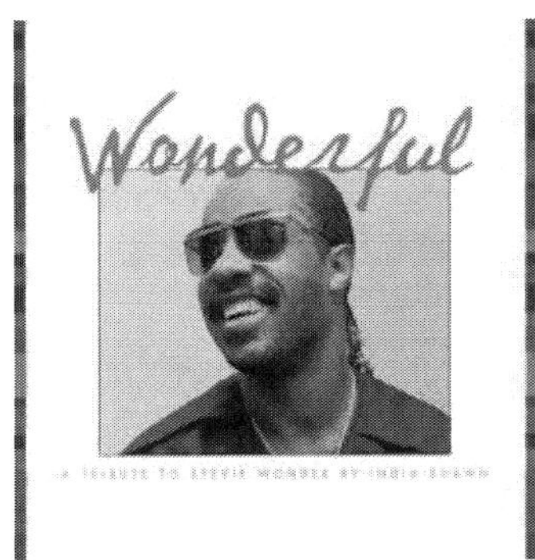

Answer: __________

148*. There were 1,260 chairs in the hall. Mr. Sandhu arranged them in 3 rows. There were 603 more chairs in the first row than the second row. The number of chairs in the second row was four times the number of chairs in the third row.

How many chairs were there in the second and third row?

Answer: __________

149. The bar graph shows the sale of T-shirts cones last week.

Monday	☆ ☆ ☆ ☆ ☆
Tuesday	☆ ☆
Wednesday	☆ ☆ ☆ ☆
Thursday	☆ ☆ ☆ ☆ ☆ ☆
Friday	☆ ☆ ☆ ☆ ☆ ☆ ☆
☆ = 4 T-shirts	

a) How many T-shirts were sold on Friday? __________

b) How many more T-shirts were sold on Friday than on Wednesday? _______

c) The number of T-shirts sold on Thursday, Friday and Monday is ____ times greater than the number of T-shirts sold on Tuesday and Wednesday.

150. The table below shows the number of ice-cream cones sold each day for a week.

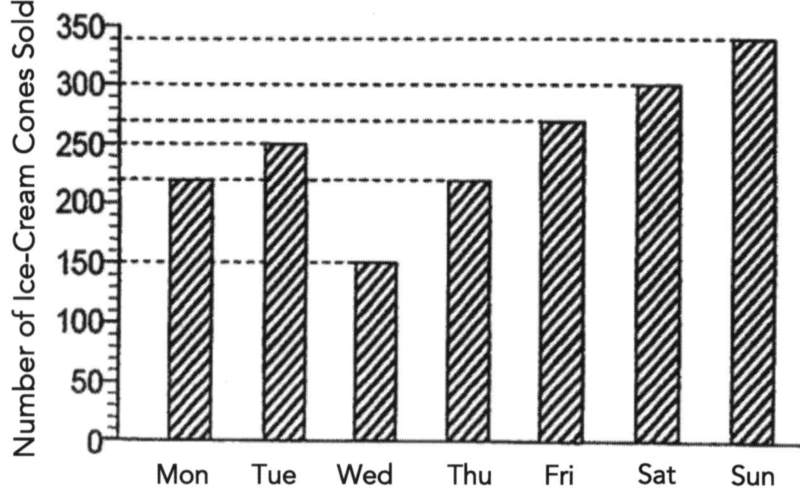

How many days were there where more than 250, but less than 325 cones sold per day?

Answer _______________

151. The following graph shows the number of tickets sold for a Katy Perry concert to different ticket purchasers (for instance, 10 families bought 2 tickets each).

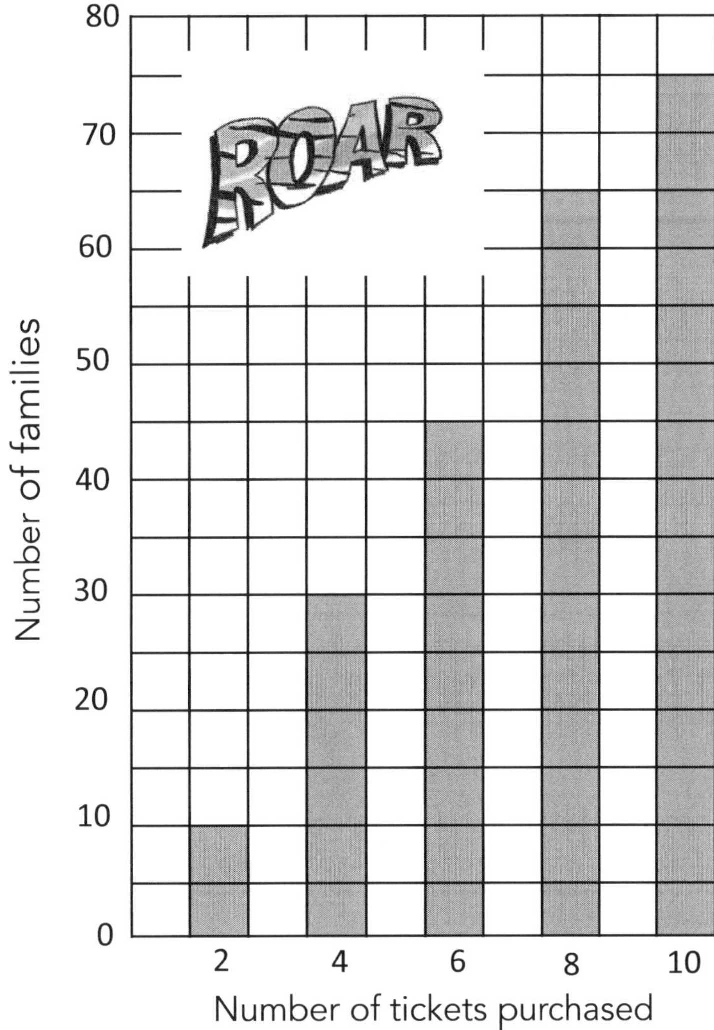

a) How many families purchased more than 5 tickets?

Answer ______________

b) If each ticket costs $128, how much money was collected in total?

Answer ______________

152. The table below shows the favorite rides taken by three classes at a amusement park. Study the table below carefully:

Class	Superman	Battle Star	Spider Ride	Ninja Twist
Renert 6A	2	20	9	10
Renert 6B	6	?	14	21
Renert 6C	4	23	6	8
Total	12	57	29	39

a) How many students in 6B chose "Battle Star" as their favorite ride?

(1) 14
(2) 20
(3) 23
(4) 43

b) Which class has the most students?

(1) 6A
(2) 6B
(3) 6C
(4) 6D

c) How many students went to the park?

(1) 137
(2) 135
(3) 127
(4) 125

BRAINTEASER

How many sheep should go where the question mark is? _____

153. The graph below shows the number of chickens sold by farmer Kehoe.

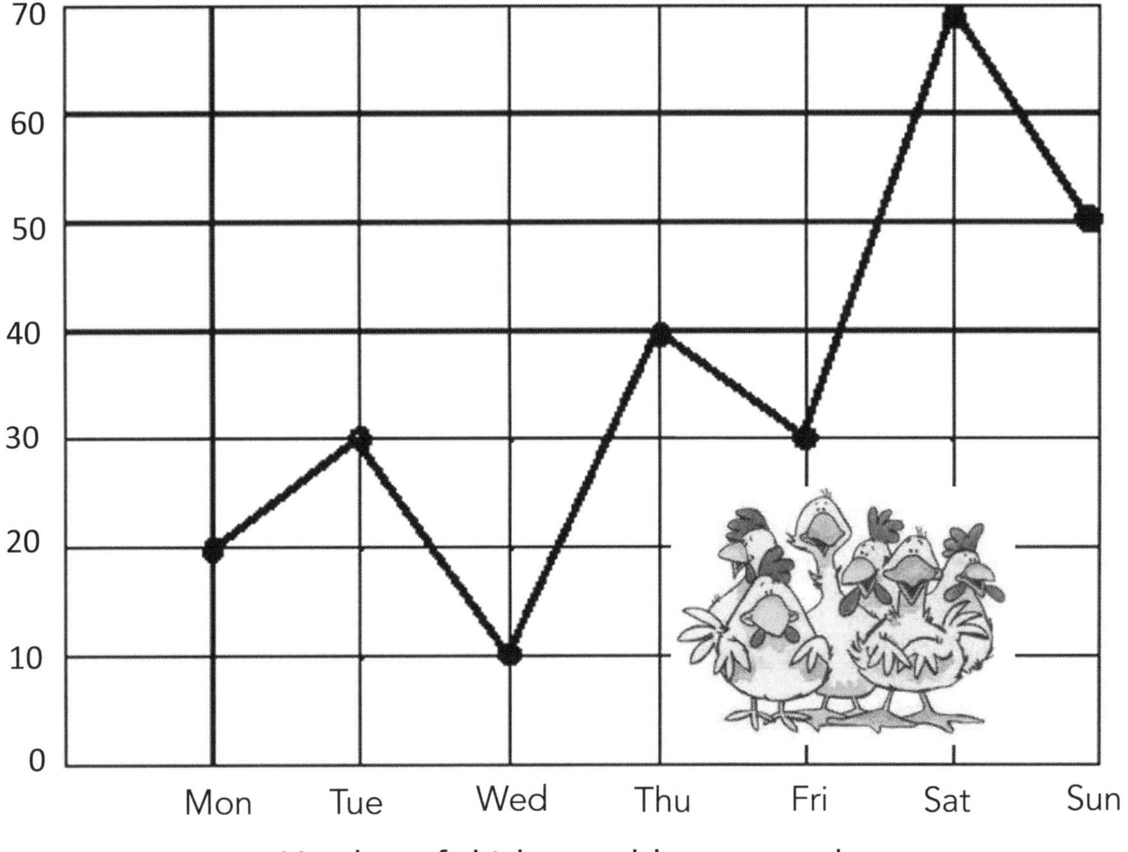

Number of chickens sold over a week

a) On what day did the greatest drop in sales occur? ________________

b) If each chicken was sold at $16.80, how much money did farmer Kehoe collect from the sale of his chickens over the weekend?

c) On what day did the greatest increase in sales occur?

BRAINTEASER

If a chicken says, "All chickens are liars" is the chicken telling the truth?

154. Use the graph to answer the questions. The graph shows the amount of rainfall over 5 months in Bora Bora in 2010.

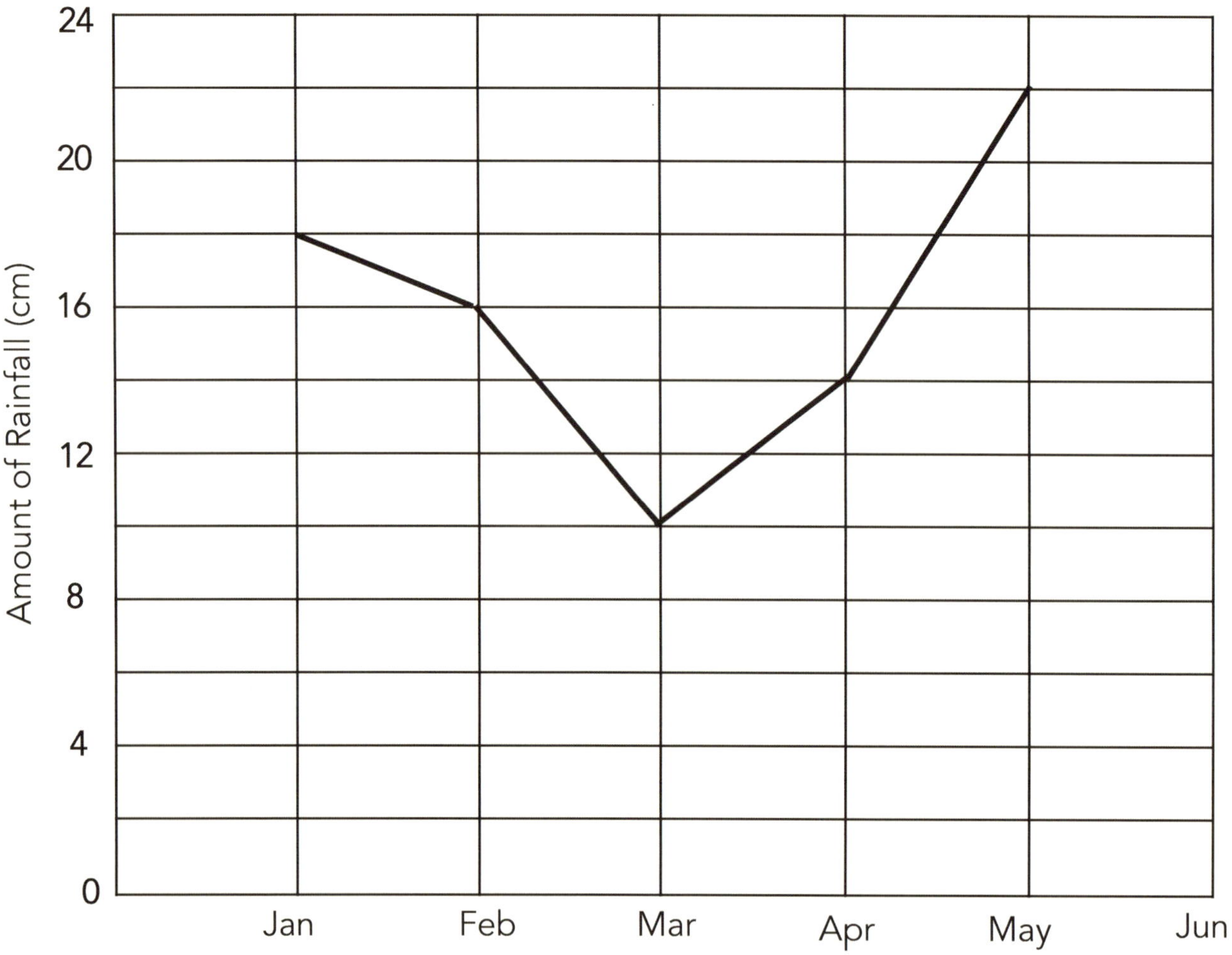

Amount of Rainfall (cm)

24
20
16
12
8
4
0

Jan Feb Mar Apr May Jun

a) What was the amount of rainfall collected in the driest month? _______________

b) A total of 100 cm of rainfall was collected in the first 6 months. Calculate the June rainfall and complete the graph.

c) What fraction of the total rainfall was recorded in April? Give your answer in the simplest form. _______________

Is it possible to predict the score at a game before it starts?

____

155. What is the missing number in the pattern below?

3546, 3476, __________, 3336, ________

156. 20 thousands + 19 hundreds + 18 tens + 17 ones = ________________

157. 20 thousands − 19 hundreds + 18 tens − 17 ones = ________________

158. At a party there are 4 boys for every 3 girls. If the number of boys and girls together is between 36 and 47, how many kids are at the party?

Answer: ______________________

159. Study the following clues and find the following 5-digit number that is made up of 5 different digits:

1. The digit in the thousands place is a prime number.
2. The thousands digit + the hundreds digit = prime number.
3. The ones digit is 4 times bigger than the hundreds digit.
4. The digit in the tens place is half the sum of its two neighbours.
5. The 5 digit number is divisible by 9.

The number is ________________.

160. A piece of string 2.30m long is cut into 3 pieces. Two are of the same length and the third one is 20cm longer than each of the equal ones. What is the length of each of the two equal pieces?

Answer: ____________

161. A notebook costs $3.45. An eraser costs 1/5 of the price of a notebook, and a sharpener costs 2/3 as much as a notebook.
What is the cost of 5 notebooks, 4 erasers and 3 sharpeners?

Answer: ____________

162. At the Calgary Winter Club 1/3 of members are men and ¼ are women. The rest are children. If there are 680 children at the club, how many women are there?

Answer: ____________

Marking Key - Guide to Parents and Markers

The reason we include a marking key at the end of each booklet is so students can tell in real time whether they understand the material and are getting the correct answers. Solving math problems without knowing if you are doing it correctly is time-wasteful, and even pointless. This is where you, the parent, can greatly help both your child, as well as the teacher.

How to do it right? Please follow these guidelines closely:

- Grab your favourite yellow highlighter.
- Place a checkmark ✓ with a pen beside any question the child gets correct.
- HIGHLIGHT with a yellow highlighter the question number of any question the child got wrong. If the question is unnumbered, you can highlight the wrong answer itself.
- Ask the child to go over their mistakes, and try to correct, to the best of their ability. If it is a careless error, the child should be able to find and correct it. If it is an error that stems from lack of understanding of how to solve the question, this is fine. We will explain the concept again to the child in class and guide him to the solution.
- We do not expect you to teach your child any of the mathematical concepts at home. This is our job, but it speeds us tremendously when the marking was done at home, so we can see very quickly where the child went wrong.
- Do NOT spoon feed solutions to your child or guide them too heavily. As instructors we always assume that a correct answer is one that the child worked out, and that if asked how they got it, they should be able to explain. Making many mistakes is part of the learning process and **there is nothing wrong with it**. As a parent you have to get very comfortable with your child making mistakes. You will speed your child up, however, by highlighting these mistakes and asking the child if they can correct them unassisted.
- Feel free to communicate with the instructor by jotting comments in the booklet and asking your child to show them to the instructor. For instance, you may write "really struggles with long division, but understands very well short division..." etc. Again, it helps our instructors a great deal in knowing what to zoom in on.
- Marking key is to use, not abuse. If the child starts copying answers wholesale and presents them as their own, explain to them how unproductive it is, and that they should not do it.

You can access the **4A digital marking key** at: https://bit.ly/3ioqR5n

IXL Recommended activities for this booklet (4A)

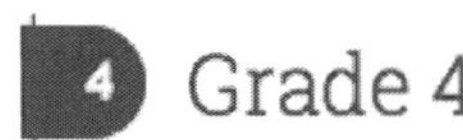

Understand Fractions
Y.6Fractions of number lines: unit fractions
Y.7Fractions of number lines
Y.8Identify fractions on number lines
Y.9Graph unit fractions on number lines
Y.10Graph fractions on number lines
Y.11Fractions of a group: word problems
Y.12Fractions of a number - unit fractions
Y.13Fractions of a number
Y.14Fractions of a number - unit fractions: word problems
Y.15Fractions of a number - word problems

Grade 4

Number sense
A.1 Place values
A.2 Convert between place values
A.3 Word names for numbers
A.4 Roman numerals
A.5 Prime and composite numbers
A.6 Rounding
A.7 Even or odd: arithmetic rules
A.8 Inequalities with number lines
A.9 Put numbers up to four digits in order
A.10 Compare numbers up to five digits

Addition
B.1 Add numbers up to five digits
B.2 Add numbers up to five digits: word problems
B.3 Addition: fill in the missing digits
B.4 Properties of addition
B.5 Add three or more numbers up to five digits each
B.6 Addition patterns over increasing place values
B.7 Choose numbers with a particular sum
B.8 Estimate sums
B.9 Estimate sums: word problems

Subtraction
C.1 Subtract numbers up to five digits
C.2 Subtract numbers up to five digits: word problems
C.3 Subtraction: fill in the missing digits
C.4 Subtraction patterns over increasing place values
C.5 Choose numbers with a particular difference
C.6 Estimate differences
C.7 Estimate differences: word problems

Multiplication
D.1 Multiplication facts to 10
D.2 Choose the multiples of a given number up to 12
D.3 Multiply 1-digit numbers by 2-digit numbers
D.4 Multiply 1-digit numbers by 2-digit numbers: word problems
D.5 Multiply 1-digit numbers by 3-digit numbers
D.6 Multiply 1-digit numbers by larger numbers
D.7 Multiplication patterns over increasing place values
D.8 Properties of multiplication
D.9 Estimate products - multiply by 1-digit numbers
D.10 Estimate products - multiply by larger numbers
D.11 Estimate products: word problems
D.12 Box multiplication
D.13 Lattice multiplication
D.14 Choose numbers with a particular product
D.15 Multiply numbers ending in zeroes
D.16 Multiply numbers ending in zeroes: word problems
D.17 Multiply three numbers
D.18 Multiply three or more numbers: word problems
D.19 Inequalities with multiplication

Division
E.1 Division facts to 10
E.2 Division facts to 10: word problems
E.3 Properties of division
E.4 Divide larger numbers
E.5 Divide larger numbers: word problems
E.6 Complete the division table
E.7 Interpret remainders
E.8 Choose numbers with a particular quotient
E.9 Divide numbers ending in zeroes
E.10 Estimate quotients
E.11 Estimate quotients: word problems
E.12 Divisibility rules
E.13 Divisibility rules: word problems
E.14 Division patterns over increasing place values
E.15 Inequalities with division

IXL Recommended activities for this booklet (4A)

4 Grade 4

Mixed operations
F.1Add, subtract, multiply and divide
F.2Addition, subtraction, multiplication and division word problems
F.3Estimate sums, differences, products and quotients: word problems
F.4Multi-step word problems
F.5Word problems with extra or missing information
F.6Solve word problems using guess-and-check
F.7Choose numbers with a particular sum, difference, product or quotient
F.8Mentally add and subtract numbers ending in zeroes
F.9Inequalities involving addition, subtraction, multiplication and division

Logical reasoning
I.1Find two numbers based on sum and difference
I.2Find two numbers based on sum, difference, product and quotient
I.3Find the order

Patterns and sequences
J.1Find the next shape in a repeating pattern
J.2Complete a repeating pattern
J.3Make a repeating pattern
J.4Find the next row in a growing pattern of shapes
J.5Complete an increasing number pattern
J.6Complete a geometric number pattern
J.7Number patterns: word problems
J.8Number patterns: mixed review

Data and graphs
L.1Read a table
L.2Interpret line graphs
L.3Create line graphs
L.4Interpret bar graphs
L.5Create bar graphs
L.6Interpret line plots
L.7Create line plots
L.8Frequency charts
L.9Stem-and-leaf plots
L.10Circle graphs
L.11Choose the best type of graph

Money
M.1Compare money amounts
M.2Round money amounts
M.3Add and subtract money amounts
M.4Making change
M.5Price lists

Units of measurement
N.1Choose the appropriate metric unit of measure
N.2Compare and convert metric units of length
N.3Compare and convert metric units of mass
N.4Compare and convert metric units of volume

Time
O.1Convert time units
O.2Add and subtract mixed time units
O.3Fractions of time units
O.4Elapsed time
O.5Find start and end times: multi-step word problems
O.6Convert between 12-hour and 24-hour time
O.7Time zones - 12-hour time
O.8Time zones - 24-hour time
O.9Transportation schedules - 12-hour time
O.10Transportation schedules - 24-hour time
O.11Time patterns

Geometry
P.1Which two-dimensional figure is being described?
P.2Identify three-dimensional figures
P.3Count vertices, edges and faces
P.4Identify faces of three-dimensional figures
P.5Which three-dimensional figure is being described?
P.6Nets of three-dimensional figures
P.7Is it a polygon?
P.8Number of sides in polygons
P.9Lines, line segments and rays
P.10Parallel, perpendicular and intersecting lines
P.11Acute, right, obtuse and straight angles
P.12Types of triangles

Geometric measurement
Q.1Perimeter
Q.2Perimeter: find the missing side lengths
Q.3Find the area of figures made of unit squares
Q.4Select figures with a given area
Q.5Select two figures with the same area
Q.6Create figures with a given area
Q.7Find the area or missing side length of a rectangle
Q.8Area and perimeter: word problems

IXL Recommended activities for this booklet (4A)

Grade 4

Understand fractions

R.1 Understand fractions: fraction bars
R.2 Understand fractions: area models
R.3 Match fractions to models
R.4 Show fractions: fraction bars
R.5 Show fractions: area models
R.6 Unit fractions: modelling word problems
R.7 Unit fractions: word problems
R.8 Fractions of a whole: modelling word problems
R.9 Fractions of a whole: word problems
R.10 Fractions of a group: word problems

Equivalent fractions

S.1 Find equivalent fractions using area models
S.2 Graph equivalent fractions on number lines
S.3 Equivalent fractions
S.4 Fractions with denominators of 10, 100 and 1000
S.5 Patterns of equivalent fractions
S.6 Write fractions in lowest terms

Compare and order fractions

T.1 Compare fractions with like numerators or denominators using models
T.2 Compare fractions with like numerators or denominators
T.3 Compare fractions using models
T.4 Compare fractions
T.5 Graph and compare fractions on number lines
T.6 Benchmark fractions
T.7 Compare fractions using benchmarks
T.8 Compare fractions in recipes
T.9 Order fractions with like numerators or denominators
T.10 Order fractions
T.11 Find smaller or larger fractions

IXL Recommended activities for this booklet (4A)

Grade 5

Place values and number sense
A.1Place values
A.2Convert between place values
A.3Compare numbers up to millions
A.4Word names for numbers
A.5Roman numerals
A.6Rounding
A.7Even or odd: arithmetic rules

Addition and subtraction
B.1Add and subtract whole numbers up to millions
B.2Add and subtract whole numbers: word problems
B.3Complete addition and subtraction sentences
B.4Fill in the missing digits
B.5Choose numbers with a particular sum or difference
B.6Properties of addition
B.7Inequalities with addition and subtraction
B.8Estimate sums and differences of whole numbers
B.9Estimate sums and differences: word problems

Multiplication
C.1Multiply by one-digit numbers
C.2Multiply by one-digit numbers: word problems
C.3Multiplication patterns over increasing place values
C.4Multiply numbers ending in zeroes
C.5Multiply numbers ending in zeroes: word problems
C.6Properties of multiplication
C.7Choose numbers with a particular product
C.8Estimate products
C.9Estimate products: word problems
C.10Box multiplication
C.11Lattice multiplication
C.12Multiply by 2-digit numbers: complete the missing steps
C.13Multiply 2-digit numbers by 2-digit numbers
C.14Multiply by 2-digit numbers: word problems
C.15Multiply three or four numbers
C.16Multiply three or four numbers: word problems
C.17Multiply 3-digit by 2-digit numbers
C.18Multiply 3-digit by 2-digit numbers: word problems
C.19Inequalities with multiplication

Division
D.1Division facts to 12
D.2Division facts to 12: word problems
D.3Divide by one-digit numbers
D.4Divide by one-digit numbers: word problems
D.5Divide by one-digit numbers: interpret remainders
D.6Estimate quotients

Division
D.7Estimate quotients: word problems
D.8Division patterns over increasing place values
D.9Divide numbers ending in zeroes
D.10Divide numbers ending in zeroes: word problems
D.11Choose numbers with a particular quotient
D.12Divide by two-digit numbers
D.13Divide by two-digit numbers: word problems

Number theory
E.1Prime and composite numbers
E.2Prime factorization
E.3Divisibility rules
E.4Divisibility rules: word problems
E.5Greatest common factor
E.6Least common multiple

Fractions and mixed numbers
J.1Show fractions: fraction bars
J.2Show fractions: area models
J.3Fractions review
J.4Fractions of a whole: word problems
J.5Fractions of a group: word problems
J.6Mixed numbers
J.7Fractions of a number
J.8Fractions of a number: word problems
J.9Arithmetic sequences with fractions
J.10Geometric sequences with fractions
J.11Round mixed numbers

Fraction equivalence and ordering
K.1Find equivalent fractions using area models
K.2Graph equivalent fractions on number lines
K.3Equivalent fractions
K.4Patterns of equivalent fractions
K.5Write fractions in lowest terms
K.6Graph and compare fractions on number lines
K.7Compare fractions
K.8Compare fractions and mixed numbers
K.9Order fractions with like denominators
K.10Order fractions with like numerators
K.11Order fractions

IXL Recommended activities for this booklet (4A)

Add and subtract fractions

L.1Decompose fractions multiple ways
L.2Add and subtract fractions with like denominators using number lines
L.3Add and subtract fractions with like denominators
L.4Add and subtract fractions with like denominators: word problems
L.5Add and subtract mixed numbers with like denominators
L.6Add and subtract mixed numbers with like denominators: word problems
L.7Add up to 4 fractions with denominators of 10 and 100
L.8Add three or more fractions
L.9Add three or more fractions: word problems
L.10Complete addition and subtraction sentences with fractions
L.11Inequalities with addition and subtraction of fractions
L.12Estimate sums and differences of mixed numbers

Multiply fractions

M.1Multiply unit fractions by whole numbers using number lines
M.2Multiply unit fractions by whole numbers using models
M.3Multiples of fractions
M.4Multiply unit fractions and whole numbers: sorting
M.5Multiply fractions by whole numbers using number lines
M.6Multiply fractions by whole numbers using models
M.7Multiply fractions and whole numbers: sorting
M.8Multiply fractions by whole numbers
M.9Multiply fractions by whole numbers: input/output tables

Mixed operations

N.1Add, subtract, multiply and divide whole numbers
N.2Add, subtract, multiply and divide whole numbers: word problems
N.3Write numerical expressions
N.4Evaluate numerical expressions
N.5Add, subtract, multiply and divide decimals
N.6Add, subtract and multiply decimals: word problems

Problem solving

O.1Multi-step word problems
O.2Word problems with extra or missing information
O.3Guess-and-check problems
O.4Find the order
O.5Use Venn diagrams to solve problems
O.6Price lists

Patterns and sequences

P.1Find the next shape in a repeating pattern
P.2Complete a repeating pattern
P.3Make a repeating pattern
P.4Find the next row in a growing pattern of shapes
P.5Complete an increasing number sequence
P.6Complete a geometric number sequence
P.7Use a rule to complete a number sequence
P.8Number sequences: word problems
P.9Number sequences: mixed review

Data and graphs

S.1Read a table
S.2Interpret line graphs
S.3Create line graphs
S.4Interpret bar graphs
S.5Create bar graphs
S.6Interpret pictographs
S.7Create pictographs
S.8Interpret histograms
S.9Create histograms
S.10Interpret line plots
S.11Create line plots
S.12Frequency charts
S.13Stem-and-leaf plots
S.14Circle graphs
S.15Choose the best type of graph

Time

U.1Convert time units
U.2Add and subtract mixed time units
U.3Elapsed time
U.4Find start and end times: word problems
U.5Convert between 12-hour and 24-hour time
U.6Time zones - 12-hour time
U.7Time zones - 24-hour time
U.8Schedules and timelines - 12-hour time
U.9Schedules - 24-hour time
U.10Time patterns

Units of measurement

V.1Choose the appropriate metric unit of measure
V.2Compare and convert metric units of length
V.3Compare and convert metric units of mass
V.4Compare and convert metric units of volume
V.5Choose the more reasonable temperature

Geometric measurement

Z.1Perimeter with whole number side lengths
Z.2Perimeter with decimal side lengths
Z.3Area of squares and rectangles
Z.4Area and perimeter of figures on grids
Z.5Use area and perimeter to determine cost

HOMEWORK TRACKING

HOMEWORK TRACKING